The Working Smarter Fieldbook | September 2010

By Jay Cross, Jane Hart, Harold Jarche, Charles Jennings & Clark Quinn

ISBN 978-0-557-68978-1

Internet Time Alliance, 30 Poppy Lane, Berkeley, California 94708 http://internettime.com

October 13, 2010

The Working **Smarter** Fieldbook

By Jay Cross, Jane Hart, Harold Jarche, Charles Jennings & Clark Quinn

Why bother?

Smart companies prosper. Clueless companies die. Brains make the difference.

Organizations that continuously exercise and improve their collective brainpower come out on top. This Fieldbook aims to show you how to create value by increasing your organization's intelligence.

Until recently, most of the collaboration and development that fuels the growth of individual and group braininess was haphazard. Our goal is to bring this activity into the sunlight and suggest ways you can take advantage of it.

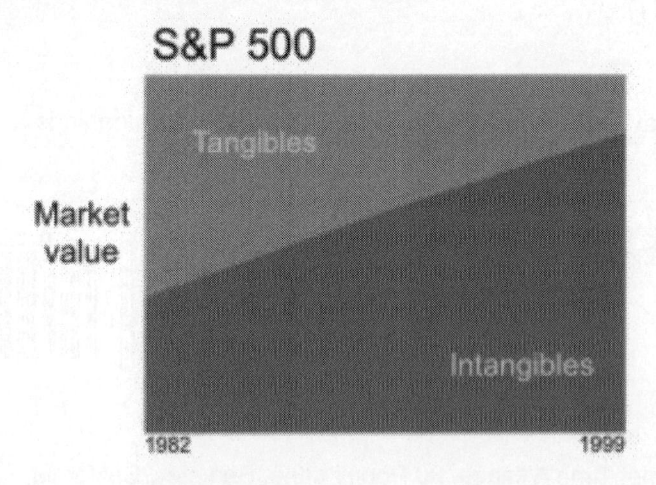

The last two decades of the 20th century witnessed a remarkable shift in American business. Investors realized that what you can't see is often more valuable than what's in plain sight.

Invisible assets like relationships and know-how count for more market value than visible assets such as plants and equipment.

We'll be exploring what to do as connections become more important than what they connect, traditional ROI fails to measure what's valuable, and street smarts trumps formal education for getting things done.

Who should read this book?

This is a book for business managers who want to build workforces that improve performance naturally, without prodding. It's a fresh look at how people become competent in their work and fulfilled in their professional lives.

In our mind's eye, we are telling these stories to hands-on managers, people with titles such as sales manager, operations supervisor, project leader, and product manager. People in IT and marketing will also profit from the stories here.

We foresee a convergence of the "people disciplines" in organizations. As the pieces of companies become densely interconnected, the differences between knowledge management, training, collaborative learning, organization development, internal communication, and social networking fade away. Anyone who invests in brainpower to improve organizational performance can benefit from the messages in *The Working Smarter Fieldbook*.

That said, this book is *not* directed to doctrinaire training directors or workshop instructors. It's impossible to learn something you think you already know. Besides, they will find our message threatening. Learning is way too important to delegate to the training department.

What can you achieve with this book?

Boosting brainpower is both a profit strategy and the key to organizational longevity.

Raising corporate IQ reduces time-to-performance, improves customer service, boosts sales, streamlines operations, and increases innovation. Intelligent organizations naturally motivate their workers to give their best. People who know how to learn effectively adapt to changing conditions as they occur.

Pragmatic and grounded in experience, this is a re-think of how upgrading an organization's brains can increase profits, spur innovation, and help businesses prosper.

What's this book about?

This *Wordle* depicts the main topics of this unbook:

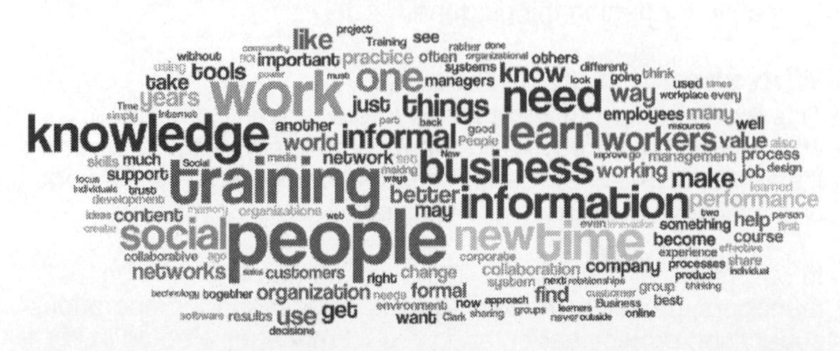

Wordles are "word clouds" generated from text. The clouds give greater prominence to words that appear more frequently in the source text. Each chapter in this version begins with a Wordle.

A toolbox

Years ago, Stewart Brand published *The Whole Earth Catalog* to provide "access to tools." It listed all manner of interesting and oddball stuff, from windmill kits to hiking sox to books like *Vibration Cooking*. The *Catalog* didn't tell readers how to live their lives; it merely described things that might help them to do their own thing. Feedback and articles submitted by readers made each edition better than its predecessor.

The Working Smarter Fieldbook follows the tradition of *The Whole Earth Catalog*. Harold, Jane, Clark, Charles, and Jay provide access to the tips, tricks, frameworks, and resources that we've used to help organizations work smarter. Our goal is to put together an irresistible package of advice.

An unbook

This is an unbook. Unbooks are never finished.

Rather than hold things back until they're "ready," unbooks come out while the ink is still wet. You have in your hands the sixth version of *Working Smarter*. Revisions come out several times a year. An unbook has the freshness of a periodical and the depth of a book. If you choose to subscribe, buy a new copy next year. You can track major changes and additions at internettime.com to see if it's worth it.

Jane Hart, Harold Jarche[1], Clark Quinn, Charles Jennings, yours truly, and other friends and colleagues collaborated to write this book. Our thoughts are inextricably intertwined. Nobody's so smart that they wouldn't do better with the help of others. In nonfiction, the concept of a single author is a conceit we can do without.

With most books, it's take it or leave it. If you have an issue with a traditional author, you can send a letter to the black hole known as a publisher. The world changes, but the book is frozen in time. That's another reason unbooks are in perpetual beta.

Expect some rough edges and redundancy in this version. Join the typo team and email us when you come across errors or confusing passages. Send feedback, large or small, to jaycross@internettime.com. Better still, become a co-author. Your input is welcome.

Join us at *http://bit.ly/avDnKO* *(http://internettimealliance.com/book)*

You can't judge a book by its cover

What's the biggest change since the June 2010 Edition? The cover.

---

[1] *Jarche* is pronounced jar-key.

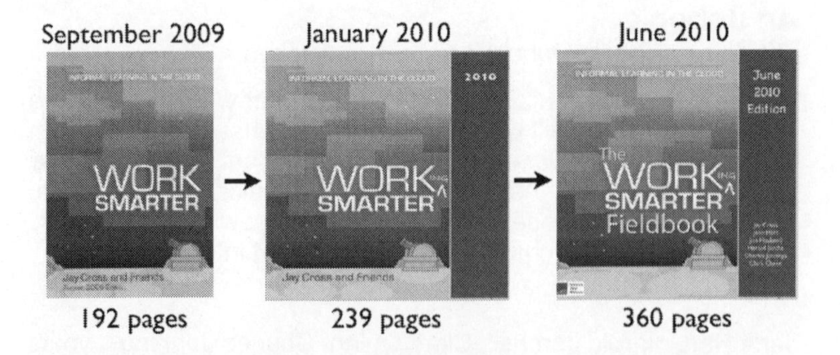

The June 2010 Fieldbook was a major upgrade, a radically different book than its January 2010 predecessor. Longer, deeper, more practical.

We wanted the cover of the June edition to express the unbook philosophy that newer, better content is being hacked together all the time.

That backfired. People saw the cover and said "I've already read it." Hence, a new cover. Pictured is the church where the father of Pablo Picasso was baptized in Malaga. May you all be Picassos in your field.

Get online

Go to: http://internettimealliance.com/book Sign up for updates. Join the club. You'll find a lot more information about working smarter.

Let's get into it. There's no time to spare. Time is all we have.

"In business, words are words; explanations are explanations, promises are promises, but only performance is reality."

Harold Geneen

September 2010 Edition

Contents

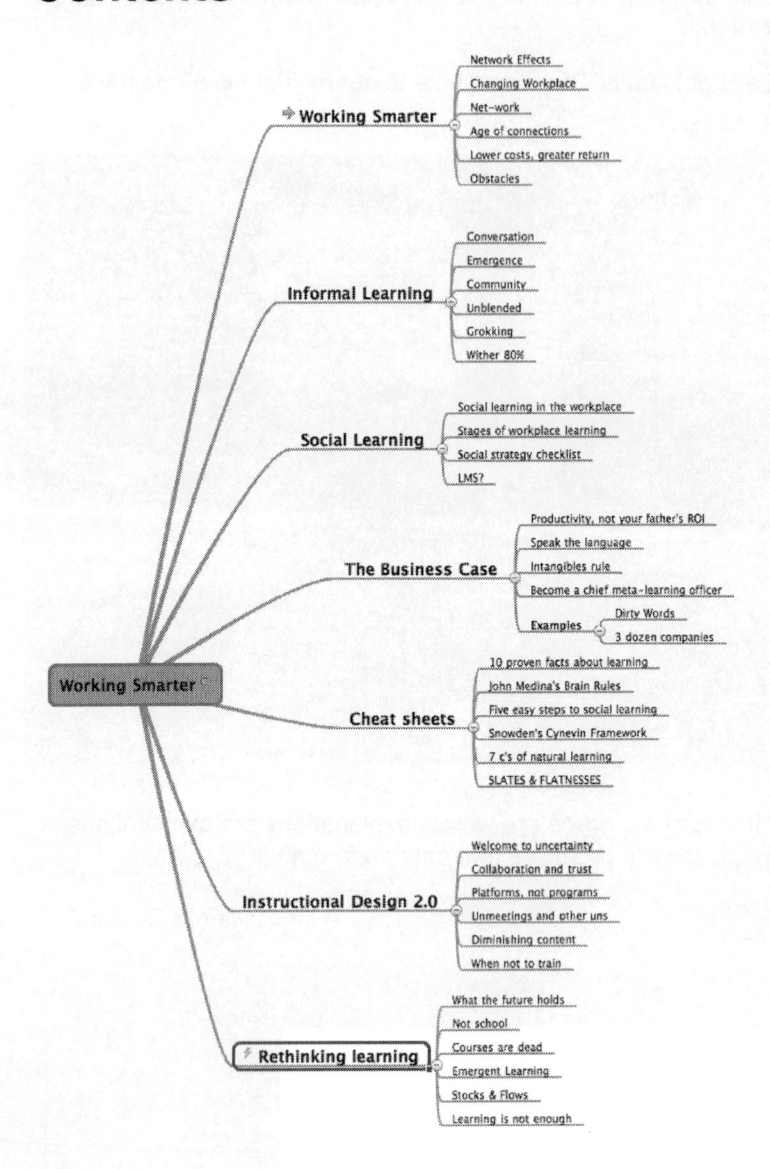
Working Smarter
Working Smarter
Network Effects
Changing Workplace
Net-work
Age of connections
Lower costs, greater return
Obstacles
Informal Learning
Conversation
Emergence
Community
Unblended
Grokking
Wither 80%
Social Learning
Social learning in the workplace
Stages of workplace learning
Social strategy checklist
LMS?
The Business Case
Productivity, not your father's ROI
Speak the language
Intangibles rule
Become a chief meta-learning officer
Examples
Dirty Words
3 dozen companies
Cheat sheets
10 proven facts about learning
John Medina's Brain Rules
Five easy steps to social learning
Snowden's Cynevin Framework
7 c's of natural learning
SLATES & FLATNESSES
Instructional Design 2.0
Welcome to uncertainty
Collaboration and trust
Platforms, not programs
Unmeetings and other uns
Diminishing content
When not to train
Rethinking learning
What the future holds
Not school
Courses are dead
Emergent Learning
Stocks & Flows
Learning is not enough

Contents

Preface

Cataclysm

The industrial age is in decline, making way for the network era. This may be a bigger change than when the Industrial Revolution eclipsed the agrarian age. That time, people moved from farms to cities. Working to the clock replaced working to the rhythm of the sun. Repetitive, mindless factory labor replaced toiling holistically with nature. Following orders replaced thinking for one's self. Slums were born; society unraveled.

Industry won't disappear, but about a third of all industrial companies probably will. The ranks of the permanently unemployed will swell. New categories of work will pop up to address network optimization, making connections, reconfiguring functions, real-time enterprise design, constructive destruction, virtual mentoring and so on. Hallowed laws, regulations, standards and memes will evaporate.

Management itself, the art of planning, organizing, deciding and controlling, will fall by the wayside. After all, planning is of little value in an unpredictable world. Organizing takes on new meaning when things self-organize. Deciding is everybody's business when networks rule. Control is a nonstarter in a bottom-up, peer-powered society.

Does it matter?

- ☐ **What's in it for me?**
- ☐ **What business are we in?**
- ☐ **Principle of materiality.**
- ☐ **Don't fret over the inconsequential.**
- ☐ **Don't sweat the small stuff.**
- ☐ **The past is a sunk cost.**

As networks continue to subvert hierarchy, successful organizations will embrace respect for the individual, flexibility and adaptation, openness and transparency, sharing and collaboration, honesty and authenticity, and real-time responsiveness and immediacy. Training becomes obsolete because it deals with a past that won't be repeated. Learning will be redefined as problem solving, achieving fit with one's environment and having the connections to deal with novel situations.

Impending doom unfreezes organizational structure to make room for reorganizing, rearranging and replacing the status quo. Survivors develop agendas for change while things are in flux. If I worked in a corporation, here's the pitch I'd give the most senior person I could get a hearing with:

"Next week, we will close the training department. We are shifting our focus from training to performance. Any remaining training staff will become mentors, coaches and facilitators who work on improving core business processes, strengthening relationships with customers and cutting costs.

Make no little plans. They have no magic to stir men's blood. *Daniel H. Burnham*

"I'm changing my title from VP of training to VP of core capabilities. My assistants will become the director of sales readiness and the director of competitive advantage, respectively. The measure of our contributions will be results, not training measures. We're scrapping the LMS posthaste. Wherever possible, we're replacing proprietary software with open source.

"All of our energies will go into peer-to-peer, self-service learning. If something doesn't dramatically improve the capabilities of our people, we won't do it. We are scrapping lengthy program development projects in favor of quick-and-dirty rapid development. We are abandoning classrooms.

"We are eliminating all travel and helping others do the same by introducing Skype and free real-time conferencing. We're setting up a corporate FAQ on a wiki to capture and distribute the information we once received from people who are no longer with us. In this and all of our efforts, we intend to work smarter, not lower our standards or quality of service.

"Recognizing that informed customers make better customers, we are opening up most of our platforms for learning to them, as well as our employees and former employees. To the extent that we help them cut costs, improve performance and implement better methods, we both win.

"Everything has a price tag. When we wring out costs, I want commitment from senior management to allocate time for people to help one another, exploit the benefits of social networks and converse with one another freely. This is a multiyear program. It will not work if we try to implement it while still doing business as usual. Burning people out is not a survival strategy.

"That is my plan for this week. If I have your support, I'll be happy to come back with a few more things next week."

Internet Time Alliance

We are six can-do practitioners with more than a century of experience managing projects, designing interventions, improving service, increasing sales, and boosting profits.

We've probably seen, explored, and used any approach to organizational and individual development you've ever been exposed to. We are web-savvy. We know what works and what doesn't.

The world has grown complex. Augmenting human intelligence draws upon interface design, neuroscience, organizational development, social networking, experiential learning, cognitive science, collaborative software, and scenario planning. Monitoring this level of complexity is beyond the reach of any one individual. That's why we formed our guild in 2009. Five heads are better than one.

We help organizations prosper with networking, performance support, and collaborative intelligence. Together, we will create a workplace that makes it easier for employees, partners, and customers to acquire skills and get things done. Many corporate advisers know business; many know the web; and many understand how organizations become smarter. Internet Time Alliance understands all three.

This Fieldblook is chock full of ideas and contributions from us all. You can see what we are thinking at:

Internet Time Alliance home: http://internettimealliance.com

Internet Time Alliance blog: http://internettime.posterous.com

Internet Time on Facebook:

Or you can track our individual pursuits:

Jay Cross	internettime.com	@jaycross
Jane Hart	c4lpt.uk	@c4lpt

Harold Jarche jarche.com @hjarche
Charles Jennings duntroon.com @charlesjennings
Clark Quinn quinnovation.com @quinnovator

Working Smarter

Our objective is to help your organization work smarter by taking advantage of its collective brainpower.

Working Smarter through Workscaping

Working smarter is the key to sustainability and continuous improvement. Knowledge work and learning to work smarter are becoming indistinguishable. The accelerating rate of change in business forces everyone in every organization to make a choice: learn while you work or become obsolete.

The infrastructure for working smarter is called a *workscape.* It's not a separate function so much as another way of looking at how we organize work. *Workscaping* helps people grow so that their organizations may prosper. *Workscapes* are pervasive. They are certainly not lodged in a training department. In fact, they may make the training department obsolete.

Organizations must stop thinking of learning as something separate from work. The further we get into what Dan Pink calls the conceptual era[2], the greater the convergence of working and learning. In many cases, they are already one and the same.

Workers in a *workscape* learn by solving problems, coming up with fresh thinking, and collaborating with colleagues. They don't learn *about* these things; they learn to *do* them.

The *workscape* is the aspect of an organization where learning and development become never-ending processes rather than one-time events. A *workscape* is a learning ecology. The *workscaping* viewpoint helps knowledge workers become more effective professionally and fulfilled personally. A sound workscape environment empowers workers to be all that they can be.

No, no, no. Learning *is* the work, not apart from the work.

Workscapes match flows of know-how with workers solving problems and getting things done. They are the aspect of workplace infrastructure that provides multiple means of solving problems, tapping collective wisdom, and collaborating with others.

Workscapes are not a new structure but rather a holistic way of looking at and reformulating existing business infrastructure. They use the same networks and social media as the business itself.

---

[2] Pink, D. (2006) *A Whole New Mind.*

Technology is never the most important part of this. Foremost are people, their motivations, emotions, attitudes, roles, their enthusiasm or lack thereof, and their innate desire to excel. Technology, be it web 2.0 or instructional design, social psychology, marketing, or intelligent systems, only supports what we're helping people to accomplish.

Got the idea? Okay, I'm going to stop putting workscape in *italics.* Think of workscapes as an inevitable part of every organization.

As business de-emphasizes industrial-era command-and-control systems to make way for agile, sense-and-respond networks, the structure of business adapts to its new environment.

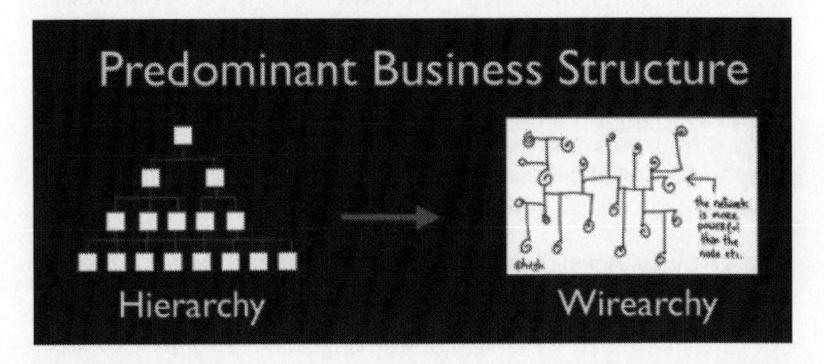

Terra Nova

England's New Forest is called *new* because it was built in 1079 by that well-known Johnny-Come-Lately, William the Conqueror. William wanted an oak forest for hunting. Timber would be required for building ships centuries later. He was thinking long term; let's follow his example.

Free yourself from day-to-day worries for a few minutes, and join us for a tour of the learning landscape five years hence, in 2015.

We will call our destination *Terra Nova*, Latin for "new world." Within five years, the world will have changed so radically, you will not recognize it. It is a new era and it is right around the corner.

- Agricultural age: manual labor by individual farmers, 8,000 BCE -

- Industrial age: machine-assisted manual labor in factories, 1760 -
- Information age: white-collar knowledge work in offices, 1949 -
- Terra Nova: creative collaborative innovation in networks, 2012 -

In the industrial age, bosses issued instructions and told workers[3] they were not paid to think. This is the ultimate in *push*, for people deal with what is pushed upon them.

In the information age, people were encouraged to think, but only "inside the box," that is, complying with narrow sets of procedures and rules. Workers were empowered - within strict bounds. Assignments still drifted down from the top. This is still primarily *push*.

In Terra Nova, Push and Pull combine to create a dynamic flow of power, authority, know-how, and trust. Change is so fast and furious that work and learning blur into one activity. Workers respond to novel situations as best they see fit, governed by organization values and gut feel.

Terra Nova is holistic, with significant decision-making power delegated to the workers themselves. "Power to the people" could be its rallying cry.

The industrial age was top-down, explicit, and focused on efficiency. By contrast, Terra Nova supplements hierarchy with networks.

---

[3] We say *workers*, not *learners*, because work is their ultimate goal; learning is but an enabler.

Worker Autonomy Increases

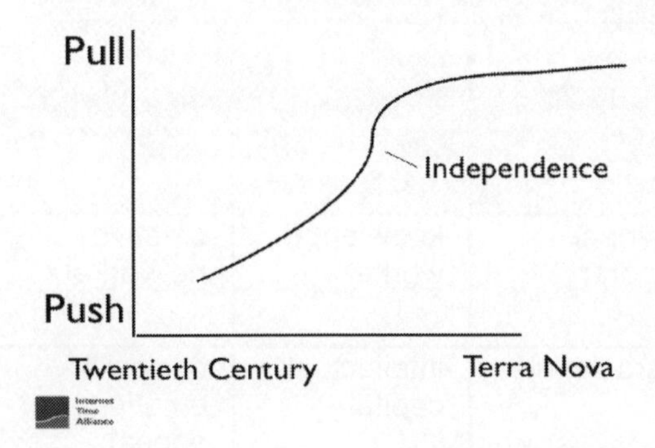

"I love to learn (pull) but I hate being trained (push)," said Winston Churchill.

We're optimistic about Terra Nova: Workers will lead organizations as well as managers and executives. No longer treated as cogs in the machine, people will have the freedom to be all that they can be - and the responsibilities that go with that freedom. Our hive mind will create unparalleled value and fulfillment.

Here are more characteristics[4] for describing the transition from one-way push to two-way pull. The lines between them are fuzzy. Old eras never die; they simply fade into the background.

[4] Inspired by Dan Pink's *A Whole New Mind* (2006)

Characteristics of Terra Nova			
	Industrial Age	Information Age	Terra Nova
worker	manual laborer	knowledge worker	creative networker
source of value	hard assets	intellectual capital	design & emotional appeal
what works	muscle & blood	left-brain logic	right-brain art
focus of attention	mindless	execution	innovation
communications media	speech	text	context
exemplars	factory labor, robber barons	MBAs, lawyers, engineers	inventors, counselors, entertainers
workflow	sequential	linear	simultaneous

Networks and connections exemplify Terra Nova. Networks crave connections. The denser the connections, the faster the cycle time. Time flies by at blinding speed. There's more progress made in one of your minutes than in one of your father's hours. One scientist[5] calculates that the 21st century will contain 20,000 20th-style years!

Isaac Newton gave us a clockwork universe where every action yielded an equal and opposite reaction. René Descartes made the case for pure logic (by taking God out of the equation.) Their

---

[5] Kurzweil, R. (2006) *The Singularity is Near*

world was predictable, precise, and tidy. We felt in control. Logic ruled.

In Terra Nova, everything is relative. As more and more people and entities interconnect, everything flows. Control is an illusion. Complex adaptive systems create butterfly effects[6] all around. In the industrial age, an exemplary worker might produce 25% more than average; now, a great engineer may create *two-hundred times* the value of an ordinary engineer. Black swans abound. The insight of a minute may reverberate for decades.

Making progress in this network age requires know-how and the motivation to apply it. Let's look at each in turn.

Motivation

People are motivated to do things because they want to make progress[7]. As Dan Pink[8] writes, "It's about satisfying workers' desire for autonomy, which stimulates their 'innate capacity for self direction[9].'" Some people want to increase the breadth of their repertoire to gain personal power. The best motivation is intrinsic. People do things for their own satisfaction, not external rewards.

The carrot-and-stick method doesn't work. In fact, external reward initiatives often backfire. Withdraw the reward and the desired behavior may stop. Also, rewards tied to performance have the potential to change play into work.

If you set high expectations of people, they usually live up to them. if you have low expectations of people, they live down to them. A person not trusted with the authority to do something can't take responsibility for doing it. 'It's not my department." A person authorized and trusted to take responsibility cannot help but do so.

---

[6] Lorenz, E. "*Does the flap of a butterfly's wings in Brazil set off a tornado in Texas?"*

[7] Amabile, T. *Creativity, Improvisation, and Organizatlons,* Harvard Business School Case Notes, 2009.

[8] Pink, D. 2010. *Drive, the Surprising Truth About What Motivates* Us

[9] O'Connel, A. 2010. *Daniel Pink's* Drive

As Will Herzberg[10], "the father of motivation theory," pointed out years ago, workers are motivated by achievement, recognition, the work itself, responsibility, promotion, and growth. This innate desire to do well can be hindered by obstacles that reduce motivation: lack of respect, poor working conditions, perceived unfairness, low pay, lack of job security, and poor relationship with supervisor.

Instructional design pioneer Robert Mager [11] proposed a manner of determining whether a roadblock was inadequate knowledge or lack of motivation. Hold a gun to her head. If she does what you ask, you're grappling with a motivation problem.

Sources of knowhow

My class at Harvard Business School has the distinction of being the last not allowed to bring portable calculators to exams. (A Bowmar 4-function calculator cost $99, a sum that kept many of us from acquiring one.) I got through by doing discounted cash now with a slide rule.

Everyone has several calculators today. They are giveaways. There's probably one in your phone. All of which makes it irrelevant to learn long division, how to take cube roots, or logarithms. Why bother? That's yesterday's know-how.

Robert Kelley at Carnegie Mellon discovered that whereas in 1986 we carried 75% of what we need to know to do our jobs in our heads, by 2006 our brains contained only about 8-10% of what we needed to know. The rest is stored in our "outboard brains" -- our laptops or, increasingly, our smart phones.

Once I had to learn most of the things required to do my job; now I need to know where to retrieve them. I search or ask people when I need to know. If I have a good network of savvy

---

[10] Herzberg, W. 1968. *One More Time, How Do You Motivate Employees?* Harvard Business Review

[11] Mager, R. 1970. *Analyzing Performance Problems. Or You Really Oughta Wanna.* Fearon Publishers

colleagues, I can ask them for advice ("social search"). "I store knowledge in my friends[12]."

Instructional designers once only designed instruction. Now they must assess the tradeoff of putting knowledge in the worker's head (learning) or putting it in an outboard brain (performance support).

[12] Karen Stephenson, as quoted by Downes http://www.downes.ca/cgi-bin/page.cgi? post-44607

Among the options available to them:

Formal	In between	Informal
Instructor-led class Workshop Video ILT Schooling Curriculum	Mentoring Conferences Simulations Interactive webinars Performance support YouTube Podcasts Books Storytelling	Hallway conversation Profiles/locators Social networking Trial & error Search Observation Asking questions Job shadowing/ rotation Collaboration, Community Study group Web jam Wikis, blogs, tweets, feeds Social bookmarking Unconferences

Searching and asking questions work best with explicit information, things that could be written down.

The subtle information that cannot be pinned down in simple sentences, for example, the emotions and nuances that make or break a sale, is tougher to transfer because "'wisdom can't be told[13]." People acquire this implicit knowledge through observing others, collaboration, and lengthy trial and error. Like blindfolded zen archery[14], mastery sometimes takes years.

---

[13] Harvard professor Charles I. Gregg. 1970. http:// www.aacu.orgipeerreviewlpr-wiOSlprwi05realitycheck.cfm

[14] Herrigel, E and Suzuki, D. 1953. *Zen and the Art of Archery*

Or course, many times we have already learned a skill through experience. Today experiential learning can be accelerated through simulation, virtual worlds, and role play.

	Formal	Informal
Control	Top-down	Laissez-faire
Delivery	Push	Pull
Duration	Hours, days, weeks	Minutes
Locus	Apart from work	Embedded in work
Author	Instructional designer, SME	Individual, the learner
Time to develop	Months, weeks	Minutes
When?	In advance	At time of need
What?	Know	Become

In the increasingly complex world we inhabit, we often confront novel situations. This requires innovation, a new way of doing things. Innovation is often the result of a mash-up of ideas, for example a rule of thumb from one discipline being applied in a new context.

What's wrong with most training?

It's just like school.[15]

[15] Roger Schank

School is not a very effective way to learn things. I know, that sounds blasphemous. That's because for sixteen or more years, you were indoctrinated. What's wrong with school? Lots.

You forget most of what you learn before you have the opportunity to use it. Human memory, if not reinforced, decays at an exponential rate. That's why you no longer remember it after taking the test[16].

- You don't get to chose what to learn; you often deem what you're studying irrelevant.
- School bears little relation to the greater world outside its walls.
- School is based on the negative assumption that you are deficient in some way, something no one wants to hear.
- School forces you to learn from an authority; you have much more faith in your peers.
- School focuses on individuals; success in real life depends largely on groups.
- School was designed for socialization and conformity; this drives stifles creativity, innovation, and initiative.
- School is walled off from the real world, making it impossible to
- experience and learn from reality.
- School teaches people to answer; it fails to teach them to question.
- Early schooling is impersonal: everyone studies the same subjects.
- Traditional college curricula was designed to prepare students to become professors or clergy, not, ahem, productive workers.
- School assumes pupils graduate; learning never ends.

Grades, the measure of performance, are related to nothing outside of school. Honor roll students and those who almost fail are equally likely to be happy, rich, or successful. It would be difficult to find a more random variable.

---

16 Ebbinghaus, H. (1885) *Oberdas Gedachtnis*

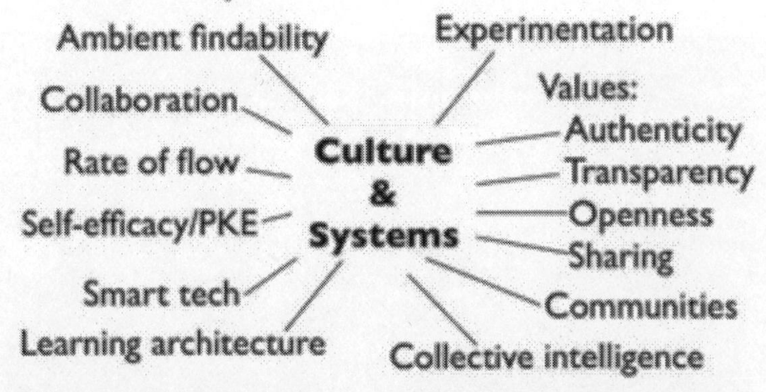

Classroom	Workscape
apart from work	embedded in work
training, push	learning, pull
programs	platform
piecemeal	holistic
events	processes
static	fluid
know things	work smarter

Times have changed. The industrial age is ending; the network era is upon us.

Nothing is predictable. Relationships have connected to everything else, the business world has become complex and become more important than individuals. Value flows to intangibles. Networks grow denser, cycle time speeds up, and everything goes faster, faster, faster. Scientist Ray Kurzweil[17]

---

[17] Kurzweil, R. 2006. *The Singularity is Near.* Penguin

says the 21st century won't contain a hundred 20th century years; it will contain 20,000 of them!

People who are spoon-fed learn nothing by the shape of the spoon.

Formal learning in school can work well when the answer is known. That's rarely the reality we live in. The world has become more complex, the answers more negotiated and emergent. Schools must prepare people to adapt, not to simply go through the motions.

School was never an efficient way to learn; it did a decent job of enforcing social control. In the industrial age, schools aped factories and Taylorism. Eliminate surprises. Embrace mass production. One size fits all. Times have changed. Traditional schooling is becoming counter-productive.[18]

It used to be the bottom of the class that dropped out; now the smart kids drop out. School is irrelevant and boring.

This is not a good model for corporations to copy, yet they do. Old habits die hard.

What we are dealing with here is more than traditional learning.

---

[18] See John Taylor Gatto's *Underground History of American Education* at www.johntaylorgatto.com

Learning is defined as the acquisition of skills or knowledge. That misses the trade-off of learning and performance support. Furthermore, organizations need more than learning: they need results. Learning is not enough; we want action.

The word *learning* has baggage. Mention learning to an executive and you can almost see them think *schooling.* Schooling, eh? That was not very effective. I'm not buying it. This is why I talk about working smarter. Or tapping into collaborative knowledge. I don't run into many people who don't want to work smarter.

A platform for working smarter

Back in the latter half of the twentieth century, a period we call the Golden Age of Training, corporations developed and delivered training programs. These programs were rigid events. Old-style training programs cannot keep pace with the future, save dealing with the fundamentals.

Today we need environments that simplify and encourage working smarter. This is where workscapes come in. Workscapes are to work as ecosystems are to events in nature. Pollution gums up the entire works. The Green movement and workscaping deal with impacts on whole systems.

We can encourage collaboration, problem-solving, and continuous improvement in a variety of ways:

- Focus on helping high performers and old hands work smarter; novices aren't the only workers who need to learn
- Set up conversation nooks and put wi-fi in the cafeteria
- Do not punish people for failed experiments (if you never fail, you're not innovating)
- Create a network that enables people to locate who knows what
- Apply the *80/20* rule to critical functions and seed communities of practice around them
- Trust people to manage their own learning and development
- Make mentoring and coaching part of everyone's job
- Use information technology to pull knowledge out of individuals and file cabinet, making it available to all
- Encourage people to narrate their work, documenting what they do to share with others
- Root out information hoarding; make sharing the norm (Some companies fire hoarders)
- Use social network analysis to locate and break bottlenecks
- Provide workers with smart phones, modern PCs, and internet access
- Seek opportunities to help customers, partners, temporary workers, alumni, and everyone else who works with the company work smarter
- Set up wikis and collaborative documents to avoid the proliferation of versions and confusion over what's current
- Look for opportunities to reduce cycle time: the world's not going any slower. Instant messenger, Twitter clones, podcasts
- Avoid duplication of effort in keeping up with news and research by providing shared information flows
- Reduce costs and increase relevance by replacing formal training programs with user-generated content
- Where possible, substitute self-service and peer learning for workshops
- Timeliness trumps perfection. Use amateur video and blogs to distribute information while it's still fresh
- Adopt best principles to outshine your organization's peers

Doing things at the workscape level enables you to improve the overall system instead of mucking about with individual programs.

Envisioning the workscape is analogous to the meta-learning view, which I've described before as "the view from the balcony" or "looking down from the helicopter." When you take in the entire vista, doing things to improve conversation, e.g. putting leather sofas in the hallways and wi-fi in the cafeteria, has lasting, systemic effects.

Payoff

Most corporate functions have been streamlined, re-engineered, fish boned , TQM'd, sigma'd, disintermediated, and squeezed until there's no slack left to cut.

Optimizing the workscape, on the other hand, is virgin territory. Simple instances of working smarter by sharing information in real time or making professional development self-service can throw millions of dollars in savings to the bottom line, for example:

- Free wiki becomes the go-to source of corporate information for 20,000 workers, eliminating $20 million a year in duplicate effort.
- Twitter-like information sharing saves wind turbine company $3 to $5 million annually
- Self-service FAQ cuts length of customer calls by 10%, improving service while shaving $3 million off payroll for temporary workers.
- In-house subscriptions to research findings saves 4,000 systems engineers two hours/week, freeing up 8,000 billable hours, expanding capacity by more than $25 million/year.
- A major consumer goods company has outsourced 50% of its R&D to customers, saving on staff and increasing innovation.
- A national telecommunications firm used performance support to reduce the rate of order entry errors from 30% to 6% (an 80% reduction) in 6 months.
- 3,000 communities of practice embedded in a major manufacturing company have generated more than $75 million in savings.
- More than 2,000 employees of Best Buy have provided more than 20,000 answers to customer queries using Twitter.
- 7,000 workers at a major insurance company are sharing information in near-real time via Twitter.

Let's examine the first of these examples. Six years ago, a product manager at Intel asked a web enthusiast in IT, "Couldn't we set up sort of an in-house Wikipedia to capture stories about our history?" When the manager called back a few weeks later to say he'd found some money for the project, the fellow in IT told him he'd already set things up. He had downloaded a free copy of Media Wiki (the same open-source wiki that powers Wikipedia) and loaded it into surplus space on a Linux box connected to the internal network.

Intelpedia[19] went viral. Two and a half years after launch, workers had posted 25,000 articles and achieved 100 million annual page views. The site contains a wide variety of content:

> Intel history (where the project started)[20]
> Groups, such as "Macs at Intel" and "Intel Sailing Club"
> Products and Technologies
> Acronyms and code names, which often differ across divisions
> Workgroup processes

An early page from Intelpedia appears on the opposite page.

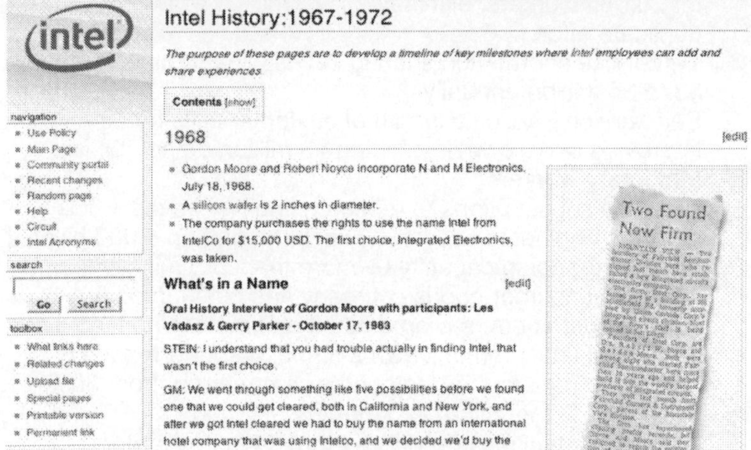

[19] Intel, Premier IT, Winter 2008. Http://ipipo.intel.com

[20] Sample Intelpedia page from Intel's Josh Bancroft http://flickr.com/photos/joshb/501483861/

All Intelpedia[21] articles on are written and maintained by Intel workers. They make an average of six edits per page that keep content fresh and accurate. "Intelpedia appears to have become the system of record for much of Intel's documented history," noted an assistant to Intel's CIO. Workers are embracing Intelpedia as the repository for Intel knowledge.

In the United States, knowledge workers typically spend a third of their time looking for information. Imagine the time 10,000 people at Intel must be saving. Plus, the information they find on Intelpedia is always the latest version, for that's all you see on a wiki!

> The truth will set you free - but first it will piss you off.

How to improve the quality of your workscape

Start *workscaping* (yes, it's also a verb) by:

- Legitimizing informal learning in your organization
- Recognizing that learning is the work and the work is learning
- Fostering trust, collaboration, and connecting with others
- Clearing out obstacles to conversation, including time and space
- Tolerating -- make that praising -- failed experiments
- Respecting the unorthodox, the surprise, the contrarian
- Helping workers learn how to (earn
- Exploiting the web and the democratization of the workforce
- Relentlessly seeking innovation

Your organization already has a workscape. If you haven't nurtured it, opportunity is passing you by.

The Learning Lifecycle

To everything there is a season. We are born, we play, we work, we teach, we die. As time goes by, we change how we learn.

A baby's every waking moment goes into figuring things out. Child's play for pre-schoolers is learning in disguise: They devote

[21] Not to be confused with Intellipedia, the wiki used by the American intelligence community to share formerly classified information.

their time to experimenting and understanding their world.

School children attend formal classes and do assignments to lay a foundation for learning the three R's, cultural memes and social norms. Few would argue that children should have to invent, say, multiplication rather than have it taught to them in school.

School children weave a mental tapestry of understanding, whereas adults patch holes in the fabric.

Upon escaping the confines of school, people go to work. Just as the high-school graduate descends from the top of one heap to the bottom of another as an entering freshman, the college graduate starts over as a new hire.

Careers are front-loaded with formal learning: orientation sessions, workshops on fundamentals and certification programs. Everyone is a novice in some areas and an expert in others. Workshops, courses and other formal instruction are appropriate for the newbie who needs the 20,000-foot view as a landscape for connecting and making sense of details.

> An invasion of armies can be resisted but not an idea whose time has come. *Victor Hugo*

Over time, informal learning becomes more prominent. Mid-career workers rarely take workshops. Collaboration, search, small-chunk simulations and other informal means are more appropriate to their needs: fine-tuning and improvising from what they already know.

Most people arrive at adulthood having built the foundation skills, mental models and working knowledge they need to get along in the world. Adults learn when they need to solve pressing problems. They don't have patience for superfluous material or rehashing what they already know. Curriculum is for kids—exploration is for adults.

Veteran workers who are savvy in the way things work are most organizations' top performers. In the factory, the best worker was perhaps twice as productive as the worst. In the knowledge economy, the best worker is hundreds of times more productive than a mediocre peer. Top performers justify special handling.

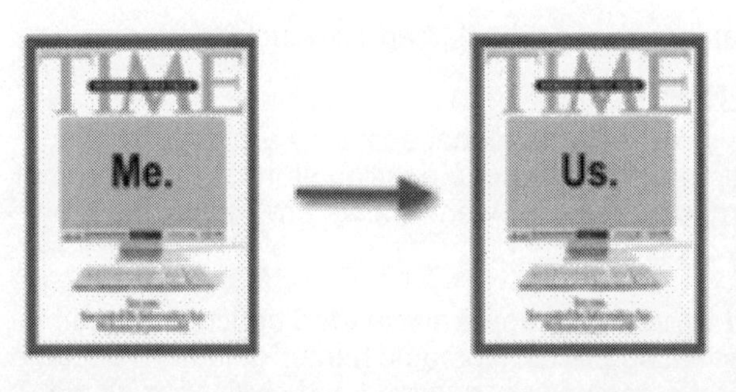

What portion of your workforce is made up of green recruits? What fraction already knows the ropes? How many are top performers? If you're like most organizations, your old hands outnumber the new recruits ten to one. The western world's workforce is aging. Yet all too often, trainers treat learners as if they were all the same.

Part of the reason organizations overemphasize training novices is an inheritance from the DNA of instructional design. Back up sixty years: The United States enters World War II with no standing army, and suddenly, millions of civilians need to learn how to fight. This sowed the seeds of what morphed into instructional systems design (ISD) in the '50s. The core methodology of ISD, the ADDIE model (analyze, design, develop, implement and evaluate), had a great run at elevating novices to basic competence.

**First we make our habits.
Then our habits make us.**

Winning World War II was such a success that corporations followed the military's example. Command-and-control hierarchies were run by officers who developed strategies to battle the competition. But times have changed, and models that once helped companies succeed now hold them back. ADDIE is not the best way to help top performers learn. ADDIE starts with a needs analysis, but experienced workers do better when they define their own needs.

Why do companies persist in putting most of their training budgets into courses, workshops, learning management systems and other things that deal primarily with getting novices up to speed? Doesn't it make more sense to invest in communications infrastructure, putting resources at workers' fingertips, and facilitating collaboration? Helping experienced workers do their jobs better has a higher payback than introductory courses.

Network Effects

The business world and the global economy are experiencing permanent climate change, not a passing storm. Things are not going to return to where they were, for we are witnessing the birth of a new order.

Ten thousand years ago, people discovered agriculture and began domesticating plants. Nomadic hunter-gatherers became farmers, formed communities, and invented civilization as we know it. The farmers learned to leverage tools in new ways and use animals to boost productivity, which enabled them to stockpile surpluses to tide them over in hard times and to trade with others.

Three hundred years ago, the steam engine replaced manual labor, and industrialists built factories for manufacturing and canals to open up trade. People migrated from farms to cities. Clock watching replaced working to the rhythm of the sun. Repetitive, mindless factory labor replaced working holistically with nature. Taking orders replaced thinking for one's self. Slums were born. In time, people harnessed electricity, laid rails, and rationalized production, providing the material wealth we enjoy today.

Man plans; God laughs.

Right now, we're moving from the industrial age to the era of networks, and once again, humanity is in turmoil. Yesterday's bedrock is today's soup. Businesses, governments, and citizens are becoming densely interconnected. The denser their connections, the faster networks cycle. Everything is relative because everything's connected. The future is unpredictable, and the survivors will be those who learn to deal with surprises as they arrive.

Cycles within cycles

Institutions	Individuals
Technology	People
Centralized	Decentralized
Formal	Informal
Rigid Structure	Recombinant
Preordained	Emergent

In the network era, we will continue to have factories, just as we still have farms. Some functions will remain hierarchical. Pockets of old-style face-to-face instruction will soldier on. It's just that the action will have shifted to where connections are active. Meaning will shift from entities to relationships.

> *"I am old enough to know that newspapers are where you get your political news and how you look for a job. I know that music comes from stores. I know that if you want to have a conversation with someone, you call them on the phone. I know that complicated things like software and encyclopedias have to be created by professionals. In the last fifteen years, I've had to unlearn every one of those things and a million others, because they have stopped being true."*
>
> *"I've become like the grown-ups arguing in my local paper about calculators; just as it took them a long time to realize that calculators were never going away, those of us old enough to remember a time before social tools became widely available are constantly playing catch-up. Meanwhile my students, many of whom are fifteen years younger than I am, don't have to unlearn those things, because they never had to learn them in the first place."*
>
> Clay Shirky, *Here Comes Everybody*

Organizations must seize the opportunity to change while things are in flux, and learn to continually adapt. It's improvisation, not scripted performance. Organizations must leap the chasm from current conditions to the brave new world, and crossing the chasm takes a bold leap. Continual learning through problem solving and collaboration is the key.

Playing by yesterday's rules: faux East German border guard

Networks are growing faster than vines in the rain forest, reaching out, and encircling the earth. Denser connections yield faster throughput. The exponential growth of networks is the underlying reason that everything in the world appears to be speeding up.

Social networks, computer networks, communications networks, and any other network you can think up are constructed of nodes and connectors and nothing more. Each new node of a network increases the value of the overall network exponentially. Connecting networks to other networks turbo-charges their growth.

New linkages distribute information and power, breaking down organizational boundaries and fiefdoms. Networks subvert hierarchy. Perhaps it took longer than we expected, but people were right when they said, "The Net changes everything."

Learning used to focus on what was in an individual's head. The individual took the test, got the degree, or earned the certificate. Now we're interconnected.

What's important is doing the job right, not what's in one person's head. The workplace is an open-book exam.

What worker doesn't have a cell phone and an internet connection? Smart companies encourage workers to use their lifelines to get help from colleagues and mine the world's knowledge from the internet.

Knowledge is power, and through networks, knowledge is being shared among workers and citizens as never before. It's power to the people as businesses embrace multiple systems of making decisions.

> *The purpose of the organization is to enable common men to do uncommon things. No organization can depend on genius; the supply is always scarce and unreliable. The test of an organization is the spirit of performance. The focus must be on the strengths of a man—on what he can do rather than what he cannot do. The focus of the organization must be on opportunities rather than problems.*
>
> Peter Drucker

Threatening as it seems to people accustomed to sitting on the top tier of hierarchies, the network era favors decentralization, democratization of the workforce, self-managed workers, peer decision-making, empowered teams, and bottom-up innovation.

In the previous commercial era, workers operated machinery to produce goods. You could see what they were doing and touch the goods they produced. Time-and-motion studies identified the one best way to do a job; training taught workers how to do it. Successful workers followed instructions: "You're not paid to think." Outcomes were predictable. Work was mechanical.

Today, workers apply knowledge to deliver services, often via networks. You can't see most of what they're doing, and their output is largely intangible. There's always a better way to do a job; learning stretches minds to cope with new situations. Successful knowledge workers are rewarded for innovation and ingenuity. These workers *are* paid to think. Change is rampant and unpredictable. Work is social.

Harold Jarche and Jay Cross at the Berlin Wall, talking about tearing down internal roadblocks to learning.

Unlike clockwork, this new net-work is a whole new space-time continuum. Results are not a function of time. When labor was manual, a great performer made 20% more widgets per hour than average; a poor performer, 20% less. Knowledge work is unpredictable, for its outputs are ideas and relationships.

A great performer may outperform the average a hundred-fold by re-inventing the business. The idea behind that re-invention may have occurred to its thinker in an instant.

Knowledge workers are often their own bosses. They manage their own time. Indeed, it's tough for a supervisor to tell when a knowledge worker is goofing off. Knowledge workers exercise their personal judgment continuously. An overseer would be a nuisance.

Knowledge workers need leaders, not managers. They need challenges, not detailed instructions. Indeed, knowledge workers resent being told what to do; they prefer being told what needs to be done. Because they are dealing with unpredictable conditions, their work is better driven by values than by rules.

Value has migrated from physical things to ideas. Thirty years ago, most of the value of publicly traded companies was vested in the tangible assets on the balance sheet, things you could see and touch, like cash, real estate, factories and equipment. Ten years later, 80% of the market value of corporations had migrated to intangibles, things like customer relationships, intellectual property, and know-how. Measurement systems that fail to take intangibles into account mistake what's easily measured for what's most important.

Progress along a career path once entailed building repertoire, that is, the skills to do the job. Increasingly, career development is a matter of becoming a professional. Professionals maintain standards, improve the practice of the profession, share worthy practices, and take pride in their work. It's not just a job.

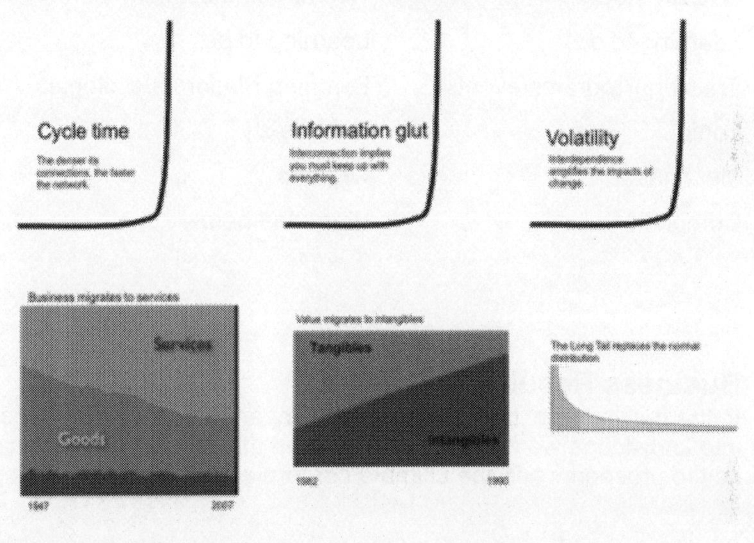

The belief that our ships are immobile, as if moored in concrete, is called learned helplessness. We see what we expect to see and are blind to possibilities beyond our expectations. Here are some eye-openers.

Old Mindset: The Age of Stuff	New Consciousness: Age of Connections
Clockwork world	Perception is reality
WYSIWYG, one reality	Many realities
“It is I.”	“We are all in this together.”
Belief in absolutes	Everything is relative
Some things are bedrock	Everything flows
People are nodes	People are connectors
World is clockwork	Time is in our heads
“We are nodes”	“We are connectors”
Learning to do	Learning to be
Training Programs/events	Learning Platforms/ecologies
Logic	Complexity
Mechanical	Organic
Completion	Perpetual beta

Business Results

In the network era, brains replace brawn, and most work evolves into knowledge work. Using your brain(s) effectively becomes the key to prosperity and the ultimate corporate survival skill.

In today's volatile, unpredictable times, brainpower and collective intelligence are the keys to corporate responsiveness and survival. While learning is ascendant, training is in decline, for workers are embracing self-service learning; they learn in the context of work, not at some training class divorced from work.

It is best to learn as we go, not go as we have learned.

Leslie Jeanne Sahler

We envision corporations where everyone is a teacher, the workplace is the classroom, performance on the job is the measure of success, and learning is the pathway to continuous improvement.

Embedding learning in work reduces overall spending while improving performance. Abandoning obsolete practices saves time and cuts costs. Relying on natural, peer-based learning improves business results.

Lower costs, greater return

Learning can be either push or pull. Push is the sort of learning you encountered in school, where authorities selected the curriculum and lessons were imposed on you. Pull describes the way you learn from Google or discovered how to kiss a lover. With pull learning, you select what you want to learn and how you want to learn it.

Pull learning is more cost-effective than push. It doesn't require as much in the way of control mechanisms, structure, and outside assistance. Furthermore, lessons learned through pull are more likely to stick because they're relevant to perceived need, delivered when required, and usually reinforced with immediate application. Pull learning delivers more bang for the buck.

Organizations that increase the ratio of pull learning to push learning can lower their overall investment in learning without sacrificing results. Given the greater payback of pull learning, the result is more return from smaller investment.

Isn't that what business is all about?

What can we do to improve this informal learning?

Managers accustomed to top-down control wring their hands at all this, saying it's not their job or there's nothing to be done or you just have to hire the right people in the first place. That's crazy talk. All kinds of interventions can improve the quality and quantity of informal learning, for instance:

Support the informal learning process:

- Provide time for informal learning on the job.
- Create useful, peer-rated FAQs and knowledge bases.
- Provide places for workers to congregate and learn.

- Supplement self-directed learning with mentors and experts.
- Set up help desks 24x7 for informal inquiries.
- Build networks, blogs, Wikis and knowledge bases to facilitate discovery.
- Use smart tech to make it easier to collaborate and network.
- Encourage cross-functional gatherings.

Help workers improve their learning skills:

- Explicitly teach workers how to learn.
- Support opportunities for meta-learning.
- Share ways others have learned subjects.
- Enlist learning coaches to encourage reflection.
- Calculate lifetime value of a learning "customer."
- Explain the know-who, know-how framework.

Create a supportive organizational culture:

- Set up a budget for informal learning. (There's no free lunch.)
- Don't confuse "informal" with "random" or "optional."
- Publish a statement of support for informal learning.
- Position learning as a growth experience.
- Conduct a learning culture audit.
- Add learning and teaching goals to job descriptions.
- Consider all-in cost of turnover and of not growing your own.
- Support innovation (which requires making failure "OK").
- Encourage learning relationships.
- Support participation in professional communities of practice.

Techniques and Patterns

Most training professionals consider instructional design the bedrock of instruction. Some go so far as to suggest that without instructional design, learning cannot take place.

Instructional design was invented around the time of World War II. Starting virtually from scratch, America had to train millions of men to be soldiers and millions of civilians to make ships and armaments. The training film was born, soon to be followed with the ADDIE model. ADDIE (analyze, design, develop, implement & evaluate) made it possible to manage the process of creating useful training programs.

Instructional purists still revere the logic of ADDIE. (It's hard to argue with the concept of planning your work, then working your plan.) But the weaknesses of ADDIE are becoming apparent:

- Training is only part of the learning equation.
- Training is generally imposed on people. Whether of not they learn is an entirely different matter.
- Learning requires motivation. (You can lead a boy to college but you can't make him think.)
- ADDIE invariably points to training as the solution.

Sometimes it's more effective to imbed the knowledge in the work than to plant it in the head of the worker.

Modern instructional design needs to focus on creating **flexible environments** that nurture learning **rather than rigid programs** that attempt to force lessons into the heads of learners.

> Give a man a fish, feed him for a day. Teach a man to fish, feed him for a lifetime.
>
> Chinese Proverb

Old-style training enraged many managers because it was separate from work. Why isn't Sally at work today? Because she's in training.

It needn't be this way, particularly since knowledge work and learning are nearly indistinguishable. Most corporate learning today can take place simultaneously with work. I call the platform where learning and work transpire a *workscape.* A major part of modern instructional design is actually *workscape design*.

Workscape designers, like landscape designers, start with the existing environment. They assess what's given, imagine a more harmonious arrangement, and prescribe additions and adjustments to accomplish it. By contrast, instructional designers are accustomed to building new programs from the ground up, like architects who begin by chopping down trees and leveling contours so they can plan from a blank sheet of paper.

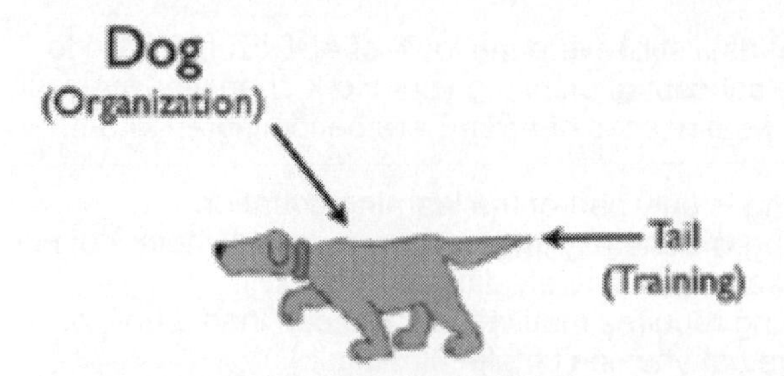

Industrial age workers created value in factories. Knowledge workers create value in workscapes. A workscape is a platform where knowledge workers collaborate, solve problems, converse, share ideas, brainstorm, learn, relate to others, talk, explain, communicate, conceptualize, tell stories, help one another, teach, serve customers, keep up to date, meet one another, forge partnerships, build communities, and distribute information.

In most cases, the knowledge work pays the freight; the informal learning comes along for the ride. If an organization is committed to Microsoft Sharepoint, IBM Lotus, or another proprietary solution for in-house communication and project management, the workscape designer will do best by tweaking that platform for optimal learning rather than trying to replace it.

An online workscape is a network tuned for learning and collaboration.

A typical workscape features these components:

- Participant profiles, expertise locators
- Information flows, feeds, subscriptions
- Information repository, archives, search engine
- Forums for written discussion by topics or by teams
- Facility for online discussion, instant messaging, video conferencing
- Unfettered access to the resources of the internet

Our current work involves figuring out how to inject best practices from adult learning theory, brain science, social psychology, business execution, and elsewhere into workscapes.

Reflection

Deep learning takes reflection. Every time you learn something, make a connection to something you already know. After attending any event, I give myself time to look over my notes, to write and to draw mind maps. Friends who took 6 a.m. flights to get back to the office won't retain nearly as much as I will.

Staying out with the same crowd all the time limits innovation and encourages groupthink. To learn new things, leave your comfort zone and sample new disciplines and cultures. Use the Web to read other countries' newspapers, other professions' journals and other people's blogs.

Imagine that your field of work is a spinning disk. Things at the center move very slowly. Innovation resides at the periphery, far from that slow, established core. The edge is where your work interacts with that of others. You've got to be edgy if you seek fresh perspective.

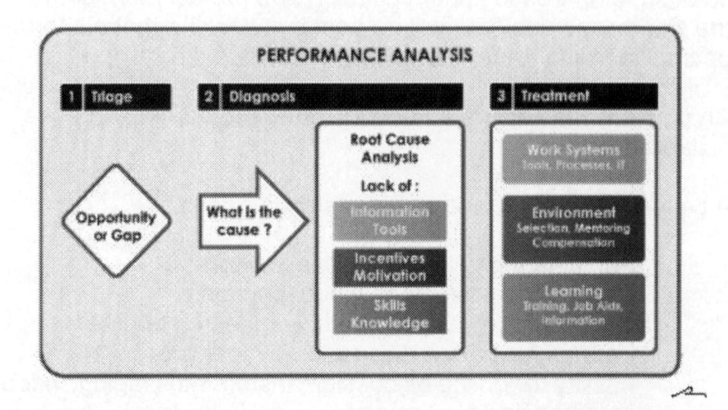

A learning pattern language

Getting things done with knowledge workers involves figuring out what you want to accomplish, collaborating with others to develop a concept, getting people on board, and proceeding holistically. This is tricky. There's no cookbook. It's not step-by-step. And your case is different from the next person's.

Because every organization is different, same-size-fits-all approaches aren't ideal for designing workscapes. A more sound approach is to mix and match components that have worked well in a variety of situations in the past to assemble up hybrid models to try on for size. Just as words can be used to create an endless variety of sentences, standard elements can be reconfigured to create very personalized workscapes. Renegade architect Christopher Alexander calls these timeless elements patterns, and we'll do the same.

Patterns are rules of thumb. Some are quite specific; others are general. A pattern describes a situation, a way of dealing with it, and a story to illustrate its application. Patterns come on many levels, from enterprise strategic intent and long-term perspective, through values like trust in workers or openness to change, to infrastructure issues such as full internet access and offering places to meet, to practical aspects of sharing stories and using collaborative software, and eventually down to common sense things like learning from one's mistakes.

Successful social learning patterns include:

- Wrapping informal learning around existing courses and workshops to improve results. Use the beginning-middle-end model, treating the formal learning as the middle element.
- Replacing instructor-led training with self-service learning. Self-service requires support to work...
- Embedding knowledge in the work via performance support to eliminate learning altogether except for learning where to find things. Often this involves replacing memorization with search of wikis, FAQs, and information repositories.
- Shift the roles of instructor and tutor to peers, colleagues, and partners.
- Share news and discoveries with others, filter the results, and cut back on the wasted effort of unguided exploration.
- Enlist a community's eyes and ears.

Here are some concrete examples of successful learning patterns:

Intel set up an organization-wide wiki for sharing information. Intelpedia runs on free, open-source software. More than 20,000 employees use it, saving more than $20 million annually by finding information fast.

T. Rowe Price put together a simple FAQ to help 1,500 seasonal tax preparers assist customers calling in for advice. This simple look-up service shaved 10% off average call time, saving $3 million in salary cost while improving accuracy and customer service.

SAP set up the SAP Developer Network now used by 1,000,000 customers to get answers to technical questions. Most queries are answered by consultants and customers vying for recognition rather than SAP employees. In addition to more than $50 million in salary savings, questions fielded by outsiders are answered more rapidly and accurately than when only SAP employees were involved.

4,000 consultants at **CGI Systems** now receive news and updates in their professional area from feeds directed to their inbox. Replacing thousands of scattered, individual efforts to keep up to date with shared information flows frees up more than $10 million in billable hours annually.

Sun Microsystems used eLearning, applied case studies, and guided experience to cut time-to-quota performance for new-hire sales people from fifteen months to six months, an increase of $3.5 billion in revenue.

U.S. Army company commanders set up blogs to share ground-level information on battlefield tactics, cutting out the Department of the Army middleman to share fresh information in hours instead of months.

(See the chapter on examples for more cases.)

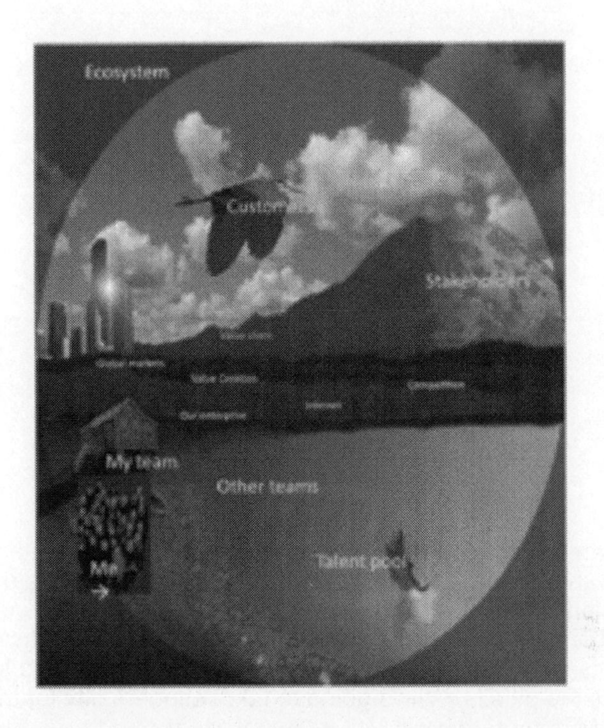

Issues
The web enables the many to wrest power from the few and helps them not only change the world but change the way the world changes. The cover of Time magazine ran a picture of a computer monitor filled with one word: You. The text underneath read, "Yes, you. You control the Information Age Welcome to your world." This is hardly the first instance of Time oversimplifying things.

There's a speed bump on the road to your world: **THEM.**

The Obstacle

They are skeptical. They fear that no matter how well-intentioned and enthusiastic its fans, this web 2.0 stuff can wait. It is a diversion from the core mission. It might backfire. It's disruptive. The ROI's not there. We need to plan first. We have to assign responsibility. We have to put controls in place. We need to assess the pitfalls. Who's going to take responsibility for this stuff? Murphy's Law will kick in. Ad infinitum.

The two-letter acronym that summarizes these arguments is **BS**. To win them over to your cause, you may want to be less direct.

"Where absolute superiority is not attainable, you must produce a relative one at the decision point by making skillful use of what you have."
Karl von Clausewisz (On War, 1832)

“We don’t have enough time.”

Human brains have not changed much in the past 20,000 years. On the savannah, evolution favored hunters who could make snap decisions. Thinking long-term didn’t matter when people lacked the language to plan ahead, the average lifespan was under 20, and all of humanity didn’t leave a carbon toe-print. Times have changed but brains have not.

Two out of three organizations tell me “Our organization is slow to change, even when it would be in our best interest.”

“He’s too busy chopping down trees to stop and sharpen his axe” exemplifies the folly of short-term thinking. You cannot postpone the inevitable. “I don’t have enough time” is a statement of priorities, not a description of the availability of time.

What’s holding us back?

Business has already squeezed the big process improvements out of its industrial systems. For many companies, the benefits of collaboration and networking are virgin territory. The upside potential is staggering: people innovating, sharing, supporting one another, all naturally and without barriers. The traditional approach has been to automate routine tasks in order to reduce cost; the new vision is to empower people to take advantage of their innate desire to share and learn.

Web 2.0, the “collaborative web,” makes file cabinets and hard drives overflowing with email obsolete. Members of a group can share information and make improvements to one copy that’s virtually available to everyone. Workers learn to remix rather than re-invent, and having everyone read from the same page overcomes the danger of mistaking obsolete information for current. Distance no longer keeps workers apart. As we remove obstacles, the time required to do anything shrivels up.

What counts

Businesses exist to create value, and the source of value resides outside the learning function. As Peter Drucker has pointed out, "Neither results nor resources exist inside the business. Both exist outside. The customer is the business."

Try to imagine a business without customers, perhaps an

insurance company on a desert island or a manufacturer that never ships. No value, right? What goes on inside an organization is just rearranging the furniture.

Training directors bemoan not being able to demonstrate significant business results. If they remain entirely within the training function, they never will, because they don't own the yardstick that measures business results. Who owns that yardstick? Generally, it's training's sponsor, the person with authority to sign off on large expenditures. This is usually a company officer who can weigh the potential returns and costs of various investments and select those likely to create the highest net value. Since the sponsor decides the economic fate of training programs, it's worthwhile to contemplate how sponsors typically make decisions.

All business decisions are relative. When assessing value, where you stand depends on where you sit. A training director may measure success in terms of lower costs and more workshops. A line manager is concerned with quarterly targets or higher revenue. A senior executive focuses on organizational flexibility and competitive advantage.

Business leaders present themselves to the world as confident, authoritative, conservative, results-oriented, deliberate, and a bit staid. It's best to leave your clown suit in the closet when you're selling a concept to executives. Be concise. When you've said your piece, ask for questions and sit down.

Managerial decision-making is generally more subjective than people recognize. ROI is often a hurdle or a means to focus preliminary cost-benefit analysis to screen out clear losers. When the time comes to make choices, gut feeling and good judgment often win out over formulas.

Training directors sometimes claim that pinpointing training outcomes is impossible because so many other things muddy the results. It is a weak argument. All business decisions are made with less-than-complete information. Waiting for "enough" information often means ceding thought leadership to the competition.

Sponsors don't usually back a project unless its economics are so compelling that they can do the math on the back of an envelope. If the odds are good that I'll get $750,000 in benefits from my $75,000 investment, I don't need four-place accuracy to decide to spend the money. This is business, not a science experiment. As a Fortune 50 company official recently told me, "We manage this place with sound bites."

What if the benefits of your proposal are not obviously compelling? Pick another project. Executives are single-minded. They care about one thing: execution. They do not start from the assumption that training is the answer. They refer to people as "customers," "employees" and "workers." (We are the only ones who call them "learners.")

Not long ago I was addressing the division training managers at a top high-tech company. I suggested they work with their sponsors to identify business requirements and gain their agreement in writing on what would constitute success or failure in a training post-mortem. To my amazement and disappointment, many of the training managers rebelled. "To do what you're asking," they said, "we'd have to understand the business." Well, duh. That was precisely what I was saying.

The way to get funding, to make significant contributions, to be recognized by management, to be promoted and to reduce the stress in your life is to make business metrics your yardstick for success and describe what you do in business terms. Here are a few examples to think about:

- Make sales force productive sooner.
- Implement strategic initiatives.
- Educate customers online.
- Increase reach into new markets.
- Decrease staff turnover.
- Reduce cycle time.
- Roll out enterprise processes.

- Speed up time-to-market.
- Keep partners in sync.
- Merge organizations effectively.

Getting Started

Traditionally, taking a holistic view of boosting brainpower falls through an organization's cracks. Nobody has been responsible for improving brainpower overall. Hence, there's plenty of low-hanging fruit, ripe for the picking. The returns from systematic workscaping are enormous.

Let's take a look at the basics of informal learning.

Jay Cross & Jane Hart

Informal Learning

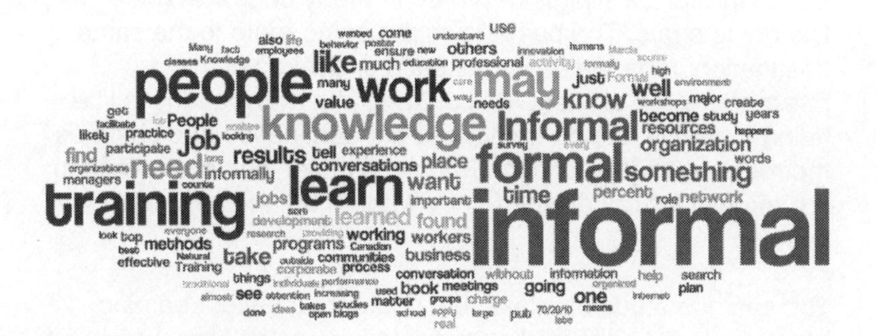

Johnny Appleseed

In the five years since the publication of Informal Learning, Jay's become the Johnny Appleseed of informal learning; he's a true believer. He didn't invent the concept. Far from it. Informal learning is older than civilization itself. His contribution has been pointing out that over-emphasis of formal learning in organizations is dysfunctional, uneconomic, bad business, and not a whole lot of fun.

Formal learning is characterized by a curriculum, i.e. content chosen by someone other than the learner. Delivered in courses or workshops or semesters or degree programs, episodes of informal learning always come to an end (although learning itself never ends.) The "completion" of a formal learning experience is generally celebrated by awarding a grade, certificate, degree, checkmark in an LMS, or other symbol.

Often, formal learning is delivered to many people at once. It's like riding a bus. The bus follows the same route to the same destination, regardless of the needs or desires of the passengers. It's efficient. By contrast, informal learning is like riding a bicycle: the rider chooses her destination and changes the route when it feels right. People who set their own direction are more likely to get where they want to be and enjoy the journey.

You can ride a bus or a bike, but not both at once. Learning, however, is not either/o. Learning is always part formal and part informal. Learning always has formal elements (a common language, shared context, fundamentals, the bedrock of culture). All learning has informal aspects (we learn "out of class," learning is social, the learner accepts or rejects what's presented formally.)

Learning is a continuum of degrees of formality. The challenge is choosing among shades of gray. People who tell me informal (or formal) learning is bad oversimplify reality; I call their thinking *bipolar*.

Jay debating the substance of informal learning at the Oxford Union, October 2010.

Permit me to answer the critics of informal learning (usually people who confuse learning and schooling).

> Question: How do we know that informal learning works?
> Answer: How did you learn to walk, to talk, to kiss a sweetheart, to be productive in society?
>
> Question: Isn't this informal learning simply an erosion of discipline and control?
> Answer: Informal means unbounded, not haphazard. It's a better way to work. If you have high expectations of people, they live up to them. Management control is largely fiction anyway.
>
> Question: What's the ROI? We're not going to do this without proof.
> Answer: Hold on. Informal learning is already the primary way your people learn their jobs. I'm suggesting that by paying attention, you can make what's going on more productive.
>
> Question: Where is the evidence that 80% of job learning is informal?
> Answer: Multiple reputable studies (see below) have come up with the 80% figure. Of course this varies by the nature of the job. More importantly, the studies predate the web. In our world of social networks and collaboration software, I'm confident the number has risen much higher than 80%.

Formal learning is ideal for novices. People without a framework and vocabulary for dealing with an area that is foreign to them can learn a lot from a formal tour. Courses and workshops are a great way to save time and avoid aimless wandering. Imagine trying to master mathematics or chemistry by hanging out around the water cooler. Better to dip into the wisdom of the ages.

Formal learning doesn't work so well for accomplished practitioners. Once people have a mental tapestry for how things work, they are looking to fill in holes in their knowledge. They want to learn what they need to know to get something done. Taking a course to learn one small item is a waste of time and an insult to a practitioner's prior learning.

By the way, this is what's behind the "informal learning paradox," the fact that corporations invest most heavily in formal learning while workers learn mostly through informal means. Corporate training focuses on novices. It's school. Schools neglect alumni; training departments neglect the experienced people, those who generate the profits.

Once upon a time, people were paid to follow instructions. We thought we could train them to do their jobs. Work is now more like improv theater. Workers have to solve problems on they fly. They confront situations no one has encountered before. They don't have the luxury of waiting to be trained; they must perform on the spot. And the only way they can keep up is by learning for themselves. Learning has become the work.

Instructional designers used to design programs. Today they need to invest in building learning environments that enable workers to take learning into their own hands.

Workers inevitably learn more in the coffee room than in the classroom.

They discover how to do their jobs through informal learning – asking the person in the next cubicle, trial-and-error, calling the help desk, working with people in the know, and joining the conversation. This is natural learning: you learn from other people when you need to be able to do something.

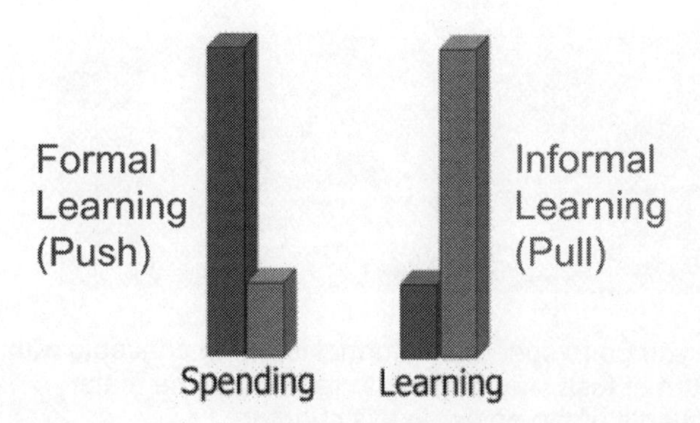

Training programs, workshops, and schools get the lion's share of the corporate budget for developing talent, despite the fact that this formal learning has almost no impact on job performance. Informal learning, the major source of knowledge transfer and innovation, is left to chance.

This chapter aims to raise your consciousness about informal learning. Learning is that which enables you to participate successfully in life, at work and in the groups that matter to you. You can't live without it.

The Informal Learning Poster

In late 2006, Pfeiffer published Jay's book, *Informal Learning: Rediscovering the Natural Pathways That Inspire Innovation and Performance*.

In league with James Macanufo at XPLANE | the visual thinking company, Jay designed a companion poster to accompany the book. Pfeiffer chose not to print it, aside from a fragment on the cover and a few outtakes.

You can see the entire poster online by clicking the image that looks like this on jaycross.com:

To get you up to speed on informal learning concepts with a minimum of fuss, Jay is going to reproduce the major components of the poster in this chapter.

INFORMAL

Informal learning is the unofficial, unscheduled, impromptu way people learn to do their jobs. Learning is adaptation. Taking advantage of the double meaning of the word network, to learn is to optimize the quality of one's networks. We learn from one another.

INFORMAL LEARNING

Learning is that which enables you to participate successfully in life, at work, and in the groups that matter to you. Informal learning is the unofficial, unscheduled, impromptu way people learn to do their jobs. Formal learning is like riding a bus: the driver decides where the bus is going; the passengers are along for the ride. Informal learning is like riding a bike: the rider chooses the destination, the speed, and the route. The rider can take a detour at a moment's notice to admire the scenery or go to the bathroom. Learning is adaptation. Taking advantage of the double meaning of the word *network,* to learn is to optimize the quality of one's networks.

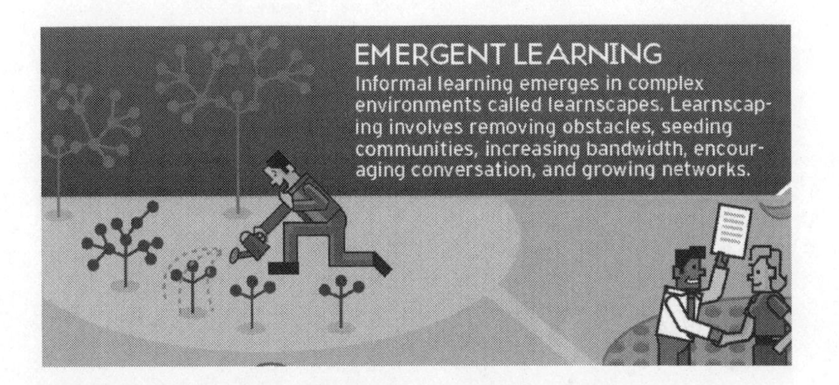

EMERGENCE

Training is something that's pushed on you; someone else is in charge. Learning is something you choose to do, whether you're being trained or not. You're in charge. Many knowledge workers will tell you, "I love to learn but I hate to be trained."

Formal learning takes place in classrooms; informal learning happens in workscapes, that is, a learning ecology. It's learning without borders.

Critics say that it's impossible to formalize informal learning and therefore informal learning is unmanageable. In fact, we don't want an executive managing learning; that's the worker's responsibility. What we want to do is optimize learning outcomes. Optimization means removing obstacles, seeding communities, increasing bandwidth, encouraging conversation, and so forth.

CONVERSATION

Conversations both create and transmit knowledge. Frequent and open conversation increases innovation and learning. Schooling planted a false notion in our heads that real learning is something you do on your own. In fact, we learn things from other people. People love to talk. Bringing them together brings excitement.

People spend most of their time at work or at home. Work is a demanding, pressure-packed, rats-in-the-maze race with the clock to get the job done. Home is a comfortable, private space for sharing time with family and individual interests. Neither work nor home, a World Café is a neutral spot where people come together to offer hospitality, enjoy comradeship, welcome diverse perspectives, and have meaningful conversations.

At Pfizer, people were so polite to one another that they avoided controversy. Conversations retreated behind closed doors. They learned to assess the motive of conversations in terms of our built-in fight or flight response. Everyone was given the right to question a response.

Business conversations at Pfizer have become forthright and open, because people have a means of critiquing the quality of their conversations. They ask, "Is the information valid? Are we making an informed choice? Are we exercising mutual control over the conversation? Or are we fighting or fleeing?"

Informal learning is like riding a bicycle: the rider chooses the destination, the speed, and the route. The rider can take a detour at a moment's notice, to admire the scenery or to help a fellow rider.

COMMUNITIES
Unless you are a hermit, you are a member of several communities of practice, although you may not have thought of it that way. Plumbers, programmers, and pastry chefs gather together to create and pass on the rules of thumb of their trade.

COMMUNITIES

Unless you are a hermit, you are a member of several communities of practice, although you may not have thought of it that way.

For a long time, I maintained that communities were organic. Like truffles, they sort of sprouted up on their own, where they wanted, and the most you could do was to nurture them by providing time and space for them to meet. Times have changed. A quarter of the world's truffles are cultivated on a plantation in Spain.

Cultivation is an apt metaphor for encouraging communities. Clark Quinn writes that the community gardener's task is to seed, feed, and weed.

Seed: you need to put in place the network tool, where individuals can register, and then create the types of connections they need. They may self-organize around roles, or tasks, or projects, or all of the above. They may need discussion forums, blogs, wikis, and IM. They may need to load, tag, and search on resources. You likely will need to preload it with resources, to ensure there's value to be found. And you'll have to ensure that there are rewards for participating and contributing. The environment needs to be there, and they have to be aware.

Feed: you can't just put in place, you have to nurture the network. People have to know what the goals are and their role. Don't tell them what to do, tell them what needs doing. You may need to quietly 'encourage' the opinion makers to participate. And the top of the food chain needs to not only anoint the process, but model the behavior as well. The top level of the group (i.e. not the CEO, but the leader of whatever group you've chosen to facilitate) needs to be active in the network. You may need to highlight what other people have said, elicit questions and answers, and take a role both within and outside the network to get it going. You may have to go in and reorganize the resources, take what's heard and make it concrete and usable. You'll undoubtedly have to facilitate the skills to take advantage of the environment. And you have to ensure there's value there for them.

Weed: you may have to help people learn how to participate. You may well find some inappropriate behavior, and help those learn what's acceptable. You'll likely have to develop, and modify, policies and procedures. You may have to take out some submitted resources and revise them for better usability. You may well have to address cultural issues that arise, when you find that participation is stunted by a lack of tolerance of diversity, no openness to new ideas, no safety for putting ideas out, and other factors that facilitate a learning organization.

As fast and easy as it is to search Google, Cisco sales engineers can pinpoint just the knowledge they're looking for. They query the in-house repository of VoDs, and the system takes them down to the exact sentences or slides of interest.

LEGO hobbyists are a community of practice. Subgroups create building standards that enable them to create large displays quickly.

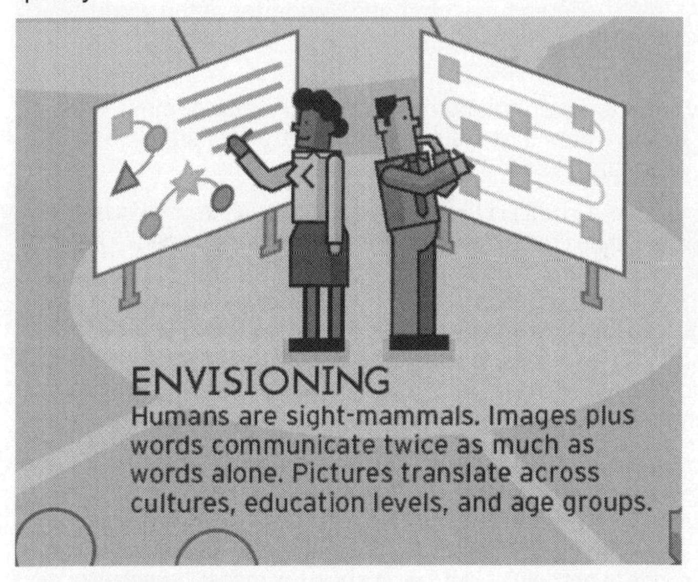

ENVISIONING

We humans are sight mammals. We learn almost twice as well from images and words as from words alone. Visual language engages both hemispheres of the brain. Pictures translate across cultures, education levels, and age groups. Yet the majority of the content of corporate learning is text. Schools spend years on verbal literacy but only hours on visual literacy. It's high time for us to open our eyes to the possibilities.

Graphics are not fluff. Consider how they can improve informal learning throughout your organization. Graphics work wonders when you need to:

- Bring deeper understanding to complex subject matter.

- Share results of dynamic meetings with others.
- Help the team see the big picture and focus attention.
- Improve the decision-making process.

UNCONFERENCES

Business meetings used to come in one flavor: dull. New approaches are creating meetings that people enjoy, often organized in scant time, and at minimal cost. These meetings are not events; there's typically activity before and after. If something is working well, why not share it with everyone? And why not keep it alive as long as you can? Successful gatherings are those where everyone participates.

There were no presentations at the first BAR Camp, no PowerPoints, no better-than-thou, no podium, and no positions carved in stone. Instead of presentations, campers had conversations. We were equals, co-discovering new ways to look at things. We sat in circles. No one was in charge because we were all in charge.

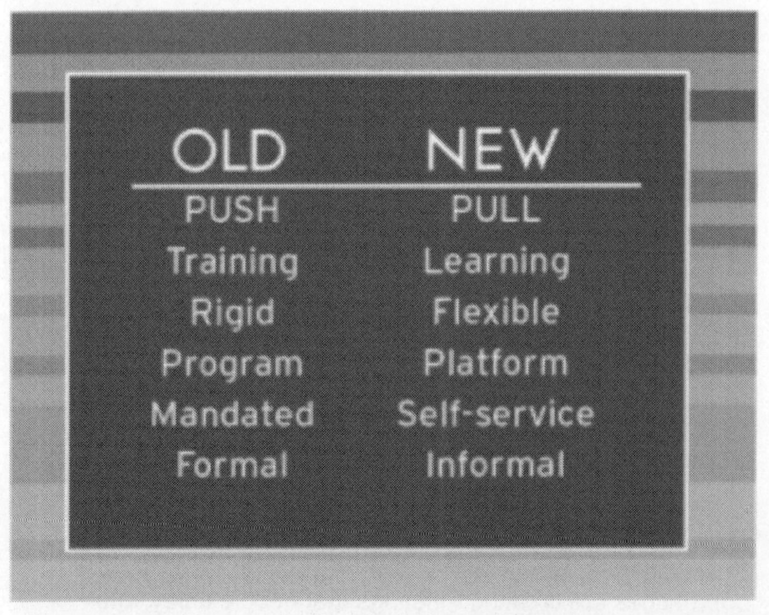
OLD
NEW
PUSH
PULL
Training
Learning
Rigid
Flexible
Program
Platform
Mandated
Self-service
Formal
Informal

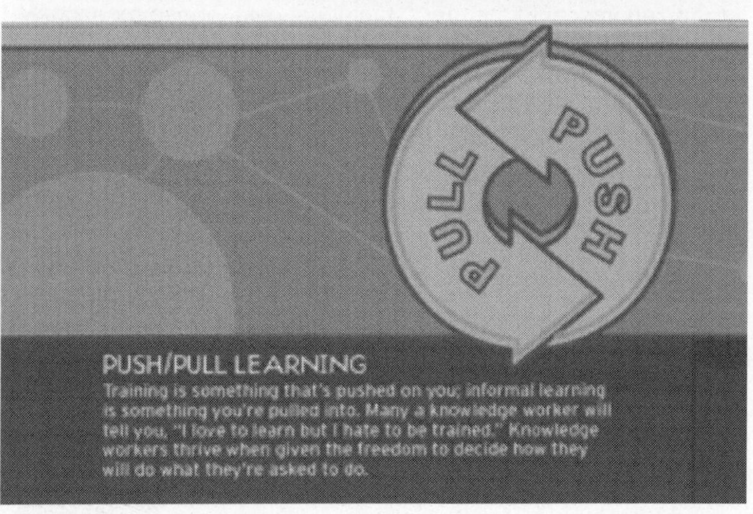
PULL
PUSH
PUSH/PULL LEARNING
Training is something that's pushed on you; informal learning is something you're pulled into. Many a knowledge worker will tell you, "I love to learn but I hate to be trained." Knowledge workers thrive when given the freedom to decide how they will do what they're asked to do.

INTERNET INSIDE
Imagine having an in-house learning and information environment as rich as the internet. You'd have blogs and search and syndication and podcasts and more. You'd also have a platform everyone already knows how to use.
ORGANIZATIONAL ANALYSIS
The informal organization does most of the work, but managers overlook it because they can't see it. Mapping the social network brings the shadow organization into the light.

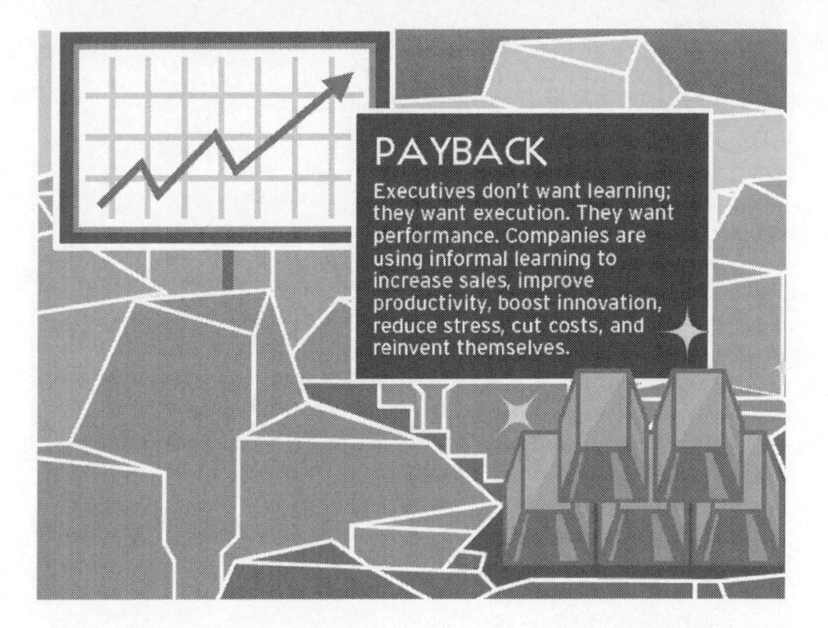

SHOW ME THE MONEY

Executives don't want learning; they want execution. They want the job done. They want performance. Informal learning is a profit strategy. Companies are applying it to:

• Increase sales by making product knowledge instantly searchable
• Improve knowledge worker productivity
• Transform an organization from near-bankruptcy to record profits
• Generate fresh ideas and increase innovation
• Reduce stress, absenteeism, and health care costs
• Invest development resources where they will have the most impact
• Increase professionalism and professional growth
• Cut costs and improve responsiveness with self-service learning

Knowledge workers demand respect and expect to be treated fairly. They thrive when given the freedom to decide how they will do what they're asked to do. They rise or fall to meet expectations.

Training managers have complained for years that senior managers don't understand the value of training. Lots of formal learning programs do not work. Maybe the executives *do* understand the value of formal training. They've determined that in its present form, it's not worth much.

Tragically, many firms have mistaken measuring activity for measuring results. Training directors measure participant satisfaction, the ability to pass tests, and demonstrations. They don't measure business results because they don't own the yardstick by which business results are measured.

Summary of Informal Learning

Appendix A of the book is a cheat-sheet. It puts informal learning in nutshell. I advise readers to start there and then to cherry-pick topics that interest them.

WORKERS LEARN MORE in the coffee room than in the classroom. They discover how to do their jobs through informal learning: talking, observing others, trial-and-error, and simply working with people in the know. Formal learning—classes and workshops—is the source of only 10 to 20 percent of what people learn at work. Corporations over-invest in formal training programs while neglecting natural, simpler informal processes.

OUT OF TIME

More happens in a minute today than in one of your great grandmother's minutes. Not only is more and more activity packed into every minute, the rate of change itself is increasing. Measured by the atomic clock, the twenty-first century will contain a hundred years. Measured by how much will happen in the twenty-first century, we will experience twenty thousand current years (Kurzweil, *The singularity is near: When humans transcend biology.*). Change itself is accelerating. People are anxious. The future is unpredictable. Companies are run by sound bites. People plan; God laughs. The traditional mode of training employees is obsolete.

CONNECTING

Reinventing the wheel, looking for information in the wrong places, and answering questions from peers consume two-thirds of the average knowledge worker's day. Slashing this waste provides a lot more time to devote to improving the business, reducing payroll, or, more likely, a bit of both.

Knowledge management is no longer the intellectual high ground it once was, by and large because it didn't work. Knowledge lives in people's heads, not in mere words. You can no more capture true knowledge in a repository than you can trap lightning in a box.

The informal organization is how most business gets done, yet executives miss it because they can't see it. Mapping social networks make the pattern clear.
It's not who you know that's important; it's who those others know.

META-LEARNING

Learning is a skill, like playing golf. The more you practice, the better your performance is, but if golfers followed the pattern of businesspeople learning, they would arrive for a match without ever having thought about the game or touched a club.

Many traditional training departments concentrate almost all of their energy on providing training to novices. That's like providing kindergarten classes to high school students to save money. In truth, the more mature learners, typically the top performers, are simply going to skip it entirely or become disgruntled.

Intuition is often more effective than logic because it calls on whole-body intelligence. It is born of relationships and patterns. It draws on the power of the unconscious mind to sort through meaningful experience as well as the immediate situation.

LEARNERS

If something improves the overall value of the ecosystem and the welfare of the individual worker, I'm in favor of it. This includes helping workers build personal strengths and overcome personal obstacles.

If your basic mental systems are out of whack, you may be working extra hard just to cope.

It should come as no surprise that workers don't like training. Most training is built atop the pessimistic assumption that trainees are deficient, and training is the cure for what's broken. Everybody wins if the starting point is, "Be all that you can be."

You may have the best thoughts in the world, but if you don't communicate them effectively, they won't help you or anyone else. I'm thinking about how you converse, tell stories, speak in public, and write.

If you're not happy, you should do something about it.

UNBLENDED

It has become trite to point out that the *e* of eLearning doesn't matter and that it's the learning that counts. I don't think the learning counts for much either. What's important is the doing that results from learning. Executives don't care about learning; they care about execution.

In 2001, training directors turned their attention to return on investment. Unfortunately, instead of learning cost-benefit analysis, people who wanted to speak the language of business studied accounting. Created long before knowledge work was invented, accounting values intangibles such as human capital at zero and counts training as an expense instead of an investment.

Consider how we managed to end up with a VCR in every classroom. Was it because teachers wanted to show nature documentaries? Hardly. Massive demand by America's seemingly endless thirst for pornography drove the unit price to $100. Smart phones, voice recognition, and virtual reality are learning tools, but learning won't drive their development. Courses are dead.

THE WEB

The Internet changed everything. In 1996, there were 16 million Internet users; in 2006 they number more than 1 billion. Google is the largest learning provider, answering thousands of inquiries every second.

Recently, I hosted a series of unworkshops on learning with blogs, wikis, and Web 2.0 tools. Why the *un*? To crush the old paradigm of workshop leader spoon-feeding participants.

Imagine having an in-house learning and information environment as rich as the Internet. You'd have blogs, search, syndication, podcasts, mash-ups, and more. You'd also have a platform just about everyone already knows how to use. CGI, a large Canadian services company is doing precisely that.

GROKKING

To *grok* is to understand profoundly through intuition or empathy.

Learning without training is alive and well. BP employees in vital positions grok their roles in an extremely complex organization digesting several mega-mergers.

JUST DO IT

Management must assign enterprise-level accountability for learning. Unless you are blessed with a rare, sensitive executive management team, you must address governance or scrap plans of getting the benefits you've been reading about.

Natural learning requires an attitude of surrender and acceptance. Informal learning is unbounded. It enables us to find a voice to take its place alongside other parts of who we are as humans. We need all of who we are to be fully engaged, outside and with inner realms to meld with larger wisdom in the world.

As work and learning become one, good learning and good work become synonymous.

Don't start with problems. Beginning with problems starts you off on the wrong path. You may solve the problem but miss a fantastic opportunity that was yours for the taking

You can find a lot more where that came from in the book *Informal Learning, Rediscovering the Natural Pathways that Inspire Innovation and Performance*. It's available on Amazon or from internettime.com.

Also, take a look at the articles and video about informal learning that appear on Jay's site (http://jaycross.com) and on the Informal Learning Blog (http://informl.com). I also recommend Marcia Conner's website (http://marciaconner.com) for an astute analysis of informal, formal, and non-formal learning.

The boss is in charge
Change is incremental
If it ain't broke, don't fix it
Fundamentals still rule
People are self-centered
What get measured gets managed
Could never sell this idea to our bosses
Back to basics
Show me proof

All of us are smarter than any of us
Traditional training dated, ineffective
Complex adaptive systems; stuff happe
Everything flows, all is relative
People are honest, seek to excel
Progress is exponential
Asymmetrical results
Controlling people is an illusion
Excited by the possibilities

Everything is rooted in a life cycle. It's young or old, evolving or dying.

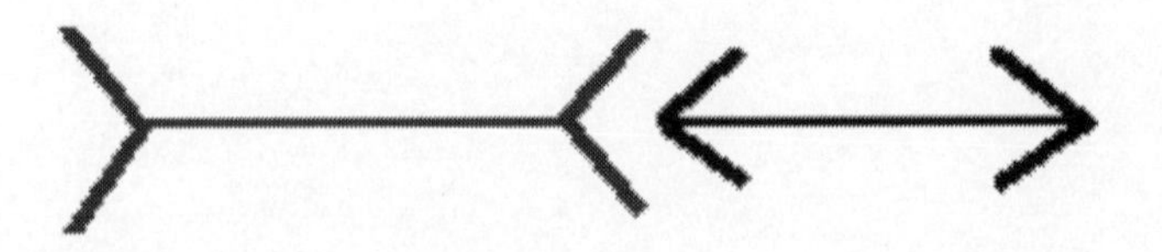

Where did the 80% come from?

Several hundred people have asked me for the source of the 80/20 ratio of formal to informal. A fair number of them are belligerent, starting out with "There is no proof..." or "This is an old wives' tale." Here's what I tell them:

I first heard that 80% of corporate learning is informal in a presentation in late 2001 by the late Peter Henschel, then Executive Director of the Institute for Research on Learning. IRL used an anthropological approach to research that enabled them to see things others were missing. Other studies, as noted below, confirm IRL's basic finding.
A word of caution is in order here. Some studies say 70%, others 80%, and some even 90%. Why? For one thing, informal learning has many definitions. Furthermore, the ratio of informal to formal learning varies with context. Learning to ride a bicycle involves a higher proportion of informal learning than learning to fly a plane. Most of us learned to use chopsticks informally but learned algebra formally.

• Marcia Conner (2005) writes that "Most learning doesn't occur in formal training programs. It happens through processes not structured or sponsored by an employer or a school. Informal learning accounts for over 75% of the learning taking place in organizations today." Marcia also notes, "In 1996, the Bureau of Labor Statistics reported that people learn 70% of what they know about their jobs informally."

• Many organizations report that 85-90% of a person's job knowledge is learned on the job and only 10-15% is learned in formal training events. (Raybould, 2000)

• In 1997, the Education Development Center, Inc., a Newton, Massachusetts-based research organization, released findings from a two-year study of corporate cultures involving Boeing, Ford Electronics, Siemens, and Motorola. One of the most noteworthy findings of the study is support for estimates from previous studies that "attempted to quantify formal training's contribution to overall job knowledge: 70 percent of what people know about their jobs, they learn informally from the people they work with." (Dobbs, 2000, pp. 52, 54)

• "Not only do employee learning programs based on informal

methods and self-study increase employee knowledge and productivity far more than more formalized methods, they also cost less, according to preliminary research by CapitalWorks LLC, a human capital management service in Williamstown, Mass. Approximately 75 percent of the skills employees use on the job were learned informally, the study found, through discussions with coworkers, asynchronous self-study (such as e-mail-based coursework), mentoring by managers and supervisors and similar methods. Only 25 percent were gained from formal training methods such as workshops, seminars and synchronous classes." (Lloyd, 2000)

• Approximately 70% of Canadians say that their most important job-related knowledge comes from other workers or learning on their own rather than employment-related courses. The National Research Network on New Approaches to Lifelong Learning (NALL) at OISE/UT surveyed 1500 Canadian adults on informal learning. Principal investigator David Livingstone, summarized the results as follows, "The major conclusion from this survey is that our organized systems of schooling and continuing education and training are like big ships floating in a sea of informal learning. If these education and training ships do not pay increasing attention to the massive amount of outside informal learning, many of them are likely to sink into Titanic irrelevancy." (Vader, 1998)

• In January 2005, an eLearning Guild survey of its members and found that "Over 70% of respondents found or sought information on their own initiative.... These results truly put more shape and depth to the 80 / 20 rule. Not only does it confirm the significant frequency of informal learning, it demonstrates that informal learning shows up in many ways: e-Learning, traditional book study, social learning, and experience."

• Canadian researcher Allen Tough, at a presentation at Ontario Institute for Studies in Education of the University of Toronto in 1999, said, "Another finding was that we were looking at all learning efforts, including 'professionally planned' or 'academic or institutional' or whatever you want to call them; formal. We found a 20/80% split. We found about 20 percent of all major learning efforts were institutionally organized, or it was like a driving school instructor or piano instructor, something like that. It was one-to-one, but it was still somebody you paid to teach you, so it was a professional formal situation. And the other 80% was informal. We didn't know what to call it. So we called it 'professional plan' and 'amateur plan', amateur being a positive word, not a put-down. That's when I came up with this idea of the iceberg as a metaphor, because so much of it is invisible, because we were surprised to find so much adult learning is sort of under the surface of the ocean as it were. You just don't see it. You could forget it's there unless you keep reminding yourself that it's there."

Princeton University Learning Philosophy

To ensure that *real* learning takes place and endures, we emphasize and encourage a holistic approach by integrating both formal and informal elements. We believe that the most effective way to learn and develop a new skill or behavior is to apply and practice it on the job and in real life situations.

Our learning and development philosophy is built upon how individuals internalize and apply what they learn based on how they acquire the knowledge. We rely on the 70/20/10 formula* that describes how learning occurs:

70% from real life and on-the-job experiences, tasks and problem solving. This is the most important aspect of any learning and development plan.
20% from feedback and from observing and working with role models.
10% from formal training.

We believe that the key elements to a successful learning process include both the "70/20/10 formula" and how individuals internalize and apply what they've learned.

Read more about the learning process.

- *70/20/10 learning concept was developed by Morgan McCall, Robert W. Eichinger, and Michael M. Lombardo at the Center for Creative Leadership and is specifically mentioned in The Career Architect Development Planner 3rd edition by Michael M. Lombardo and Robert W. Eichinger.*

How Managers Learn (in their own words) by Peter Caseboe (2010). "By far the most frequent and effective learning activity is having a frequent chat with a colleague. 82% of managers will consult a colleague at least once a month, and 83% say it is either very or fairly effective as a means of helping them perform their role when faced with an unfamiliar challenge." "In terms of the most frequently used methods of learning to support a manager, our survey showed the top five to be:

- informal chat with colleagues
- use of search engines
- trial and error
- on-the-job instruction
- use of professional literature"

Anoother European example:

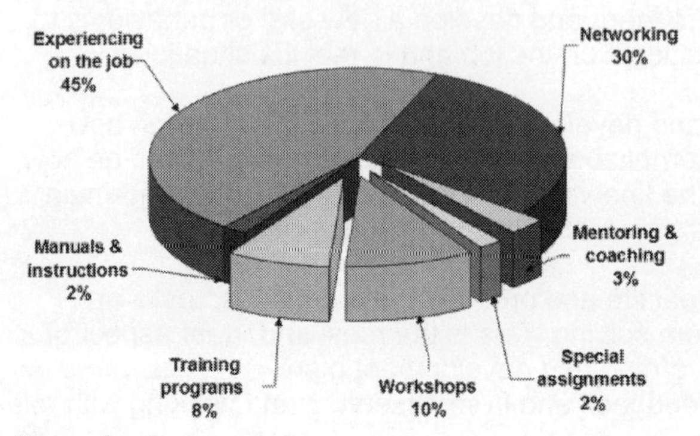

Sara Lee

Bear in mind that the 80% and 20% are *averages*. Rough averages. The lesson is that people learn a lot more about their work informally than formally. Classes are generally overrated; the wisdom of experience is frequently undervalued. Novices are going to learn a greater proportion formally; veterans will rely more on informal learning. Formal works best with explicit; informal is best for tacit.

FORMAL 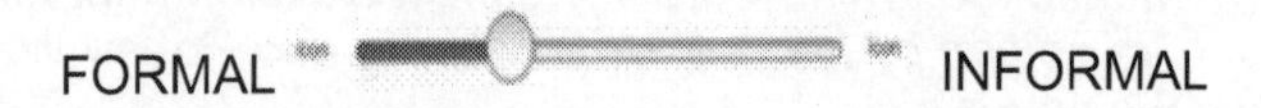 INFORMAL

When you dig down into the details, you'll find that all learning is part formal and part informal. The only thing worth discussing is the degree of formality or informality, for it's never either/or.

What Would Ivan Illich Do?
[The next few pages summarize a presentation Jay delivered in Sao Paolo on informal learning and the philosophy of radical Austrian priest Ivan Illich.]

The watchword for today is CHANGE. Our world has been turned upside down by the acceleration of time. (One of your minutes contains as much activity as thousands of your grandmother's minutes.) The dense interconnections between ourselves and our environment have rendered our simple world complex. The certainty of the clockwork world of Newton has been replaced with unpredictability emerging from the collisions of complex interactive systems. The industrial age is in its death throes and in its place a network era is arising.

The Changing Nature of Plants in Business

Ivan Illich, the radical Austrian priest who called for "deschooling society" is more important to thinking about how people learn now than when he was active forty years ago. Illich thought school got in the way of learning, saying "We have come to realize that for most men the right to learn is curtailed by the obligation to attend school."

He contended that "Schools are designed on the assumption that there is a secret to everything in life... and that only teachers can properly reveal these secrets."

Rather than establishing schools and training based on what people should learn, Illich (and I) would begin by providing access to the materials and people who can help them learn what they want to know. Illich again, "New educational institutions would facilitate access for the learner: to allow him to look into the windows of the control room or the parliament if he cannot get in my the door."

Re-reading Illich's *Deschooling Society*[22] to prepare for the event at Vivo, I was astounded at how closely Illich's thinking (before the advent of the internet) parallels my own.

Separated at birth?

For Illich, giving people permission to learn things for themselves was a fundamental human right. For people engaged in business today, self-directed learning is the only way to keep pace with change; it's become a business survival skill.

Example of Illich Principles in Action: The University of Phoenix In 1976, John Sperling recruited me to develop the business program for what became the University of Phoenix.

---

[22] Illich, I. Deschooling Society, 1971. http://www.preservenet.com/theory/Illich/Deschooling/intro.html

Sperling's core goal was "to meet the needs of working and underserved students by giving them the chance to earn a college degree. Flexible scheduling, faculty with real-world knowledge and a consistent and effective curriculum design can help make higher education accessible to everyone."

Like Illich, Sperling sought provide access that would enable people to learn for themselves. Years later, he told me that when he conceived the University of Phoenix, not a single college bookstore in America was open after 5:00 pm, cutting adult students out of the source of textbooks.

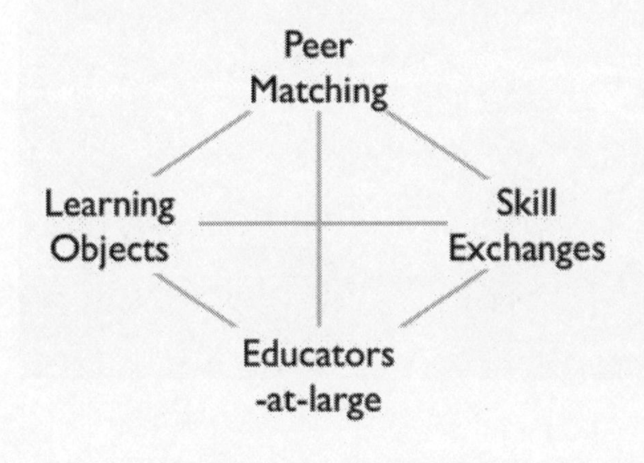

Illich called for four types of opportunity networks: learning objects, peer matching, skills exchanges, and educators-at-large.

The University of Phoenix created these networks by focusing study around a live project, welcoming students of all ages (average age was 35), using the workplace itself as a source of learning, and using successful business practitioners to teach instead of academics.

Twenty years later, Phoenix had become the largest private university in the United States. Three years after that, enrollment topped 100,000 students. Three more years and enrollment was 200,000 students.

Examples of Illich Principles in the Business Context
In the last twenty years of the twentieth century, the market valuation of public companies flipped from tangibles (things you could see, like plants and money in the bank) to intangibles (invisible things like relationships, know-how, and a compelling vision.)

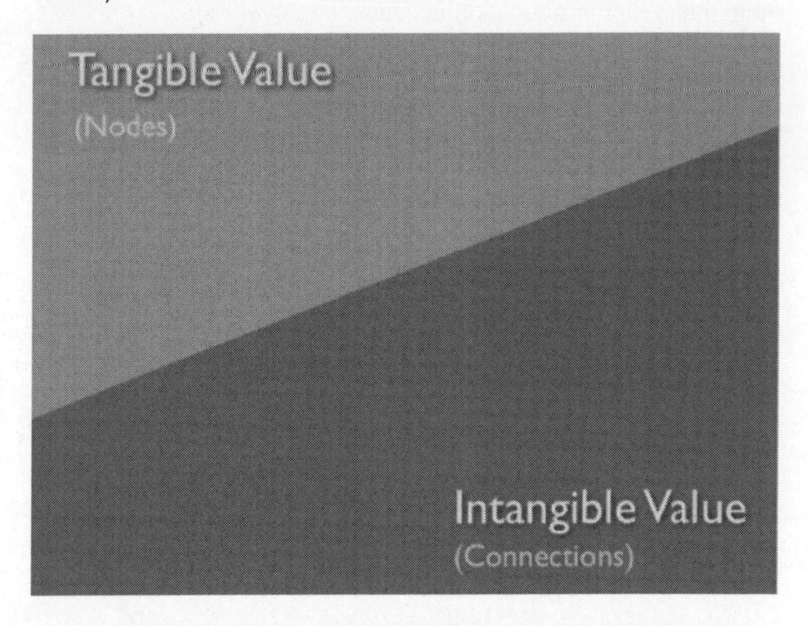

This astounding reversal came up when, immediately following my presentation, I enjoyed the privilege of talking with Roberto Oliveria de Lima, Vivo's visionary president and CEO. We conversed about what business Vivo is in. Hardware and communications technology were not mentioned. Instead, we spoke of intangibles such as providing 57 million customers with networks that will improve the quality of their lives. Planning for the World Cup to be hosted by Brazil, Vivo's focus is on how the facilities can benefit society after the last goal is kicked.

The very nature of work is changing. Until recently, people were paid to follow instructions. Doing what you were told was the rule for workers wearing white collars as well as those wearing blue. Now, we are asking people to do what Dan Pink[23] calls "conceptual work." Workers are solving problems whose answers don't appear in the rule books. People do jobs that cannot be described in traditional job descriptions.

Surviving in this new world means that learning becomes the work. Everyone needs easy access to learning objects, knowledgable collaborators, and veteran performers. Truth be told, this is a bigger challenge than what we used to think of as learning. I call it working smarter.

British Telecom is working smarter. A few years ago, its training department could not keep up with the flow of new products. They stopped developing costly courses to be delivered by instructors around the globe. In their place, they put inexpensive video cams. When a new product is released, they record a question-and-answer session with the product manager or other expert. The video goes up shortly after it was produced. Illich would say British Telecom is offering learning objects to its workforce.

Remember that Illich was writing about networks before we had networks as we know them today. Yet if you envision a Craigslist shopping center for skills, it would be close to his vision of peer matching. For example, I need information about publishing in ePub (i.e. iPad) electronic book format. My blog carries a notice of what I'm looking for and directs other interested parties to join my discussion board to swap ideas.

Finding the right person for skill exchanges used to be impossible in the U.S. intelligence community. Everything was secret unless you could demonstrate a "need to know." People working for the CIA were unaware of what people were doing on

---

[23] Pink, Dan. *A Whole New Mind*, 2006. Riverhead Trade Press.

similar projects at the NSA, the FBI, the Defense Intelligence Agency, and so forth. The tragedy of 9/11 was one outcome of people being caught unawares because they were not working together.

The intelligence agencies put together blogs and a wiki to share information widely. We assumed that analysts would go after knowledge that way. As it turned out, the facts were secondary. More importantly, analysts now had a means to find out who was working in their area of interest. This led to phone calls and lunch meetings, creating what Illich would think of as skill exchanges.

Four thousands software engineers working for a large technology infrastructure consulting firm in Canada used to keep up with their field individually. An engineer would read technical journals, attend conferences, and prowl the web for new applications. Reinventing the wheel was inefficient and costly.

The company selected a dozen thought leaders with the organization, gave them a day a week to keep up with developments in their specialities, and assigned them writers who would send out intelligence updates no more than twice a week. Engineers are now less likely to miss vital changes or to misinterpret the information they receive.

Eliminating duplicate effort freed up more than $100 million in annual consulting capacity.

Vivo Call Center Training Staff

The program of learning conversations in the call centers of Vivo is another example of applying the genius of Ivan Illich. In a separate session, I met with two dozen call center training managers who have been implementing a means of learning through peer-to-peer conversation in lieu of formal training. The structure was set up by Papagallo[24], a performance improvement consultant working with Vivo.

How did the call center workers take to the new form of learning? They loved it. They began learning from one another. The culture changed from discouraging questions to championing them. Workers got up to speed more quickly. Initial observations suggest that job satisfaction is on the rise. (Turnover is the bugaboo of all call centers. The demeaning nature and low prestige of the work create dissatisfaction from the get-go.)

Call center staff are becoming more engaged in their work. People brag about new discoveries. Learning conversations are pouring over into the workscape.

Learn like a child

"Don't limit a child to your own learning, for he was born in another time." Rabbinical Saying. Photo: children reporters at Vivo's Second Symposium on Learning.

The people who learned the most at the Rede Vivo Educação were probably the several dozen children who documented the event.

After my talk, they cornered me. Two were interviewers. Another held a pocket video cam. Someone else held the voice recorder.

---

24 http://papagallis.com.br/

A third person snapped photos. They asked what I thought about people no longer spending significant time in libraries, I replied that libraries have their place, but that we've blessed to have so many other sources.

The famed debates about whether Brittanica has more substance than Wikipedia, how did I feel about that? Brittanica never has fresh material, but Wikipedia is perpetually being updated. Wikipedia reports on Lady Gaga, Botox, and the world situation.

They asked why the internet useful for learning. Absent the net, they would never have heard of such things.

With the net, they can connect to people and information from around the world.

I told them about young people doing very professional interviews like theirs whom I'd met in Seattle. Nothing was holding back their learning.

Iliich would have been ecstatic. These kids were out of the classroom, making inquiries of the real world.

They are going to live a much different lives that those of us who were taught to stay in our place.

Learning Ecologies[25]

Instructional designers and training departments used to think their job was to prepare and develop courses. That doesn't work

---

[25] For more information, see jaycross.com. Check the Informal Learning Page.

very well today. Instead, designers and trainers should be leveraging learning platforms.

Wordles[26] are graphics that size words according to their frequency in a piece of text. The wordle that follows describes traditional instructional design and course-building. What matters most appears to be instruction, design, learning, model, cognitive, and theory.

Instructional design 1.0

26 See http://wordle.net

Learning ecology design

This wordle captures the essence of a chapter on Instructional design 2.0 in the Working Smarter Fieldbook[27].

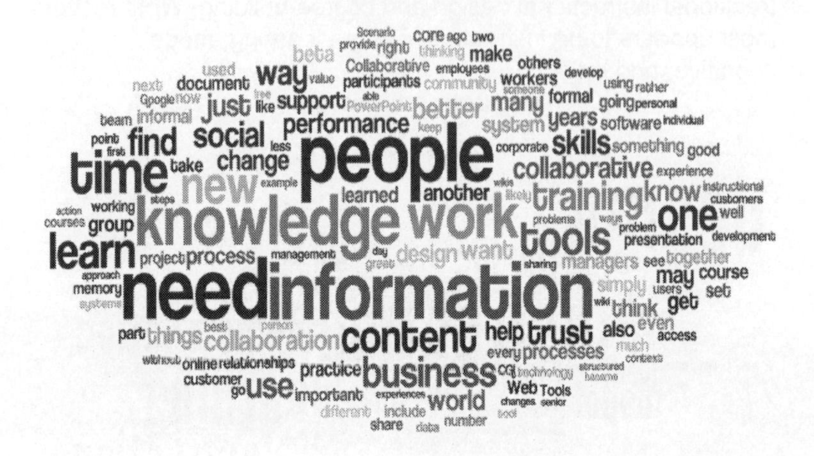

What matters most in this view of the future: people, information, work, need, time.

Ivan Illich would be happy with our progress.

[27] Cross, et alia. The Working Smarter Fieldbook, June 2010. http://www.internettime.com/excerpts-from-work-smarter-informal-learning-in-the-cloud/

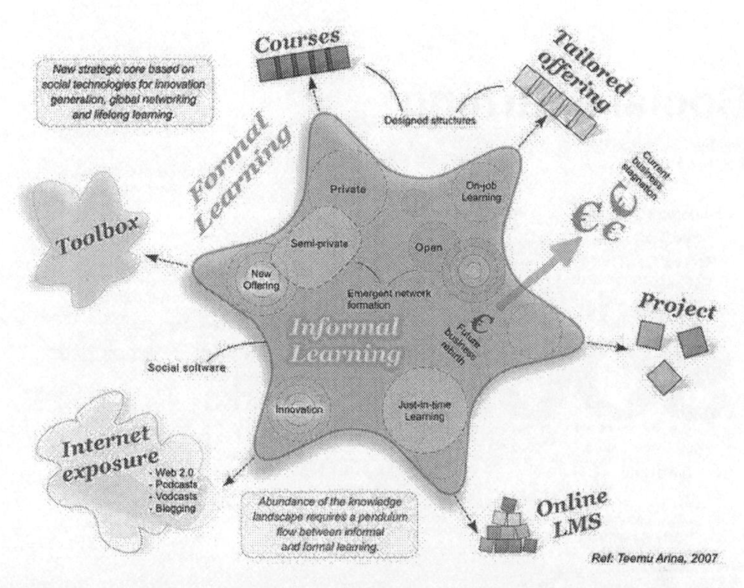

Our friend Teemu Arina asks, “How would organizations look if they put informal learning at the center of things?”

Social Learning

Social Learning in the Workplace Today

The emergence of social media tools in the 2000s has changed the face of the Web; allowing individuals to create content in a variety of formats, make connections with people, share information and experiences and/or collaborate on different activities. It is now clear from the statistics, presented in Erik Qualman's video, Social Media Revolution in August 2009, that a huge number of people are using these tools in their daily lives.

This year's Top 100 Tools for Learning 2009 was also dominated by social media tools; the Top 10 including Slideshare, Wordpress, Google Docs, YouTube, Google Reader and Delicious, with Twitter ranking No 1 on the list. Often those looking at the list remark that "*these aren't learning tools - just everyday tools*" whilst others ask "*how can Twitter (or any social media tool in fact) be used for learning?"* As the use of social media for learning - aka "social learning" - becomes a hot topic, is it, as Maish Nichani succinctly put it on his blog posting from the DevLearn conference in the US in November 2009, a matter of just *"get social and you'll learn"?*

To answer these questions, I spent some time analysing the Top 10 Tools lists of learning professionals, and identified over 100 examples of the use of different social media tools for learning. I also began to collate documented examples of the use of different social media for workplace learning.

From these two lists it became clear that social media was being used for many different types of learning. Whereas it has recently become fashionable to differentiate learning as either "formal" or "informal" - terms which have now become mis-used if not abused, identified 5 different categories of social learning.

1. Formal Structured Learning
2. Personal Directed Learning
3. Group Directed Learning
4. Intra-Organisational Learning
5. Accidental & Serendipitous Learning

Here below is an analysis of these 5 categories of learning, with examples of how social media is being used.

Formal Structured Learning (FSL)

Learning = being taught or trained

For many people, this is how they define "learning". This is formal education and training; classes, workshops, etc - either face-to-face or online which are "pushed" to the learner. Examples of the use of social media for formal structured learning include:

- Building a collaborative library of course links in a social bookmarking tool (like Delicious)
- Educators creating course/class blogs and learners writing learning (b)logs (using e.g. Wordpress or Blogger)
- Using wikis (like Wikispaces or Wetpaint) to create collaborative course learning spaces where all learners can participate.
-

It is clear that workplace training is still very much focused on the creation and delivery of expert-generated content (albeit more rapidly than before), and any social functionality that exists, is often just "added-on" to an online course. Whereas in education (schools, colleges, universities etc), the social aspect is much more integrated into the course and classroom, and in some cases a fully collaborative approach to learning is employed so that the learner is a full and active participant in the learning.

Learning management systems (LMS) are pretty commonplace in most corporates, however most have little or no social functionality so that this is often provided by externally hosted social media tools. Educational course management systems (CMS) and virtual learning environments (VLE) on the other hand, have more social functionality within them (e.g. Moodle). But, there is also a growing educational trend to move away from systems that manage and control the formal learning process in such formal (see the recent ALT-C debate The VLE is dead), and many educators are therefore heavy users of public social media tools in their teaching and learning.

Nevertheless, social Learning in this context is defined as using social media for formal education and training.

However, in the workplace employees "learn" - that is find out, hear about or discover things in many other ways which have nothing to do with being trained or taught by anyone as part of their daily working lives - in much more informal ways, as described below.

Personal Directed Learning (PDL)

Learning = finding things out for or by yourself

This is where individuals organise and manage their own personal or professional learning, that is they find and make use of both informational and instructional content as well as connect with people to address their own learning and performance problems.

It is becoming clear that many people are making substantial use of social media tools in this respect, for instance:

- By joining social networks (e.g. Facebook or LinkedIn) to interact with others, ask and answer questions, start discussions and build a personal or professional network
- By using a micro-blogging service (like Twitter), in the same way, to share their own daily information, as well as follow people that share tips, guidelines and tools
- By using an RSS reader to subscribe to blog and web feeds to keep up date with what is happening in their field of interest

Whereas education has for some time now recognised the importance of personal learning, the concept is not generally encouraged or supported within workplace learning for a number of reasons that will be discussed later. Nevertheless, a large number of employees are making significant use of (free) public social media tools to do just this (although they may not refer to this as "personal learning"), particularly as (a) the resources they access and the people they connect with, are often outside their own organisation and (b) because there are generally no enterprise tools to support this type of activity.

Group Directed Learning (GDL)

Learning = working with a team or other group of people to solve your problems

This is where groups of individuals learn and work together, e.g. in work teams, on projects, in study groups, or a coaching/ mentoring activity. GDL is an extension of PDL, where groups use social media tools to build their own Shared Learning Environments to share information, resources and experiences with one another, for example:

- The use of group spaces (like Google Groups) or social network tools (like Facebook, LinkedIn or Ning) to store and share ideas, experiences, resources and contacts
- The use of collaborative tools to work together on common documents, (e.g. Google Docs or wikis like Wetpaint or Wikispaces) or to brainstorm together (using mindmapping tools like bubbl.us and Mindmeister)
- The use of social bookmarking tools (like Diigo) to create group bookmarks.

Whereas group work is a common educational activity, CMS/VLE generally don't support the creation of group spaces by students themselves, so self-organising groups of students use a variety of public tools to provide the functionality they need to work and learn together. Within an organisational context, those working in teams and on projects also have resorted to the use of hosted group space tools, as once again there are often no enterprise tools to support this type of activity.

Intra-Organisational Learning (IOL)

Learning = learning from everyone in the organisation

For organisations, there is the bigger "organisational learning" picture. This is where employees share information and resources with others throughout the organisation, and generally keep each other up to date and up to speed on strategic and other internal initiatives and activities. Examples of the use of social media for intra-organisational learning include:

- The use of a private micro-blogging service where colleagues can keep each other updated in real-time with their news and activities
- File sharing across the organisations where employees create, find and view podcasts, documents, etc and discuss, rate and debate the content (using enterprise social intranet)
- The creation of an organisational community or network where employees can establish contact with colleagues (who may be remotely located) as well as enable easy communication and collaboration between them.
-

Although it seems obvious to state that employees need to be kept up to date with what's happening both inside and outside the organisation, "training" is often used to patch up issues of poor communication of strategy, projects, processes etc. However, some organisations are beginning to put in place internal platforms for employees to share news, resources etc with other another, as well as improve communication between employees. These enterprise systems are generally either hosted internally or managed by providers to ensure privacy and security.

Accidental & Serendipitous Learning (ASL)

Learning = acquiring knowledge without realising it

This is where individuals learn without consciously realising it, and is also known as incidental or random learning, or even "learning at the water cooler". Although accidental learning can take place in any of the above scenarios as well as in other personal or professional settings, some individuals like to take advantage of possible serendipitous learning that might occur using social media, e.g.

- Finding out about new things using a micro-blogging service (like Twitter) or a social networking site (like Facebook or LinedIn)
- Finding links to resources in a social bookmarking site (like Delicious or Stumbleupon) that can help prompt ideas and creativity.
-

Organisations don't normally concern themselves with this type of learning as they simply can't measure it. But it is important to understand that it happens.

Thoughts for the future for L&D in 2010

Here now are some thoughts for Learning & Development departments and professionals, active in workplace learning, arising from the points made in Part 1.

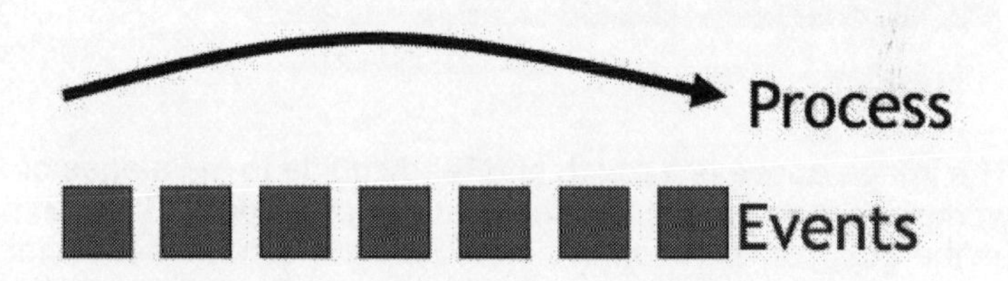

Stages of workplace learning

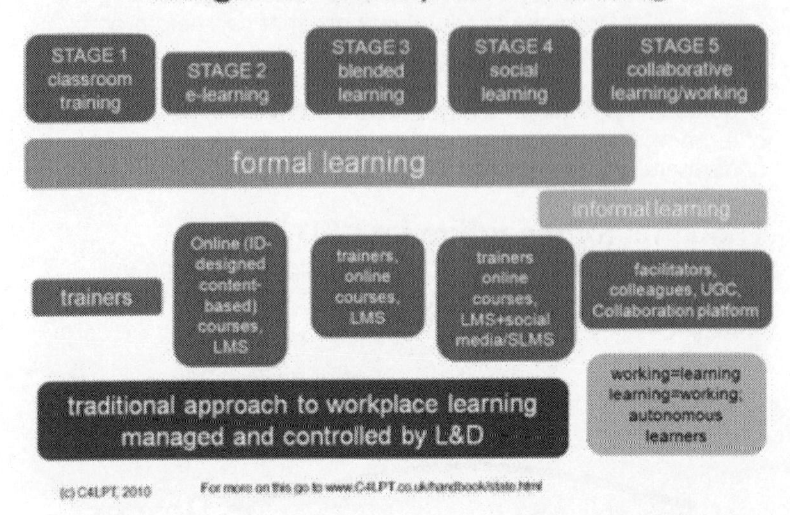

The image above is a rough and ready guide to the stages of workplace learning. Most organisations are around Stage 3, but as the L&D conversation circles around the concepts of social and informal learning, some are drifting into Stage, 4 - which is simply adding-on social (and even informal) functionality to the traditional model of learning.

Organisational L&D departments, in the main, focus on **TRAINING** i.e. creating, delivering and managing formal structured learning (FSL) and it is true there will always be a need for formal learning, e.g. bringing new people up to speed on a body of knowledge.

It has been shown that formal structured learning (FSL) accounts for only a tiny percentage of an individual's learning within an organisation (estimated around 20%). In fact the more mature the learner, the less dependence they need on formal learning. Social technologies also allow self-organising individuals and groups to address their own learning, performance and business problems ***in their own ways*** - much more speedily than L&D can normally solve a problem (by designing, delivering and managing a formal course or workshop).

L&D therefore needs to decide whether they want to remained focused on training or play a part in the wider arena of organisational "learning", and be prepared to support all its forms rather than manage solely formal learning - and move into Stage 5. Adopting an integrated enterprise-wide approach to organisational learning such as this is not just about the technology, but will require a new mindset for L&D.

(A note on the Stages of Workplace Learning; you don't need to go through all the stages to reach Stage 5, even those still stuck at Stage 1, could simply leapfrog to the future.)

New mindset for L&D

One of the key features of this new mindset is recognising that self-directed learning is nowadays just as an important part of learning within an organisation as formal learning.

When Harold Jarche, my colleague in the Internet Time Alliance, took my 5 categories of learning (described in Part 1) and built the diagram below to make sense of them for potential clients, he noted:

"What jumped out at me after the fact, and I've highlighted in red, is that social media for learning requires a lot of self-directed learning, either individually or as a participant in a group/ organization"

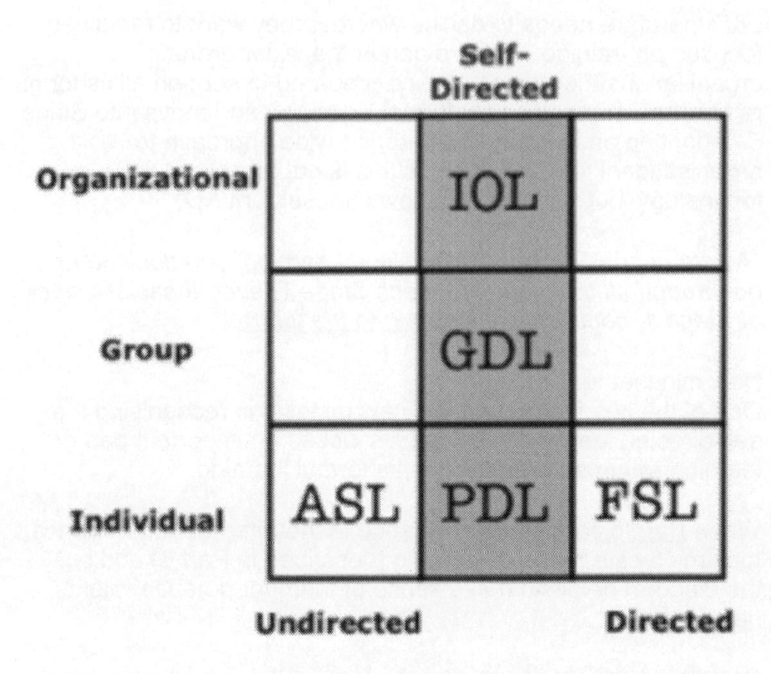

When we presented this diagram at a conference event recently, at least one L&D manager's response was: *"We can't let people direct their own learning. How do we know they are learning the right things"* However, as as can be seen from Part 1 above, individuals are *already* organising their own and their groups' learning and this will continue to happen, so L&D needs to take account of this, rather than dismiss it. In fact, a recent article, Agile Learning, Thriving in the New Economy, in CLO Managzine, explains why it should be actively encouraged:

"As competitive environments increase in speed, complexity and volatility, organizations and individuals are compelled toward a dynamic learning mindset. Dynamic learning is defined as rapid, adaptive, collaborative and self-directed learning at the moment of need."

The authors of the article, Timothy R Clark and Conrad A Gottfredson, go on to say

"It may be time for learning organizations to take a step back and offer new "learn how to learn" solutions. Even millennials, who

are natural swimmers in social networking and digital media, don't necessarily know how to learn in the digital domain.

Dan Pink's book Drive: the surprising truth about what motivates us, explains what drives (i.e. motivates) high performance in organisations, and this is also very relevant for learning. For example:

"Human beings have an innate drive to be autonomous, self-determined and connected to one another. And when that drive is liberated, people achieve more and live richer lives. ..

"The opposite of autonomy is control. And since they sit at different poles of the behavioral compass, they point us to different destinations. Control leads to compliance; autonomy leads to engagement."

"It means resisting the attempt to control people - and instead doing everything we can to reawaken their deep sense of autonomy"

"A sense of autonomy has a powerful effect on individual performance and attitude. According to a cluster of recent behavioural studies, autonomous motivation promotes greater conceptual understand, better grades, enhanced persistence at school and in sporting activities, higher productivity, less burnout and greater levels of psychological well-being."

What does this mean for L&D? That it is time to concern themselves more with supporting and enabling employees become dynamic, agile, self-directed, independent, interdependent, **autonomous,** earners and less with creating and controlling learning for dependent learners.

Helping employees become autonomous "smart" learners includes supporting them acquire a set of trusted resources and networks, using the most appropriate tools; and having the right mix of skills to make effective use of the tools and (re)sources.

Note, this does **not** mean building lots more learning content nor implementing a traditional "command and control" (social) learning (management) system where everyone's learning is tracked, monitored and managed, but rather providing an open, and enabling environment for individuals and groups to support their own learning and performance needs.

New toolset
(Social) learning activity take many forms within an organisation, as described above. In terms of the systems in use within an organisation, the tools and systems that support social learning are largely hosted outside the organisation, and there is often no cohesive approach to tying the different types of learning together.

However, some organisations are adopting an enterprise-wide integrated, social, collaboration platform or environment, which supports the different types of learning AND working *within* an organisation. A private and secure environment like this ensures that employees are less distracted by the perceived trivial content of public social networks, and addresses many of the concerns organisations have with the use of public social media tools, e.g. the potential risk of embarrassment for both employees and businesses. However some individuals may still want/need to make use of external social media tools to connect with professional colleagues outside the organisation, and of course for their own personal purposes. A diagrammatic view of enterprise learning systems might look like this:

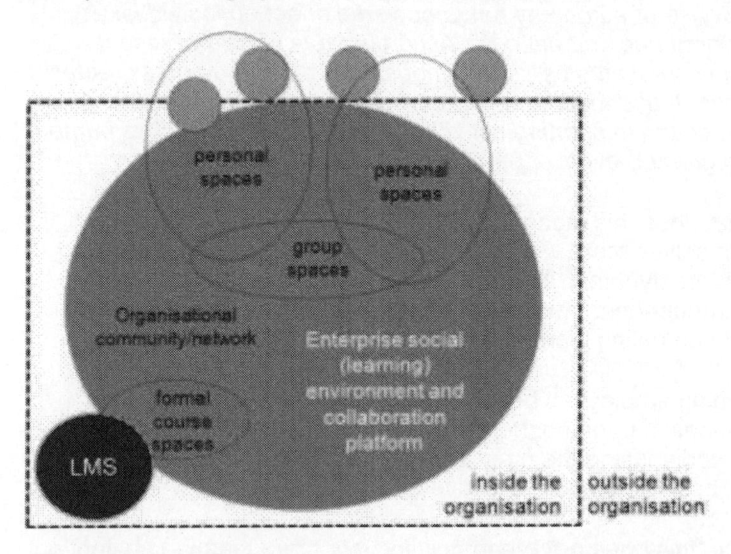

Note this type of environment does NOT track, manage or monitor working or learning, but simply provides an open infrastructure that enables communication, collaboration and information sharing - and hence supports all the 5 types of organisational learning.

Any system that claims to "manage informal learning" is a learning management system, since once you start to "manage informal learning" it becomes "formal learning" as in a LMS the learning of the learners is still under the control of the organisation.

Informal learning, is by its very nature under the control of the individuals concerned. So, all you can do is to **encourage, support and enable informal learning**, and to do that requires providing an open infrastructure that allows individuals and groups to have control of their own learning/working and set up own personal and/or group spaces and use the social tools within that environment as best suits their own needs.

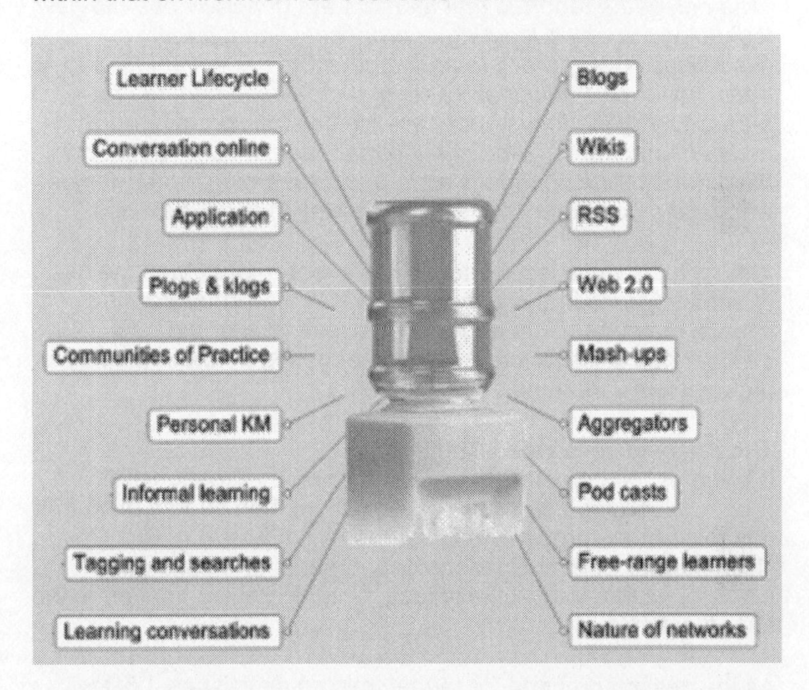

A number of L&D departments recognise the importance of such an open social collaboration platform and where they are driving the implementation within an organisation, it is often referred to as a **social learning environment.** However, were it is Bus Ops or IT that drive the implementation of an enterprise collaboration platform ,it is generally referred to as **Enterprise 2.0 software**. But inn essence these platforms are one and the same thing.

New skill set

These new approaches to learning will also requires a new set of skills for the L&D professional. A recent press release from LINE following a European corporate forum stated:

"Skills issues among those delivering learning and development within organisations are a bigger block to adoption of new learning technologies than either board-level management or learner acceptance."

The press release went on to say ..

"The delegates reported that learners are generally open to new technology-enabled learning approaches, and top team executives now appreciate and understand the advantages they offer. However, traditional learning and development teams, particularly those focused on face-to-face training, are more resistant and training and change management are required in these areas. The change is a big one for learning professionals, who face a complete upheaval in the way they do their jobs."

Although the skills issue cited in this press release was the use of virtual classrooms and webinar events for formal learning events, the statements above are no less true for the new mindset and skills required towards adopting a new approach to organisational learning advocated here.

The risk of avoiding the issues

If it seems too complex for L&D to take on the "responsibility" for enabling learning across the organisation, then bear in mind that this role will the probably be assumed by others, e.g. Bus Ops, IT or Internal Communications departments as their own interests widen. If this takes place, what is likely to happen to the L&D function?

As the desire and need for formal training diminishes, L&D will probably become more and more marginalized. Or as Karl Kapp and Tony Driscoll put it in their recent book, *Learning in 3D:*

"The biggest loss in opportunity for the learning function lies in the fact that it has rejected informal learning.

2010 is therefore the year for L&D to change that and take action!

Do you want to improve or transform workplace learning?
This diagram from Cisco's Learning from the Extremes (PDF) document about transforming schools, is very relevant to workplace learning - particularly with regard to the use of social media.

	Formal Learning	Informal Learning
Sustaining Innovation	IMPROVE	SUPPLEMENT
Disruptive Innovation	REINVENT	TRANSFORM

Simply implementing social media tools won't transform learning; although this will certainly go some way towards helping to ***improve*** and ***supplement*** workplace learning.

In order to ***reinvent*** formal learning ALSO requires a re-thinking of the existing provision of formal learning, but to go further and to ***transform*** learning requires a complete NEW mindset in understanding the role of "learning" in an organisation, - and to appreciate that, as my colleague, Harold Jarche in the Internet Time Alliance says "*learning=working; working=learning*".

Hugh McLeod

So, for social learning to be successfully implemented in an organisation it is not just about adding in the new tools or platforms but also about acquiring a new mindset and new skillset for both learning professionals and individuals.

The table on the following page summarises the key considerations.

State of Social Learning in the Workplace

<table>
<tr><th></th><th>Formal Structured Learning</th><th>Personal Directed Learning</th><th>Group Directed Learning</th><th>Intra-Org Learning</th><th>Accidental & Serendipitous Learning</th></tr>
<tr><td rowspan="3">New mindset</td><td colspan="5">working=learning; learning=working</td></tr>
<tr><td rowspan="2">not the answer to every problem: appropriate only in certain circumstances

content > collaboration

UGC = acceptable

today's "new" learners need new approaches</td><td colspan="4">informal learning is already happening - it needs to be enabled, supported and encouraged - but not designed or managed

learner control > learner autonomy</td></tr>
<tr><td>autonomous, independent, self-directed learners are essential in an agile organisation</td><td colspan="2">autonomous, interdependent learners are essential in an agile organisation</td><td>serendipitous learning is an acceptable learning strategy</td></tr>
<tr><td rowspan="3">New skillset</td><td>new social learning design models

new facilitator skills</td><td>development of autonomous learner skills</td><td>group and team working/ learning skills</td><td>↓</td><td>locating where ASL is likely to take place</td></tr>
<tr><td colspan="5">sharing, collaboration and cooperation skills</td></tr>
<tr><td colspan="5">(appropriate) use of social technologies</td></tr>
<tr><td>New tools</td><td colspan="5">(appropriate) application of social technologies</td></tr>
<tr><td>Aggregated toolsets</td><td>social LMS</td><td>personal learning environments/ networks</td><td>group spaces</td><td>↓</td><td>internal and external networks</td></tr>
<tr><td>New platform</td><td colspan="5">Enterprise-wide Social & Collaboration Platform</td></tr>
</table>

A framework for social learning in the enterprise

The social learning revolution has only just begun. Corporations that understand the value of knowledge sharing, teamwork, informal learning and joint problem solving are investing heavily in collaboration technology and are reaping the early rewards.

- Jay Cross

Harold Jarche in Las Vegas

Why is social learning important for today's enterprise? George Siemens has succinctly explained the importance of social learning in the context of today's workplace:

There is a growing demand for the ability to connect to others. It is with each other that we can make sense, and this is social. Organizations, in order to function, need to encourage social exchanges and social learning due to faster rates of business and technological changes. Social experience is adaptive by nature and a social learning mindset enables better feedback on environmental changes back to the organization.

The Internet has fundamentally changed how we communicate on a scale as large as the printing press or the advent of written language. Charles Jennings explains why we need to move away from a focus on knowledge transfer and acquisition, an approach rooted in Plato's academy:

We are moving to the world of the sons of Socrates, where dialogue and guidance are key competencies. It is a world where the capability to find information and turn it into knowledge at the point-of-need provides the key competitive advantage, where knowing the right people to ask the right questions of is more likely to lead to success than any amount of internally-held knowledge and skill.

Our relationship with knowledge is changing as our work becomes more intangible and complex. Notice how most value in today's marketplace is intangible, with Google's multi-billion dollar valuation an example of value in non-tangible processes that could be deflated with the development of a better search algorithm. Non-physical assets comprise about 80 percent of the value of Standard & Poor's 500 US companies in leading industries.

From replaceable human resources to dynamic social groups
The manner in which we prepare people for work is based on the Taylorist perspective that there is only one way to do a job and that the person doing the work needs to conform to job requirements [F.W. Taylor, The Principles of Scientific Management, 1911]. Individual training, the core of corporate learning and development, is based on the premise that jobs are constant and those who fill them are interchangeable.

However, when you look at the modern organization, it is moving to a model of constant change, whether through mergers and acquisitions or as quick-start web-enabled networks. For the human resources department, the question becomes one of preparing people for jobs that don't even exist. For example, the role of online community manager, a fast-growing field today, barely existed five years ago. Individual training for job preparation requires a stable work environment, a luxury no one has any more.

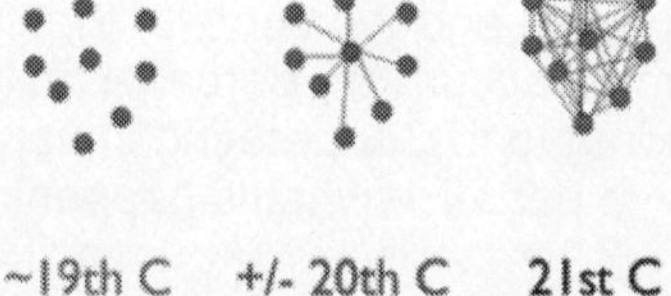

A collective, social learning approach, on the other hand, takes the perspective that learning and work happen as groups and how the group is connected (the network) is more important than any individual node within it.

MIT's Peter Senge has made some important clarifications on terms we often use in looking at work, job classifications and training to support them.

Knowledge: the capacity for effective action. "Know how" is the only aspect of knowledge that really matters in life.

Practitioner: someone who is accountable for producing results.

Learning may be an individual activity but if it remains within the individual it is of no value whatsoever to the organization. Acting on knowledge, as a practitioner (work performance) is all that matters. So why are organizations in the individual learning (training) business anyway? Individuals should be directing their own learning. Organizations should focus on results.

Individual learning in organizations is basically irrelevant because work is almost never done by one person. All organizational value is created by teams and networks. Furthermore, learning may be generated in teams but even this type of knowledge comes and goes. Learning really spreads through social networks. Social networks are the primary conduit for effective organizational performance. Blocking, or circumventing, social networks slows learning, reduces effectiveness and may in the end kill the organization.

Social learning is how groups work and share knowledge to become better practitioners. Organizations should focus on enabling practitioners to produce results by supporting learning through social networks. The rest is just window dressing. Over a century ago, Charles Darwin helped us understand the importance of adaptation and the concept that those who survive are the ones who most accurately perceive their environment and successfully adapt to it. Cooperating in networks can increase our ability to perceive what is happening.

Making social learning work

Jon Husband's working definition of "Wirearchy" is "a dynamic two-way flow of power and authority, based on knowledge, trust, credibility and a focus on results, enabled by interconnected people and technology". We are seeing increasing examples of this on the edges of the modern enterprise. World Blu's annual listing of our most democratic workplaces continues to grow and gain attention. Google's dedicated time-off for private projects, given to its engineers, promotes non-directed learning and collaboration. Zappos directly engages with its customers on Twitter, fostering higher levels of two-way trust. As customers, suppliers and competitors become more networked, being more wirearchical will be a business imperative.

Wirearchies inherently require trust, and trusted relationships are powerful allies in getting things done in organizations. Trust is also an essential component of social learning. Just because we have the technical networks does not mean that learning will automatically happen. Communications without trust are just noise, not accepted and never internalized by the recipients.

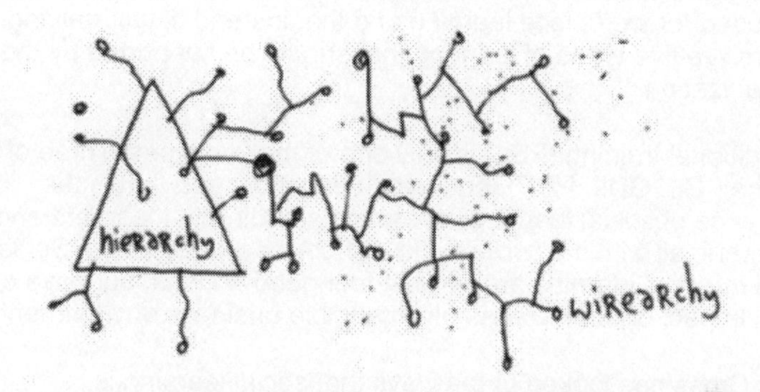

Here are some ways to make social learning work in the enterprise:

- Think and act at a macro level (what to do) and leave the micro (how to do it) to each worker or team. The little stuff is changing too fast.
- Engage with Web media and understand how they work. The Web is too important to be left to the information technology department, communications staff or outside vendors.
- Use social media to make work easier or more effective. Use them to solve problems for work teams and groups.
- Make traditional management obsolete. Teach people how to fish and move on to the next challenge. If the organization is maintaining a steady state then it has failed to evolve with the environment.

Analyzing social learning

Most 20th century workplaces had two types of learning: formal learning through training and informal learning (about 80% according to research) which just happened by accident or the result of observation, conversation and time in the job. This focus on formal training, for skills and knowledge, missed out on our social nature. Business has always been social, especially at the higher levels of management and with ubiquitous access to networks, this is once again part of everyone's work. In the global village, we are all interconnected.

Earlier in this chapter, Jane Hart showed how social media can be used for workplace learning and that instead of just training, there are five types of learning that should be supported by the organization.

Traditional training (FSL) is only one of the five types. Three of these (IOL, GDL, PDF) require self-direction, and that is the essence of social learning: becoming self-directed learners and workers, all within a two-way flow of power and authority. Social and informal learning are not just feel-good notions, but have a real impact on an increasingly intangible business environment.

Jay Cross has looked at the ways that social learning is becoming real and developed this table to highlight some of the workplace changes he is observing:

Social Learning Gets Real

Past	Future
Subject matter experts	Subject matter networks
Need to know	Need to share
Curriculum	Competency
Clockwork, predictable	Complexity, surprising
Stocks	Flow
Clock time	Time-to-accomplishment
Worker-centric	Team-centric

Jay **Cross** November 2009

Implementing social learning

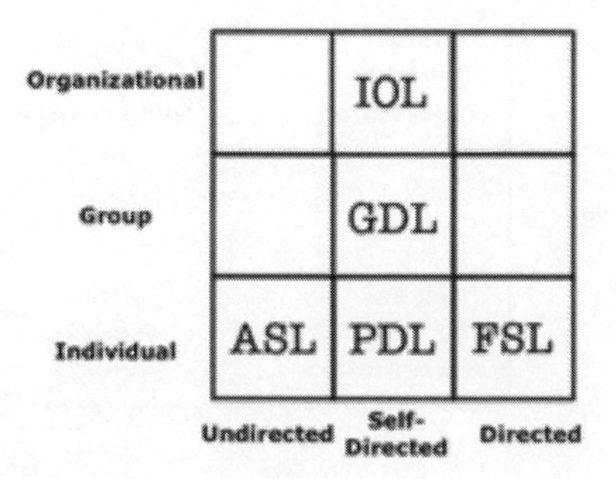

The Results of Connecting

Our workplaces are becoming interconnected because technology has enabled communication networks on a worldwide scale. This means that systemic changes are sensed almost immediately. Reaction times and feedback loops have to get faster and more effective. We need to know who to ask for advice right now but that requires a level of trust and trusted relationships take time to nurture. Our default action is to turn to our friends and trusted colleagues; those people with whom we've shared experiences. Therefore, we need to share more of our work experiences in order to grow those trusted networks. This is social learning and it is critical for networked organizational effectiveness.

Our current models for managing people, training and knowledge-sharing are insufficient for a workplace that demands emergent practices just to keep up. Formal training has only ever addressed 20% of workplace learning and this was acceptable when the work environment was merely complicated. Knowledge workers today need to connect with others to co-solve problems. Sharing tacit knowledge through conversations is an essential component of knowledge work. Social media enable adaptation, and the development of emergent practices, through conversations.

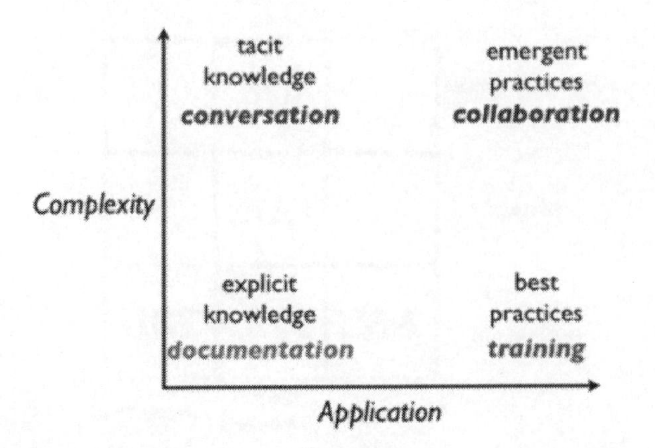

If not now, when?

Our debrief of January's Learning Technologies conferences, both Jane and Charles reported that many attendees are only just starting to shift to delivering some eLearning. Social and informal learning are not on their radar.

Lots of training directors have yet to grasp the concepts of learning through collaboration, the power of social networks, and less is more. Bear in mind that people who attend Learning Technologies are the leading edge. If they are just beginning the journey away from the classroom, imagine what things are like for those who don't attend!

Americans should not feel smug because their brethren in the U.K. don't get it. "New data on e-learning usage do not signal the death of the classroom. And despite some of the buzz, the direction of e-learning has not shifted much over the past several years," report Allison Rossett and James Marshall in an article in T+D magazine.

Reading between the lines, I suspect that many organizations are accustomed to progressing one step at a time. They expect gradual, comfortable change. One step a year seems a break-neck pace.

Incrementalism is the worst enemy of innovation. We're playing a new game now and it's fruitless to follow yesterday's rules.

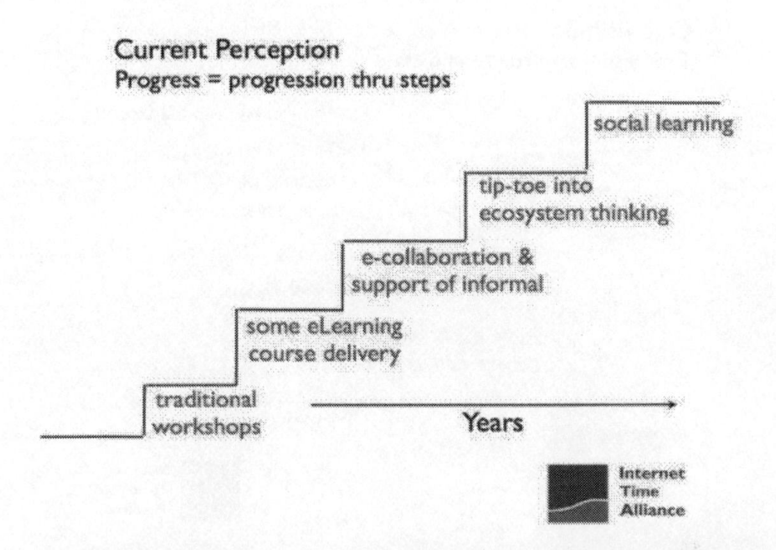

Business is dancing to an ever-faster metronome. Cycle times for product design, manufacturing, and deployment are shorter and shorter. The pace of change itself is picking up. The future is unpredictable. Our old models of training can no longer keep up. They're racing along so fast that the wheels are falling off.

As the environment becomes more complex, linear approaches are giving way to emergent behavior. People take different paths to learn what they need to do. Our task is to prepare them for things we don't even see coming!

The fundamental shift toward informal learning is taking place on internet time. Instead of plodding along step by step, Internet Time Alliance is encouraging organizations to leap over the intervening steps and adopt social and informal learning patterns immediately. Our model looks like this:

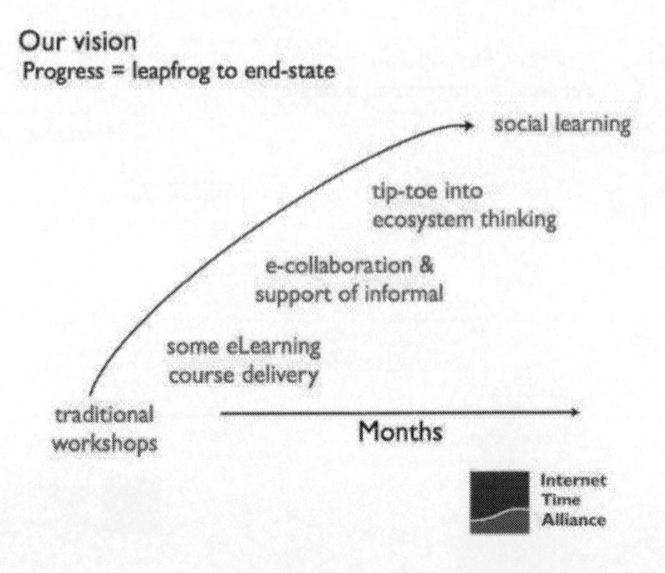

Our proposal is analogous to implementing telephone service in developing countries. In much of the developing world, fixed telephone infrastructure is poor. In 2008, India had only 3.3 fixed telephone lines per 100 and Nigeria 0.9 lines per 100 inhabitants. Rather than planting telephone poles and stringing copper wire, developing countries are going straight to mobile. Fixed telephone infrastructure is costly to set up, while wireless technology is cheap to deploy.*

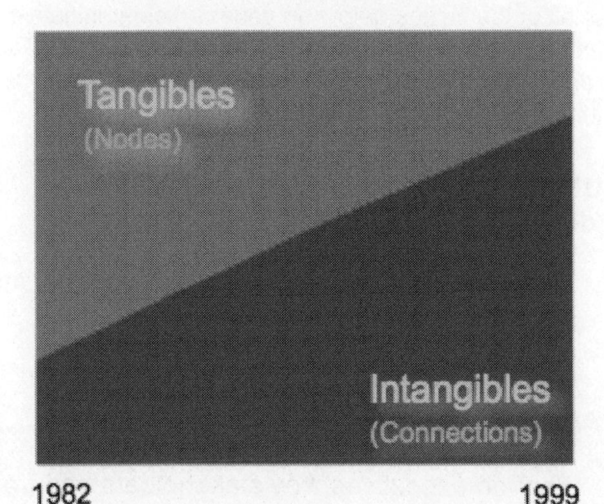

Courses, delivered in-person or online, are the phone poles and copper wires of learning technology.

Are you laying land lines or going directly to wireless?

Social Learning Strategy Checklist

By Kevin D. Jones and Dave Wilkins

Source

Organizational adoption of social media as a comprehensive learning strategy is one part software rollout, one part transformational change, and one part large scale corporate initiative. Depending on your initial focus, it might involve a single cohort group, your whole company, your partners or suppliers, your clients, or even the public at large. Regardless of your scope, there are a number of critical items that you must address in order to achieve success. While you may not need to address all of the issues below on your particular initiative, you should at least consider the implications and issues for each item below, and where necessary, develop a plan of action to address those that are relevant to your situation.

Culture

What do you want it to be? What is it today?

- ☐ Openness vs. planning? Where is your balance point?
- ☐ Autonomy and self-direction vs. top-down mandates? Where is your balance point?
- ☐ What do executives, key stakeholders and "rank-and-file" think about social media and sharing?
- ☐ What are your organizational attitudes about transparency?
- ☐ To what extent do learners take personal responsibility and accountability for their learning?

Approach and Methods

What "kind" of Social Learning models are you pursuing? How do they integrate?

- ☐ Codified?
- ☐ Collaborative?
- ☐ Emergent?
- ☐ What kinds of social learning interventions do you need?

- ☐ Do you need focused Communities of Practice or decentralized social learning that is part of all learning experiences? Or both?
- ☐ Will you pursue a federated model and use best-of-breed from multiple provides with a single or multiple aggregation points?
- ☐ Will you use a unified suite that offers core social media applications, such as SharePoint or Jive?
- ☐ How will your social media elements interact with your Learning Management System?
- ☐ If "social learning" happens outside the LMS, what will happen where?
- ☐ If "social learning" happens outside the LMS, how will you see a unified view of learner activity?
- ☐ Where will you keep the "profile" of record to avoid having multiple learner profiles across multiple systems?
- ☐ If you use a federated approach or multiple systems in any way, how will ensure that learners can discover people through content, content through people, content through content, and people through people across your systems?
- ☐ If you use a federated approach or multiple systems, how will you search?
- ☐ If you use a federated approach or multiple systems, how will develop recommendation, reward, and recognition strategies?
- ☐ If you use a suite approach, how will you address gaps – missing wiki, missing microblog etc…?

Planning

Who owns what? How will get from point A to point B? How will you mitigate risk?

- ☐ What kinds of social media are already being used in the organization?
- ☐ For what purpose?
- ☐ Who owns them?
- ☐ What kinds of learning communities do you want to help along through hands-on nurturing?
- ☐ What kinds of learning communities do you want to more proactively manage and plan?
- ☐ What are the problems you are trying to solve?
- ☐ Who is your target member for your community?
- ☐ What are the problems your community members are trying to solve?
- ☐ If the problems are solved, what does success look like?
- ☐ If the problems are solved, what is the impact of success?
- ☐ What is your Social Learning Policy?
- ☐ What is your plan when these policies are breached?
- ☐ What is in your Miss Manners Guide to Social Learning?
- ☐ Who is on your Social Learning Governance Board – IT, Legal, CLO etc…?

- ☐ How will social learning activities factor into key performance indicators and performance reviews?
- ☐ What does IT own? Some suggestions: security issues, archiving, technical issues, deployment, options, aggregation, report consolidation, integration fulfillment, report fulfillment.
- ☐ What does Learning own? Some suggestions: strategy, cultural readiness, "tools" training, moderation, member management, community management, programming, integration requirements, reporting fulfillment with built-in reporting tools.
- ☐ What does Legal and Compliance own? Some suggestions: archival strategy, social media storage requirements, approval strategies for sensitive content (which might be all content), member management and "flagging" policies, reporting requirements for all of the above.
- ☐ Who will support your organization's use of social media? Technical support? IT? Learning?
- ☐ What is your start point in terms of participants and technologies?
- ☐ What is the long-term rollout plan? What social media tools will be turned on when? When you do turn on new functionality, what is the trigger – time, membership, activity?
- ☐ Will you organize content topically, hierarchically by division, unit etc…, or by functional area?
- ☐ What is your launch strategy to drive participation? (more below)

- ☐ What is your moderation strategy?
- ☐ What is your reporting strategy?
- ☐ Who will own your programming schedule?
- ☐ How will you identify champions and key influencers prior to roll-out and on an on-going basis?
- ☐ Who will be responsible for defining content categories and the overall ontology of your social learning content?
- ☐ What is end of life or end game for your learning community? Does the community evolve into something else? Is it archived? Is there a planned obsolescence because it's a one-off in response to external factors what will change?

Launch Activities

How will you quickly achieve critical mass? How will you sustain and grow the initiative over time?

- ☐ What other corporate initiative(s) is the launch point tied to?
- ☐ How will you drive traffic and participation in the "early days"? Some suggestions: competitions, rewards, "forcing" through changed process, well-planned programming schedules, middle management expectations, senior level management modeling, social media events – wiki barn raising, live chats, team video jams etc…
- ☐ Who will be responsible for enforcing your policy and procedure changes? For example, if learners are not supposed to answer questions of each

other via email, but through the wiki or an FAQ discussion board, who will be responsible for enforcing the change?

- ☐ Who will be responsible for "seeding" content before go-live?
- ☐ Who will communicate the launch?
- ☐ How will you ensure that learners have the necessary skills and tools to participate in the conversation and sharing? Things to consider: training on the social media tools, training on social media concepts, lots of early recognition and praise.

Technical Stuff, Legal, Compliance

How will this effort fit into existing corporate governance strategies?

- ☐ What is your security plan to prevent unauthorized viewing of sensitive data?
- ☐ What is your data recovery plan in the event of corruption, server failure etc…?
- ☐ What is your plan to communicate the security so that users can help safeguard sensitive content while feeling secure enough to freely share within the defined parameters of the site?
- ☐ What is your records retention policy?
- ☐ What is your content permissions policy?
- ☐ Do you need a "contact" permission policy to prevent your SME's or other experts from being overwhelmed?

- ☐ Do you have a "Do not discuss via Social Media" list? What is it and how will it be communicated?
- ☐ What kinds of topics require "pre-approval" before posting live to the site?
- ☐ What kinds of topics must include "report violation" options after they go live?
- ☐ Do you have a list of keywords that should be redacted or replaced?
- ☐ Do you have a keyword list that should trigger notification to SMEs, Legal or Compliance personnel?
- ☐ What is your reaction plan to a breach of policy? Who owns it? Who enforces it?

Learning Communities in the Extended Enterprise

Planning for community members who are "outside" the company walls…

- ☐ If you have external audiences, suppliers, partners, clients, etc… in addition to internal audiences, what is your plan for all of the above for your external audiences?
- ☐ What is your strategy for leveraging public social media channels?
- ☐ Is the Learning group the lead or is Marketing, Customer Support, Product Management, etc…?

- ☐ How will your social learning strategies compliment your marketing, customer support, product, etc… strategies?
- ☐ How will you leverage content between various constituents?
- ☐ Do you need to have "blended" areas where clients, employees, suppliers etc… co-mingle in a shared space with access to shared content?
- ☐ What role do your external members play in community management, programming or moderation?

Community Management

How will you manage and grow your community over time?

- ☐ Who will be in charge of community management?
- ☐ What is your moderation strategy?
- ☐ Who is responsible for moderation?
- ☐ How many months in advance will you publish your programming schedule?
- ☐ How will you reward and recognize key contributors in ways that increase internal motivation?
- ☐ What sort of member management policies do you need?
- ☐ Who enforces member management?
- ☐ What role will senior leaders play in contributing to the learning community?

- ☐ How will you market your successes and the growing value of the content?
- ☐ How will you promote new content, new members, new groups, and new topics?

Professional Development, Skills, Competencies

What kinds of skills and competencies do you need to develop as a learning professional?

- ☐ Become a Social Media tools maven – wiki, video, podcast, blogging, microblogging, etc…
- ☐ Understand key concepts of Social and Cultural Anthropology
- ☐ Understand key concepts related to Team Building and Team Dynamics
- ☐ Understand key concepts in Social Psychology
- ☐ Understand key issues of self-efficacy as it relates to social media: trust, belonging, self-confidence, self-direction, motivation, skills
- ☐ Knowledge of moderation strategies and key moderation concepts like seeding, facilitating, autonomy, respect, and flow
- ☐ Knowledge of key community management strategies including programming, reward and recognition models, advertising and awareness campaigns, member management
- ☐ Ongoing professional development by networking outside the company through social learning

The Business Case

What keeps executives awake at night

Sustainability. Organizations must adapt or die. Companies that keep repeating what has worked before are headed to hell in a hand-basket.

Senior managers are asking "What can we do to take advantage of change rather than be ravaged by it? How can we become an agile, innovative survivor?"

Today's executives grew up in a business world managed by industrial-age rules. Many pay unquestioned allegiance to the vestiges of the industrial paradigm. They believe in hierarchical organization structures, top-down control, information hoarding, lack of collaboration, rigidity, formality, competition, and undervaluing intangibles. In the opposite corner, most network age business people support flat organizations, shared responsibility, information sharing, extreme collaboration, flexibility, informality, cooperation, and the importance of social capital and reputation.

We can be a bridge from the old way to the new by repositioning what we've already been doing. The informal meme fits the service environment. eLearning is clearly a carrier. If there was ever a need for wisdom, this is it. And with wetware replacing hardware, open source is part of the mix.

Results Even a CFO Can Love

Networks arise when isolated entities link to one another. Improvements in communications technology (e.g. the invention of language, writing, printing, mass communication, computer networks) encourage connections. The denser its interconnections, the shorter a network's cycle time. Speed begets speed.

The connections that knit us together make us interdependent. Because other members of the network impact what you do, you lose even the illusion of control. The future becomes unpredictable.

Natural Evolution of Networks

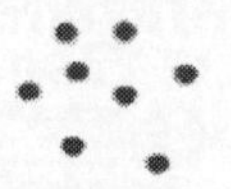
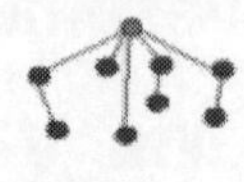
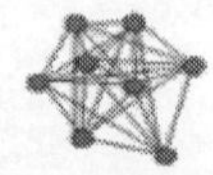

Humans	Bands	Kingdoms	Democracies
Computing	Mainframes	Client/ server	Internet
Business	Sole proprietor	Franchise	Business web
Learning	One-on-one	Classroom	Informal

Factory workers were once paid for what they produced. In a mechanized system, the slowest worker produced about the same amount as the fastest. If workers produced one widget an hour, paying by the hour was equivalent to paying by the widget. It was also simpler to measure. Managers became accustomed to equating time with production.

For the knowledge worker, time on the job is often unrelated to output. Google's recruiters figure that an exemplary engineer can create 200 times more value than an average engineer. It hardly seems fair to pay by the hour.

Visualize the workflow of a physical job: Produce, produce, produce, produce, produce, produce, produce, produce, produce.

Now visualize the workflow of a creative knowledge worker: Nothing, nothing, nothing, nothing, **flash of brilliance**, nothing, nothing, nothing.

That single moment of brilliance may be more valuable than

years of production.

That flash becomes visible in internet time. A year of internet time is roughly equivalent to seven years of calendar time. The term came into being because in its first year, Netscape was said to accomplish what had taken others at least seven years. (The firm has since imploded at an accelerated pace as well.) Internet time is a generalization, like a New York minute, the idea being that there's fast time in additional to regular time.

A businessperson with a watch knows what time it is; a businessperson with two watches does not. Most managers tell time with industrial age watches, acting as if internet time does not exist and missing opportunities left and right.

Opportunities abound because the world now moves on ideas instead of things. Value has migrated from tangible assets you could see and touch to intangible assets such as ideas, relationships, patterns, and reputation. Twenty-seven years ago, intangible assets accounted for a little more than a third of the valuation of U.S. companies; ten years ago, more than 80% of that value was intangible.

In the world of intangibles, quality trumps quantity. You can build a relationship or develop an idea in a fraction of the time it took to build a factory. Furthermore, some efforts yield out-sized rewards. As in nature, for every action, there may be an unequal and totally unexpected reaction. The butterfly that flaps its wings in the Amazon is perhaps the catalyst for Hurricane Katrina.

Chief Learning Officers consider themselves enlightened if they provide workers with a month of training per year. This would have been generous when the pace of business allowed for three-martini lunches and the nature of work rarely changed. Today everyone is busy every waking moment, figures things out for themselves, and deals with increasingly complex situations. Routine tasks crowd out reflection and innovation.

Reading email for hours on end is a waste of time. Some creative workers would produce more value were they required to dedicate eleven months of the year to learning and one month to innovation and decision-making.

At the dawn of the network age, managers enjoyed the luxury of annual planning. They communicated the firm's goals to the training department, which in turn translated those goals into workshops, learning management systems, and so forth. Back then, the past resembled the future closely enough that driving by the rearview mirror was feasible. Today's rapid changes require responsive driving skills. The road is being built a little way ahead and may take a turn we don't expect.

Today's managers have scenarios and possibilities, not single-track plans. This calls for new models. Meta-learning and flexible infrastructure are becoming more important than individual topics. Learning-to-be will supplant learning-to-know.

Legend has it that Napoleon gave the order to plant trees along the main thoroughfares of the Empire to shelter soldiers from summer heat. His lieutenants protested that the trees would take decades to mature. Napoleon replied, "Better get started right away."

Speak the Language of Business

When you plan to pitch a learning and development investment or decision to someone with the power to sign checks, you may be unsure what to say. If so, ask yourself one question; it will help you find the right approach.

That question is this: What would Andrew do?

Andrew Carnegie was born in 1835 in Dunfermline, Scotland. The industrial revolution put his father, a weaver, out of work and drove his family into poverty.

Andrew immigrated to America as a teenager and joined the Pennsylvania Railroad at 18. He took out a bank loan and invested in sleeping cars. Six years later, he was named superintendent of railroad's western division. Two years after that, he invested his sleeping car profits in an oil company. At age thirty, he founded a company to build bridges of iron instead of wood.

In 1875, Carnegie opened his first steel plant. Fourteen years later, he was earning $25 million a year from steel. In 1901, Carnegie sold his empire to J.P. Morgan for $480 million, becoming the richest man in the world. He spent the rest of his days a philanthropist.

Andrew Carnegie was the quintessential hard nosed businessman. Your objective will often be to do convince Andrew what you say/do is worthy of investment. When in doubt about ROI, just ask yourself "What would Andrew Carnegie do?"

YOUR SPONSOR

Metrics are measurements that matter. The internal customer for metrics is your sponsor. Your sponsor is the person who pays the bills. I assume your sponsor is a business person. It might be a committee of business people. When you talk with a business person, you must talk like they do. Executives only care about training as it relates to execution. Their interest is in moving the corporation forward. You should share that interest. That is what they pay you for.

Sponsors are responsible for championing the case for change (i.e., the vision), visibly representing the change (i.e, walk-the-talk), and providing reassurance and confidence (i.e., the implementation plan).

A couple of years ago, we were leading a webinar for representatives of several dozen training departments at a Fortune 50 high-tech company. Someone interrupted with a question when we were saying that trainers need to be aware of corporate objectives and rate their contributions by their impact on the business. "Wouldn't that require us to understand how the business worked?" he asked. Yes, of course. How could you do your job right without knowing where the corporation was headed? Several others jumped in, saying essentially that organizational success and helping meet strategic objectives was "not my job."

The days when corporations were larded up with layer upon layer of management whose job was to translate strategic imperatives from above into job descriptions and projects down below are long gone. Now all of us are supposed to sing from the same hymnal without the intermediaries.

If you work for a public company, define your job in terms of the issues described in your firm's annual report. Getting ahead in business requires forming solid working relationships with your sponsor and the other stakeholders it is your duty to support.

So before you go any further, ask yourself these questions. First, who is your sponsor? And second, who are your important stakeholders? Once you know the answers to these questions, you are ready to proceed. Without them, you cannot progress.

You and your sponsor
Keep your sponsor informed. Ask people where they bank, and they'll tell you where they keep their current account. This holds true even if their relationship with their mortgage banker is fifty times larger. Frequency is sometimes more important than quantity.

Monitoring things early-on may enable you to make mid-course corrections.

The responsibilities you share

We'll get businesslike right away. Peter Drucker is hailed as the father of management. He is a business guru's guru. Drucker singled out eight characteristics of effective executives.

These are precisely how you and your sponsor are going to address metrics.

- They asked, "What needs to be done?"
- They asked, "What is right for the enterprise?"
- They developed action plans.
- They took responsibility for decisions.
- They took responsibility for communicating.
- They were focused on opportunities rather than problems.
- They ran productive meetings.
- They thought and said "we" rather than "I."

The Metrics Cycle

There's no cookie-cutter formula for applying metrics, but there is an underlying process.

Generally, you'll follow these five steps to identify, agree upon, assess, and use metrics. This is not rocket science. It's the same process you already use to accomplish a lot of things in life. Let's briefly consider each step.

1. State Desired Outcome. Results do not exist inside the training department. In fact, results do not exist within the business. Results come from outside the business. Imagine a no-nonsense businessperson, say, GE's former boss, Jack Welch. If you can explain yourself to Jack, you've mastered this step.

2. Agree How To Measure. The only valid metrics for corporate learning are business metrics. Examples are increased sales, shorter time to market, fewer rejects, and lower costs. How do you decide what measures to apply? You don't: that's the responsibility of your business sponsor, the person who signs the

Learning Practices Survey

Following a major success or failure, we take time to reflect on what we've learned from it.

Learning Practices Survey

Our organization is slow to change, even when it would be in our best interest.

checks. Together you agree on what's to be done and how you'll measure success or failure. Once you've settled on the project and its metrics, get it in writing.

3. Execute Project(s). The projects could be training and/or an incentive bonus plan and/or more advertising. Training programmes are often part of a larger scheme, and it's fruitless to try to isolate them. In fact, savvy training directors look for major corporate initiatives they can hitch a ride on.

4. Assess Results. You must evaluate the impact of your efforts with the measures you set up back in step 2. In other words, you are not allowed to mimic Charlie Brown, who would shoot an arrow and then paint the target around it. Why stick with the measures you came up with before? Because that's how to maintain credibility with your sponsor. You can bring up unforeseen outcomes or anecdotal evidence, so long as you follow up on those original methods first.

5. Begin Anew. The only thing worse than learning from experience is not learning from experience. Your post-mortem on the completed project should include a section titled "What to do better next time." This is where you start the cycle anew.

Don't just talk like a business person; become one

In an article in T +D Magazine titled *A Seat at the Table*, Kevin Oakes, then president of SumTotal Systems, masterfully described how speaking the language of business is one of the biggest skill gaps in the learning profession. Kevin quotes two respected industry figures, John Cone, the former CLO of Dell Computers, and Pat Crull, then CLO of ToysRUs, that hammer home the point. Here are their original words.

> "Learning professionals who have the ear of senior management come to the table to talk about business results, not learning pedagogy. They understand the drivers of the business, how the executives think, and the metrics that mean the most to them.
>
> They talk about business outcomes, not learning enablers. And they talk about their business using real business language and real data. They talk about revenue, expense, productivity, customer satisfaction, and other quantifiable stuff that business people care about. They've learned that every conversation had better include information about money or time saved, revenue or new business generated, or customer problems solved."
>
> *John Cone*

> "During my presentation (at an industry conference), I stated that as a CLO, I see myself as an officer of the corporation. I worry about improving shareowner value. If it doesn't make a difference to the bottom line, then my work has little of no value. At that point, a woman in the audience got up from her seat and left the room."
>
> "Later, during the Q&A section of our presentation, someone who was sitting next to the woman who had left, stood up and said, "Do you know what she said right before she exited? That she didn't get into the training and development field to worry about the bottom line." I was stunned. To me, that summed up the biggest problem in our profession today."
>
> *Pat Crull*

In summary, to “earn a seat at the table” where the business managers sit, you must:

- Speak the language of business
- Behave like an officer of the corporation
- Think like a business person
- Act like a businessperson.

Informal Learning: A Sound Investment

It's all a matter of learning, but it's not the sort of learning that is the province of training departments, workshops and classrooms. At work we learn more in the break room than in the classroom. We discover how to do our jobs through informal learning—observing others, asking the person in the next cubicle, calling the help desk, trial and error and simply working with people in the know. Formal learning—classes and workshops and online events—is the source of only 10 percent to 20 percent of what we learn at work.

Informal learning is effective because it is personal. The individual calls the shots. The learner is responsible. It's real. How different from formal learning, which is imposed by someone else. Workers are pulled to informal learning; formal learning is pushed at them.

Nonetheless, organizations invest most of their training budgets in formal learning. This stands common sense on its head: Invest your resources where they'll have the least impact.

Many learners today are not self-directed—they are waiting for directions. It's time to tell them that the rules have changed. It's in their self-interest to become proactive learning opportunists. Their reluctance is hardly surprising. Most training is built on the pessimistic assumption that the trainees are deficient. Training's job is to fix what's broken rather than make what's good better. Consequences include:

- Ineffective negative reinforcement.
- Unmotivated learners.
- Learner disengagement, unrewarded curiosity, spurned creativity.
- Training instead of learning.
- Focus on fixing the individual rather than optimizing the team.

Several years ago, the late Peter Henschel, then director of the Institute for Research on Learning, posed an important question: If three-quarters of learning in corporations is informal, can we afford to leave it to chance?

Push Learning	Pull Learning
Passive student	Active learner
Others set curriculum	Learner defines content
Courses, workshops	Conversation & discovery

Grades
Obedience
Learn on your own
Unchanging knowledge

Competence
Independence
Learn in Group
Web 2.0

ROI is in the mind of the beholder
Consider these three valid but different perspectives on what's important.

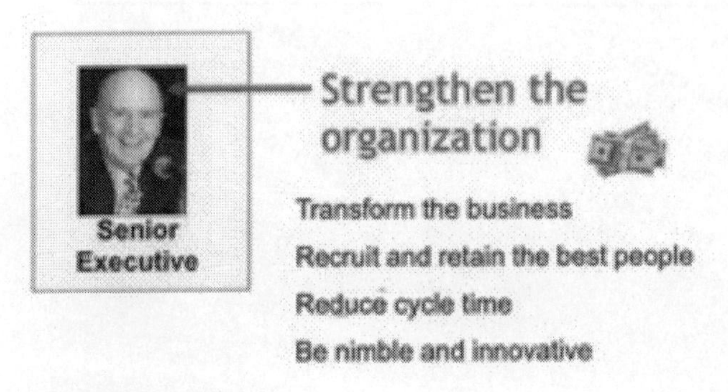

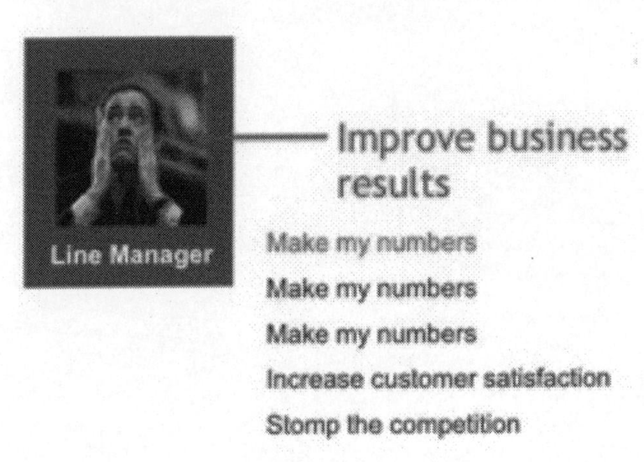

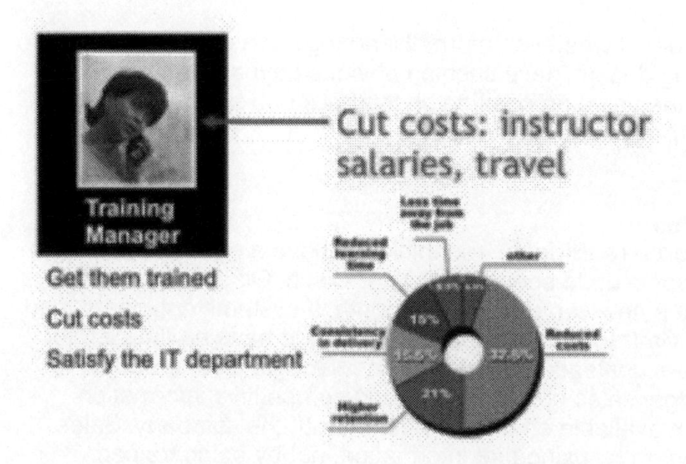

The Business Case for Soft Numbers

First of all, understand that you're not buying informal learning. It's already going on in your organization. In fact, three-quarters of the learning on and about how to do one's job is informal.

The natural learning that occurs outside of classes and workshops is vital but it probably flies under your corporate radar. No manager is accountable; no department is committed to making improvements; there's no identifiable budget. Hence, one of the most important functions in an organization, keeping up with skills to prosper in the future, is left largely to chance.

Don't get tricked by the word *informal*. Informal learning is not "do your own thing." Rather, it often begins with values, goals, and challenges. The workers have more say-so in choosing how to accomplish them, and they are usually more demanding on themselves than you would ever conceive of being.

Second of all, a persuasive business case focuses on outcomes, not activities. The measure of success or failure is business metrics, not training metrics. The only meaningful way to assess any form of learning is performance. Are workers doing their jobs well? Is their work challenging? Are workers committed to becoming "all they can be?" These are the determinants of true ROI.

Third, since no one has been re-engineering informal learning, or even thinking about it, identifying applications is akin to being the first to enter an orchard that has never been picked. Low-hanging fruit is in abundance.

Remember, if whatever informal learning intervention you are proposing doesn't have such an obvious payback that you can explain the value proposition on the back of a napkin, pick another project.

Examples

Sales force readiness. You think you have a problem keeping sales people up to speed? Consider Cisco. On average, Cisco acquires a new company every month. If systems engineers tried to learn via traditional methods, they would have no time left for customers. Instead of training, Cisco "Google-ized" product knowledge, sales presentations, and competitive information, making it available on demand throughout the company. Sales people learn by using that information, not by being trained.

Benefits: better-informed sales force, more competence on sales calls, more cross-selling, better presentations, easier to bring partners up to speed, avoid cost of product training.

Eliminate bureaucracy. Knowledge workers waste a third of their time looking for information and identifying the right people to talk with. They often spend more time recreating information hidden in someone else's file cabinet than creating original material. I just heard about a company where the workers think doing their email is the work; that's how they spend almost all of their time. Expert locators, bottom-up knowledge management, instant messaging, organization-wide wikis, and organizational network analysis all attack this plaque in the organizational arteries.

Benefits: speed flow of information, cut time wasted searching for answers, streamline organizational process, cut email by half, cease re-inventing the wheel, increase worker throughput 20% to 30%.

Conversation. Conversation is easily the most important learning technology ever invented. Conversations carry news, create meaning, foster cooperation, and spark innovation. Encouraging open, honest conversation through work space design, setting ground rules for conversing productively, and baking conversation into the corporate culture spread intellectual capital, improve cooperation, and strengthen personal relationships.

Benefits: faster cycle time, improved problem-solving, more time on mission, higher morale, lower turnover...

Measurement

"Ah, Jay," you ask, "but how do you measure it? What's the ROI? How am I going to sell this to the boss? How do you prove results?"

In brief, you measure the impact of informal learning the same way you measure the impact of any investment in the organization: by its outcomes. Are people able to do their jobs? Are they challenged? Are they working in top form?

Hold your breath a moment, for some of you will choke on this one: ROI and accounting are inappropriate measures of performance. ROI is a relic of the industrial era, when assets were tangible and repetition was the path to success in the factory. Today, the intangible assets you cannot see are far more valuable than those you can.

Google's market capitalization, what investors think it's worth, is $157 billion. Google's fixed assets (cash, securities, receivables, plant, property, and equipment) are carried on the balance sheet at $20 billion. So where's the missing $137 billion? Intangibles such as reputation, know-how, and customer relationships.

Look at the world through the eyes of a senior executive. What's better, (1) looking at how you use the fixed assets or (2) increasing shareholder value (even though its components are tough to separate out? ROI assumes training is a cost, not an investment. Whether someone has learned to do their job or not doesn't show up in the numbers because ROI overlooks the worker's ability to execute.

This morning, someone asked me how to measure informal learning with an LMS. Another proposed using questionnaires to capture the amount of time people spent on informal learning. Folks, this is like trying to tell time with a thermometer. Any results you get are guaranteed to be worthless.

Intangibles Rule

What do learning, love, patents, trust, intelligence, loyalty, brand reputation and fear of snakes have in common? You cannot see or touch them — they are intangible.

When Pacioli invented double-entry bookkeeping to measure shipping in Venice 500 years ago, intangibles didn't count for anything. Of course, the stock prices of companies such as Google indicate things have changed in our times.

Yet, business managers still act as if something invisible is worthless because it can't be seen and sized up. Vestiges of Industrial Age thinking about value live on inside corporate walls. ROI is a useful concept, but it's not if you leave out the intangibles.

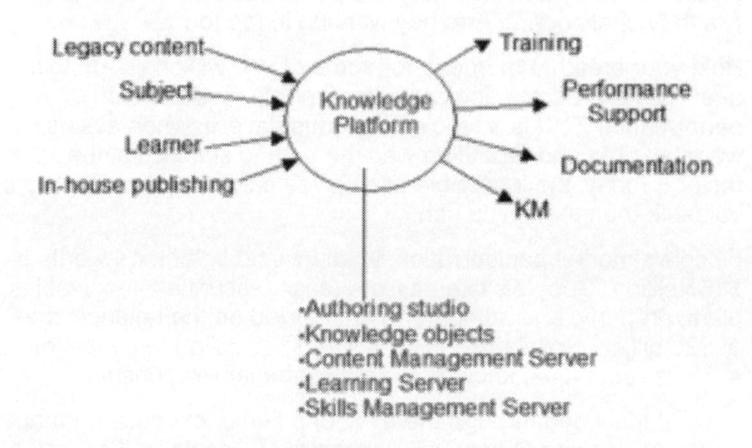

Measuring intangibles involves making judgment calls, so managers often exclude these factors from their calculations. These people tote up the numbers for things they can see and count, and then they list intangibles on the side, as if this keeps their calculations pure. This is nonsense.

If someone in San Francisco asks me the distance to Los Angeles, and I don't have a precise answer, I neither put the question in the parking lot for another day nor say it's some unspecified distance away.

No, I say it's about 400 miles. Or six hours via Interstate 5 in a Lamborghini or two leisurely days down Highway 1 along the coast, with mandatory stops at Point Lobos and Big Sur.

An approximate answer is better than no answer. The same holds true for intangibles.

In spite of their apparently indiscernible nature, intangibles are very real.

For example, what's the value of having a 50 percent chance of

receiving a fee of $100,000? It's .50 x $100,000 = $50,000. Using this logic, the return from a $100,000 deal that your sales force has 50 percent odds of landing because of its recent training is an expected return of $50,000.

That might be, say the critics, but how can you say learning caused the result? Maybe it was a new bonus system that went into effect at the same time. Maybe our products were better than the competition's. Maybe it was sun spots.

Once again, it's a judgment call, most likely the judgment of the person with authority to write checks to fund learning. Or not.

Learning in organizations is not a science experiment under controlled conditions in the lab. Cause and effect in business is never precise unless it is preceded with the phrase "other things being equal." Trust me, in the real world, other things are never equal. Reality emerges from the interaction of complex adaptive forces. Stuff happens.

"Sure, Jay," you say. "This is logical, but you can't manage what you can't measure."

Actually, the old can't-manage-can't-measure meme is totally wrong. Executives manage unmeasured things all the time. As John Wanamaker, the famous Philadelphia retailer, said, "I know that half my advertising budget does nothing for the business, but I don't know which half." All managers make decisions under conditions of uncertainty.

There is no free lunch.

Decision-making involves placing bets on the future. Decisions are more often guided by intuition and judgment than by numbers. As the investment prospectus reminds us, "Past success is no guarantee of future performance."

A lot of the measurement of learning these days lulls learning leaders into thinking they know what's going on. In most cases, they need to think again.

Why Waste Money and Resources on Training?

There's one simple truth that CEOs, CFOs and other executives should understand about training. This truth would save their organisations large amounts of money - and saving money is an important consideration for most executives, particularly in the current economic climate.

The simple truth is this:

> **A huge amount of money is wasted on training for system, process and product rollouts and upgrades. There are better ways of ensuring your employees have the capability to perform.**

Instructor-led, or classroom, training (ILT) is a particularly costly activity that is deployed for almost every system, process or product roll-out by many organisations worldwide. ILT is expensive and not effective.

More recently eLearning has been used for this type of training. It is cheaper, but eLearning courses are not very effective either. eLearning for system, process or product roll-out needs to be cut down as well.

The cost of inefficient methods

The amount of time, effort and money spent on formal ILT training prior to rollout or upgrade of enterprise platforms (particularly ERM and CRM systems), processes, and other new software systems and products is huge. Of the US$134 billion the American Society of Training & Development (ASTD) reported as being spent on employee learning and development in the USA in 2007 (the latest figure available) a very conservative estimate is that at least 5% is spent on this type of system, process and product training. That's more than US$6 billion every year that could be used much more effectively or saved.

Many CEOs, CFOs, business executives, Human Resources (HR) and Learning and Development (L&D) people just don't seem to get it. CEOs, CFOs and executives can be excused. They rely on their senior HR and L&D specialists for guidance as to the most effective and efficient learning approaches that should be used. However HR and L&D staff can't be excused. There is concrete evidence that shows front-loaded training in these situations is almost invariably ineffective and does not deliver value for money. Many HR and L&D specialists who are aware of this fact often simply put their heads down and continue on regardless.

The behaviour of these HR and L&D specialists tends to remind one of the remarkable insight of the author Aldous Huxley when he wrote "*I see the best, but it's the worse that I pursue*". Maybe most managers and L&D people are secretly drinking Huxley's soma – the hallucinogen in his novel *Brave New World* – "*half a gramme for a half-holiday, a gramme for a week-end, two grammes for a trip to the gorgeous East, three for a dark eternity on the moon*"

Training for task and process-based activity has no value

The evidence has been available for some time that formal training on detailed task and process-based activities in advance of the need to carry out the task or use the process is essentially useless.

Both the logic and the available evidence point to the fact that the traditional training approach deployed my many ('most') organisations and offered as a service by a myriad of training suppliers across the globe is both inefficient and fundamentally ineffective and of little use in ensuring readiness. However the cry "we're rolling out a new system, so we have to train all the users" is one of the most commonly heard whenever a new system rollout is planned.

It may feel comforting to attend a class prior to rollout of your shiny new enterprise, HR or Financial system, or the new processes to align with some legislative or legal directive. Participants may feel that they've learned something. However the evidence indicates differently. It suggests that you may as well throw the money spent on these activities out the window. Actually, a better option would be to spend your diminishing budget on approaches that do work. Not only would new rollouts and upgrades come into use more smoothly, but am prepared to guarantee that it would leave budget over for other uses or to offer up as savings (perish the thought!)

The evidence

Where is the evidence that the usual systems and product training approach simply doesn't work or is, at best, sub-optimal?

Well, anyone who has ever been involved in the process of training for rollout and upgrade has been faced with this dilemma. As rollout or go-live happens, users demand re-training or simply call the help desk in large numbers. The pattern in the diagram below is commonly repeated. So it helps to be aware of some fundamental truths about this flawed model.

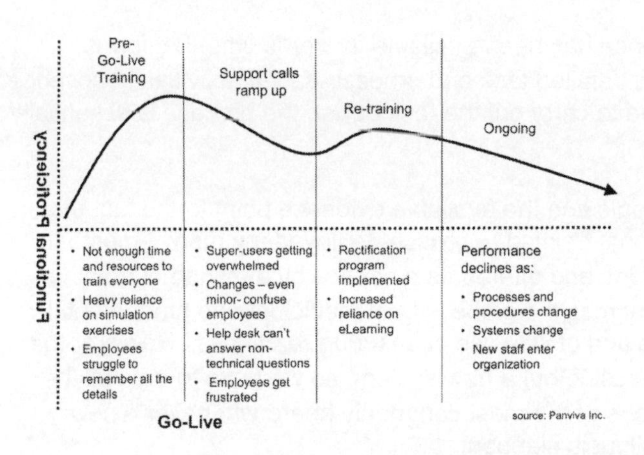

Truth 1: Too much information for any human to remember

Most pre go-live training is delivered through ILT or eLearning and is content-heavy. Instructional designers and subject matter experts usually feel the need to cover every possible eventuality in the training and load courses with scenarios, examples and other 'just-in-case' content.

During my own 30-year training and development career I have seen many PowerPoint decks of 200-300 slides prepared for delivery over 2-3 days in classroom courses for enterprise system rollouts and upgrades. Few humans can recall anywhere near that amount of information for later use, or even a fraction of it. Possibly if they have photographic memories they can do so, but planning for employees with photographic memories is not really a sensible strategy for instructional designers. Those of us without photographic memories simply park most of what we do remember at the end of the session in the 'clear out overnight' part of our brains.

We may also be presented with support material running to 200-300 pages printed in full colour to augment the training (I've seen it many times). However, all those expensively-produced user guides and manuals are a waste of the Earth's limited natural resources. They tend to be too detailed, linear in nature, full of screen grabs that the user will never refer to, impossible to navigate, and the last thing people reach for when they need help in using a new system or process.

People are far more likely to reach for the telephone and call the Help Desk than to use a printed manual. And who could blame them? Training user guides are quintessentially 'shelfware'. Usually the only time they are taken off the shelf is to be thrown into a bin during a clear-out, an office move or when the employee is moving to work with another organisation or is retiring.

Truth 2: Too much time between the training and performance

Embedding knowledge in short-term memory and in long-term memory are two very different processes. The neurological processes that build long-term memory – involving chemicals in the brain such as serotonin, cyclic AMP, and specific binding proteins – are different from the processes that allow us to recall information from short-term memory. Even the information that can be recalled immediately after training - and that's been shown as likely to be a small amount - will be lost if it isn't reinforced within a few hours.

The degradation in transfer from short-term to long-term memory was demonstrated more than 120 years ago in 1885. Hermann Ebbinghaus' famous experiment and resulting 'forgetting curve' showed that most forgetting occurred very shortly after completion of learning with around 50% forgotten after 40 minutes.

Ebbinghaus also demonstrated the beneficial effects of practice, particularly distributed practice ('spacing'), as a means to convert 'lossy' short-term memory into more persistent long-term memory.

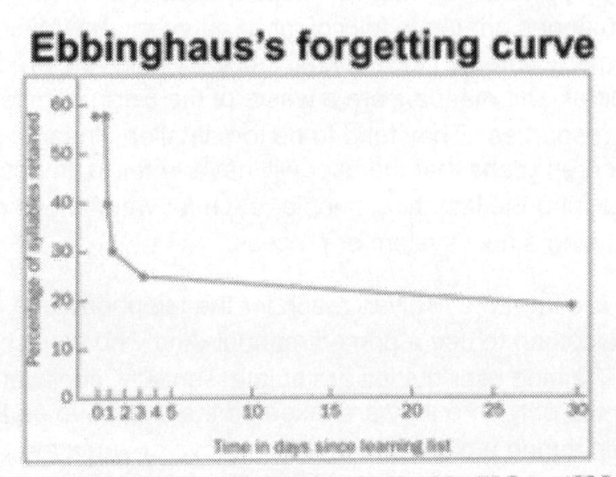

Source: Adapted from Ebbinghaus, H., Memory: A contribution to experimental psychology (H.A. Ruger and C.E. Bussenius, trans.). 1885/1913. Teacher's College Press, Columbia University, New York.

We know that of the most important aids to any learning is practice. Practice and reinforcement are required for our brains to build the new and persistent connections and patterns of long-term memory that will result in behaviour change.

The importance of practice in the process of learning can't be stressed too much. Do we think Tiger Woods' brain retains the details of how to arrange his body so as to be able to hit a golf ball 400 yards or more without lots of practice and reinforcement? Anyone who develops proficiency needs to practice, practice again, and then practice some more. Not just sports people, but any person who needs to develop an ability to carry out any task that is in any way complex, whether it's applying financial formulae, performing micro-surgery or supporting a product or service.

Unfortunately, most process and product training offers only cursory practice opportunities. There's usually not enough time allowed for extensive practice as there's so much 'knowledge' to impart, or there is no access to the system/product prior to rollout and any practice that does occur is often on some cut-down system, the 'training' servers or a simple simulation.

Truth 3: Post-Training Drop-Off has a Major Impact

Post-training drop-off is another reason why formal pre-rollout training simply can never be the most effective approach to developing user competence.

Harold Stolovitch & Erica Keeps carried out some very interesting research on desired vs. actual knowledge acquisition and performance improvement. The data from their research uncovered some important facts about human memory and processing. The graph below shows the results.

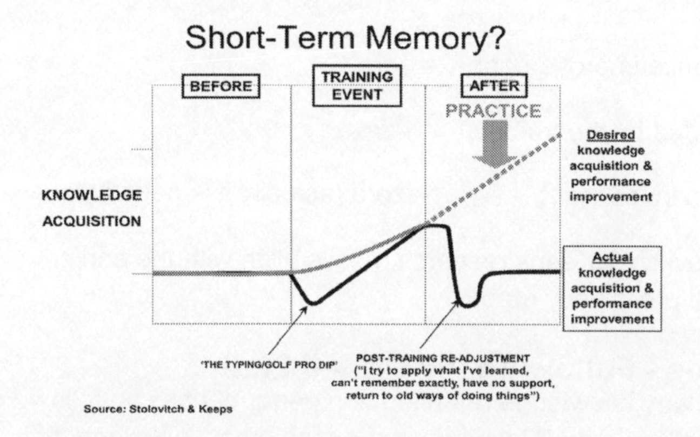

Following an initial dip during the training event (the 'typing/golf pro dip') - where performance drops as new ways of carrying out tasks are tried out and tested - knowledge and performance then improve during the training session. The individual walks out the door knowing more than they did prior to the training session and usually with higher levels of task performance than when they started the training.

Then the problems start.

The drop-off following the training event (called the 'post-training re-adjustment' by Stolovitch and Keeps) can kick-in very quickly, maybe in a matter of a few hours if there's no opportunity to reinforce and practice. So, you finish a day's training course, go home, sleep, and by the next morning a lot of what you had 'learned' has been cleaned out of your short-term memory. Bingo!

Then, next day you get back to your workplace and try to implement what you garnered in the class. The trouble is you can't remember exactly what to do, you don't have any support (that trainer who you called over to prompt you when you went through the exercises in class yesterday isn't there today and the user guide is unfathomable), so you try a few things, find they don't work (unless you're lucky) and then you simply go back to doing what you did previously.

The result?

Performance improvement = zero

Value added by the training = zero

Return on investment = zero (actually it is negative)

The Stolovitch & Keeps research results align with the earlier functional proficiency graph.

Upwards - Following the Dotted Line

The only way knowledge retention and performance can follow the dotted line in the Stolovitch and Keeps graph is if plenty of reinforcement and practice immediately follows the training. Even better if this is accompanied by some form of support – from line managers setting goals and monitoring performance, from subject matter experts (SMEs) providing on-demand advice and support, or even from learning professionals providing workplace coaching.

Unfortunately, all this rarely happens, in spite of all best intentions.

An even better (and certainly cheaper) option is simply to cut out the training altogether and replace it with a support environment from the start.

Performance Support Trumps Training Every Time

There are some very good ePSS (electronic Performance Support Systems) and BPG (Business Process Guidance) tools available now. They are economic and generally straightforward to implement and they trump training every time for supporting learning and the development of competence in using defined processes found in ERP and CRM systems and other software products and business processes.

Just Like a GPS System

ePSS/BPG tools provide context-sensitive help at the point-of-need and "*act like a GPS system rather than a roadmap*" as David Frenkel the CEO of Panviva Inc., the company that produces the very impressive SupportPoint BPG tool explains. "When you're learning to follow a process you just want to know the next 2-3 steps you need to take. You don't want, or need, to remember the entire 20-30 process steps and all the options" Frenkel says. I think he's absolutely right and it's a good analogy.

A GPS in your vehicle tells you that you need to 'turn left at the next intersection' or 'take a right turn then keep straight ahead'. It instructs incrementally. It doesn't tell you every turn you'll need to take on the journey when you first set out.

When there's no access to GPS and the driver has to revert to a map (and doesn't have a flesh-and-blood GPS sitting beside them reading the map and instructing in small increments) they will tend to read and memorise just the next 2-4 turns on the journey and then stop and re-read the map to get the next set of instructions. Job done, destination reached.

With ePSS or BPG support, functional proficiency is maintained through an ongoing cycle of learning and reinforcement in the workplace (see diagram below). Any training that is carried out before go-live or release of an upgrade is brief and focused on core concepts and changes. New or changed tasks are not included. These are supported as part of the process of 'doing' rather than in any formal instruction.

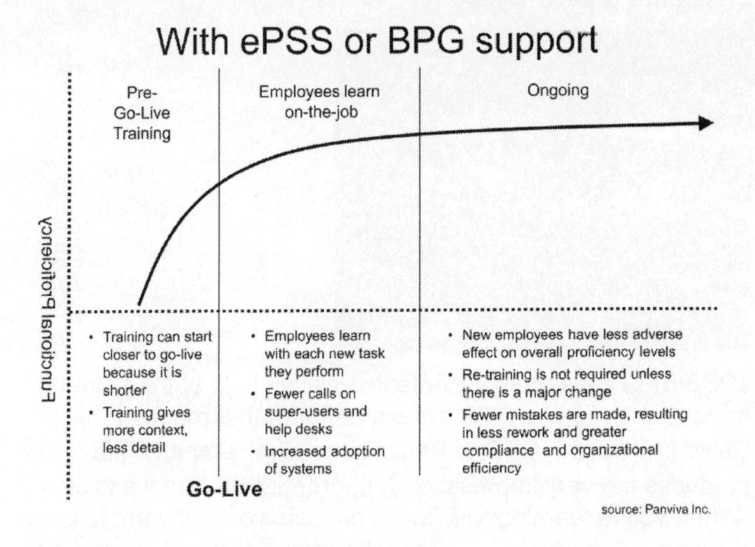

So the questions remain:

Why don't many organisations, business leaders, CFOs, COOs, middle managers, project managers, and HR and L&D folk wake up to the failings of using the wrong approaches to achieve their required outcomes?

Why are billions of $/£/€/¥ spent every year training employees on using systems, processes and products in this way when there is ample evidence to prove that it simply doesn't work?

Sadly, I think the answer may lie in Aldous Huxley's statement. *"I see the best, but it's the worse that I pursue"*.

The facts and the research findings are clear. The failings of formal training for systems, process and product and the lack of the opportunity for 'real' experience and practice in most formal training design has been highlighted over the past decade and more. For the past 30 years research has indicated that only somewhere between 10% and 30% of all formal training results in changed behaviour and improved performance in the workplace, with results tending towards 10% (Baldwin, Ford & Weissbein; Ford & Robinson et. al.). For more than100 years we have known about the limitations of memory and the 'forgetting curve'.

Yet we still to continue 'see the best but pursue the worse'.

However, I think that we will look back in 10 years time, when the majority of support for the rollout of new systems, processes and products is being carried out through on-the-job performance support in one way or another and wonder why we didn't see the best and pursue it earlier.

Decisions, decisions. Business decisions.

To "earn a seat at the table" where the business managers sit, you must:

1. Speak the language of business
2. Behave like an officer of the corporation
3. Think like a business person
4. Act like a business person

This applies to any corporation, in both the public and private sectors. It is vital to understand how a business person makes decisions – and in particular the weight they give (or not) to numbers and facts when doing so. It is equally vital to understand that different officers of your corporation will approach decisions about learning in very different ways depending on their circumstances.

Business is about making sound decisions. Every business decision is a trade-off. (If there's no trade-off, it's a no-brainer.) An important corollary: There is no free lunch. List the pro's of doing something and the con's of doing something else. Be aware of what you're trading off when making a decision. Every trade-off is a risk. That doesn't mean you should shy away from risk. Quite the contrary, for no risk means no reward. A decision-maker who disregards risk is a fool, a pauper, or both.

Fortune favors the bold. An astute businessperson seeks the most lucrative balance of risk and reward. Every business decision is made with less than perfect information, and every decision entails taking a risk. Most investment decisions trade off risk and reward.

Every business decision is made with less than perfect information, and every decision entails taking a risk. Most investment decisions trade off risk and reward. The way to make sound decisions is to judge when you have enough information to move ahead and when the level of risk is acceptable. He who hesitates is lost. Saying "We don't have enough information" is not an acceptable excuse. If the timing is not right, it would be better to say, "The downside is losing $500,000, and we can't identify the range of probability around that occurring any finer than 25% to 75%."

When you talk about the bottom line, you damn well better know what it is. I don't mean to insult your intelligence, so permit me to explain that I didn't understand the difference between profit and revenue until I took a correspondence course in accounting five years after graduating from college. If you are not fully fluent with terms like revenue, earnings, cost, cash flow, margin, and value, take a look at here and get a friend to explain the workings of the basic business model.

THE ENVIRONMENT OF BUSINESS

Everything is relative, including evidence and "hard numbers." An executive, a manager, a training director, and a worker each have different but valid ways of evaluating the effectiveness of learning.

People see what they focus on; they don't see what's really there. An alcoholic sees the liquor stores other people breeze by. A foodie always remembers whether or not she has eaten at a particular restaurant. A top executive sees long-term trends; a factory labourer sees the clock. (Training directors see learners; everyone else sees workers or employees.)

Let's walk in the shoes of different people and see what they notice.

Knowledge Workers

The knowledge worker's objective is to learn what it takes to do the best she can. The learned worker enjoys the fulfillment of a job well done, the rewards that go with high performance, and the accumulation of marketable skills. Today's workers are out for themselves. Not selfishly but realistically. Free agents. They recognize that their careers will last many times longer than their employer. Our market driven world drives people to increase their personal marketability. Incoming workers are more demanding than previous generations. They have no patience for irrelevant exercises, be they useless curriculum or teaching what they already know. Their watchwords are "Don't waste my time" and "Less is more."

A great industrial worker might be half again as productive as his middle-of-the road peer. A great knowledge worker can be several hundred times as productive as his peer. These people need the room to excel. They want their organizations to give them the dots but they want to connect the dots for themselves. Workers want learning that is 'pull', i.e. they find and use what they feel they need, instead of 'push', i.e. someone else decides the subject matter for them.

The incoming generation of knowledge workers demand opportunities to learn through their work; otherwise, they will pick up and go elsewhere.

Training Directors

In the industrial age, the worker was told she was not paid to think. In the knowledge era, workers are paid to think. And they need to keep current with a buzz of things racing by.Workers expect to learn things in small chunks. Learning has shifted from something outside of work to something embedded in work. Stand-up instruction is giving way to peer learning.

The training director's objective is to help his sponsors achieve their goals. Sponsors? Usually this is the people with the authority and wherewithal to sign the checks. Training cannot rate itself; it doesn't own the yardstick.

Business managers set objectives; training directors help achieve them. 'Proof' that training is working is when sponsors believe it is.

Pity the training director. There's more and more to learn. The old training they're accustomed to doesn't work well any more. They must interpret business needs into learning opportunities. And even as knowledge workers take responsibility for their own learning, the training director is likely to be held accountable when learners' performance is underwhelming.

Typical assessment measures – the four or five levels – are at best pieces of a much larger puzzle. "Level Four" will always be out of reach because the instruments of measurement belong to another level in the organization.

The shift from training (we tell you what to learn) to learning (you decide what to learn) increases the scope of the director's job from classes, workshops, and tests to the broad array of networks, communities, meta-learning, and learning culture.

You live your life as if everything is a miracle or nothing's a miracle; for the training director, the sky's the limit or the job is untenable. Today's training director must gain control by giving control.

Here are some things one might add to any training director's job description:

• Supporting the informal learning process

• Creating useful, peer-rated FAQs and knowledge bases

• Supplementing self-directed learning with mentors and experts

• Using smart tech to make it easier for workers to collaborate and network

• Encouraging cross-functional gatherings

• Helping workers learn how to improve their learning skills

• Explicitly teaching workers how to learn

• Enlisting learning coaches to encourage reflection

• Calculating life-time value of a learning "customer"

• Explaining the know-who, know-how framework

• Creating a supportive organizational culture

• Setting up a budget for informal learning (There's no free lunch.)

• Positioning learning as a growth experience

• Conduct a learning culture audit

• Adding learning and teaching goals to job descriptions

• Encouraging learning relationships

• Supporting participation in professional communities of practice

Managers

Getting things done is the role of managers. Meeting this quarter's numbers is the number one priority. "Long-term" means one year. Great execution merits a great bonus and more rapid promotion. Execution is judged by relative success in meeting planned objectives.

Common measures are gain in market share, increased revenue, customer satisfaction, and other business metrics. The manager does not necessarily care what it takes to hit the numbers. If people could gain new skills by popping smart pills instead of training, pharmaceuticals would push training aside. Sometimes the numbers are even manufactured.

A couple of hundred years ago, the factory system kicked off the industrial revolution. The need for coordinated action led to working hours, the urban workforce, specialization of jobs, the quest for efficiency, and the separation of management and workers. In the west, the educational system adopted German methods of schooling soldiers to convert feisty farmers and hunters into obedient factory workers.

Great ideas have a life cycle. They grow from obscurity among enthusiasts and fanatics to nearly universal acceptance and eventually to decline, as the world passes them by. Business managers cling to ROI and conventional training because they are known entities, not because they are right. These conceptual blinders retard the pace of progress.

The word processor is mightier than the particle beam weapon. *George Carlin*

We recently toured a corporate headquarters where staying late at work was prized by managers. Time on the job was thought to be correlated with output when the job is tending an assembly line. In knowledge work, overwork leads to stress and a reduction in cognitive acumen. It's better to have a team that leaves on time to exercise than one that is chained to its desks.

Executive management

Top management is led by what creates value for stakeholders. This generally involves innovation, staying power, adherence to corporate values, and sufficient organizational flexibility to keep ahead of the speed of change. Shareholder confidence along these dimensions fuels market capitalization.When investors judge that the firm can innovate, improve, and grow, the value of its shares increases, as does the take-home pay of the executive.

All learning, informal or formal and anything in between, should be evaluated with the same metric: whether people who participate in it are doing the job.

Executives realize that competing successfully in business requires teams of inspired employees – mentally equipped to make sound decisions on the fly; able to execute good ideas in a snap; and proactive when it comes to taking initiatives and bringing innovation.

Being on the front line dealing with customers, these employees don't have time to run every idea up the management flagpole. Leaders want to field a team that's in the game and ahead of the crowd. They want to pile on innovation that meshes smoothly with what people already know. They want organizations that make bold moves and respond to change as if by instinct. The overall goal: an environment where people learn faster and better than the competition.

Getting there takes more than a lavish investment in training. Time is frequently more important than money." "We are moving from a world in which the big eat the small to a world in which the fast eat the slow," says Klaus Schwab, director of the World Economic Forum.

Let's look at how senior decisions are really made. The staff has shopped various projects around, gathered the figures, done due diligence on suppliers, run the numbers, assessed the impact of changes in the marketplace, and prepared terse summaries for each scenario. Six business cases for new investments, bound with a clear sheet up front, rest in a pile on the coffee table at the executive vice president's weekend cabin. (This is going on simultaneously at the CEO's place by the lake, the COO's condo, and a few other spots.)

A couple of projects are no-brainers; these are so integral to the organization's mission, giving a go-ahead is a mere formality.

Projects that enter new territory, eLearning for example, warrant more detailed consideration. If you were to eavesdrop on the executive's internal thought processes, you'd hear something like this:

[Inner dialog] *"Good Heavens, this effort is going to cost us $8 million and change. But our people are our hope for the future. The analysis shows that we're already spending nearly that much on training. I wonder what Mikey thinks. The ROI is better than building another fab plant but some of the underlying numbers are soft. Of course there's no guarantee that the fab plant wouldn't be another white elephant when it comes on stream in three years. The breeze is picking up outside. I bet it rains tonight. Without eLearning, we'll never become an eBusiness. Some of our systems are pretty creaky right now and would benefit from streamlining. We need to shrink cycle times throughout our organization. This eLearning infrastructure would give Charlie a platform for broadcasting and reinforcing his message about transforming our organization. The Net Discounted Cash Flow is $2 million better than if we took this on ourselves. And the real problem there is that our IT staff would be swamped. And this would wait in line behind the other mission critical projects they're working on. Keeping up with eLearning is not a core activity for us; we should outsource as much of it as we can. I wonder what Charlie thinks. The ballgame comes on in about ten minutes. Where do I come out on this one? I'm optimistic about the potential. It feels right. I'll back it at the Executive Committee Meeting on Monday. I better call the wife to let her know I arrived safely. I could use a slug of single malt about now…."*

Don't believe it? Most senior executives have more faith in gut feel than numbers. The numbers are input. The decision is broader than that.

Five years ago, an Information Week survey revealed that "more companies are justifying their ventures not in terms of ROI but in terms of strategic goals… Creating or maintaining a competitive edge was cited most often as the reason for deploying a business application."

Decision making at work is as much about what the heart says (based on experience and values) as the head (dictated by the numbers). To give yourself a chance to lead on learning in your organization you need to understand and appeal to both – at all levels.

The Future of the Training Department

Prior to the 20th Century, training per se did not exist outside the special needs of the church and the military. Now the training department may be at the end of its life cycle. Join us for a brief look back at the pre-training world and some thoughts about what may lay ahead.

Before the advent of the industrial age, work was local and industry meant cottage industry. People had vocations, not jobs. Sometimes guilds helped apprentices learn by doing things under the eye of a master, but there weren't any trainers involved.

About three hundred years ago, work became an organizational matter. Factories require groups of people working together. To coordinate their activities, groups needed a shared understanding of who is doing what. Orders from the top of the organization kept everyone on the same page. Managers showed workers how to do things and made sure they were doing them the right way. A little training went on, but there still weren't any full-time trainers.

Twentieth century limited

Fast forward to the 20th century. The pace of progress is unrelenting. Clocks measure working hours instead of the sun. Railroads and communications links span the globe. Competition fuels change. Efficiency becomes paramount. Frederick Taylor used time-and-motion studies to find the one best way to do individual pieces of work, and his Principles of Scientific Management became the bible for maximizing efficiency.

Training was *invented* in the first half of the 20th Century. GE started its corporate schools. NCR delivered the first sales training. Factory schools appeared in Europe. Mayo discovered the Hawthorne Effect, opening the study of motivation. B.F. Skinner constructed teaching machines. The U.S. military formalized instruction to train millions of soldiers for World War II. ASTD was born.

The second half of the 20th Century was arguably the Golden Age of Training. Every corporation worth its salt opened a training department. Xerox Learning, DDI, Forum Corporation, and hundreds of other "instructional systems companies" sprung up. Thousands upon thousands of trainers attended conferences to learn about new approaches like programmed instruction, behavior modeling, roleplay, certification, interactive multimedia, sensitivity training. corporate universities, and Learning Organizations. Training was good; efficient training was better.

Most of this training activity assumed that you could prepare people for the future by training them in what had worked in the past. Yesterday's best practices were the appropriate prescription for tomorrow's ills. That works when the world is stable, and things remain the same over time.

Century 21

At this point in the 21st Century, the game is changing once again. Complexity, or maybe our appreciation of it, has rendered the world unpredictable, so the orientation of learning is shifting from past (efficiency, best practice) to future (creative response, innovation). Workplace learning is morphing from blocks of training followed by working to a merger of work and learning: they are becoming the same thing. Change is continuous, so learning must be continuous. To justify its existence from here on, a training department must shift direction in three areas:

* Embracing complexity and adaptation to uncertainty

* Inverting the structural pyramid

* Adopting new models of learning

Complexity (Cynefin)	Social (TIMN)	Practices (Cynefin)	Group Work
Chaotic	Tribal	Novel	Action
Simple	+Institutional	Best	Co-ordination
Complicated	+Markets	Good	Collaboration
Complex	+Networks	Emergent	Co-operation

Embracing complexity

Nothing is for sure any more. Consultant and management theorist Dave Snowden has come up with a framework for management practice in complex environments.

Snowden's Cynefin framework has been used in the study of management practice. It can also help us make decisions for our organizations. Understanding what type of environment we are working in (Simple, Complicated, Complex or Chaotic) lets us frame our actions. When the environment is complex, the relationship between cause and effect can only be perceived in retrospect, but not in advance, the approach is to Probe – Sense – Respond and we can sense emergent practice.

From the Cynefin perspective best practices are only suitable for simple environments and good practices are inadequate in responding to constant change. Both approaches look to the past for inspiration, or as Marshall McLuhan wrote, "We look at the present through a rear-view mirror. We march backwards into the future."

Most of our environments are complex so first we need to probe, or take action, and then sense the results of our actions (Probe-Sense-Respond). This approach has already been adopted by Web services, where beta releases are launched and tested before they are finalized. For example, Google's ubiquitous GMail service is still in beta. The phrase, "we are living in a beta world" is increasingly being used outside the Web services domain.

In complex environments it no longer works to sit back and see what will happen. By the time we realize what's happening, it will be too late to take action. Here are some practical examples for learning professionals:

1. **PROBE**: Prototype; Field test; Accept Life in Beta; Welcome small failures

2. **SENSE**: Listen; Enable conversations; Look for patterns; Learn together

3. **RESPOND**: Support the work; Connect people; Share experiences; Develop tools

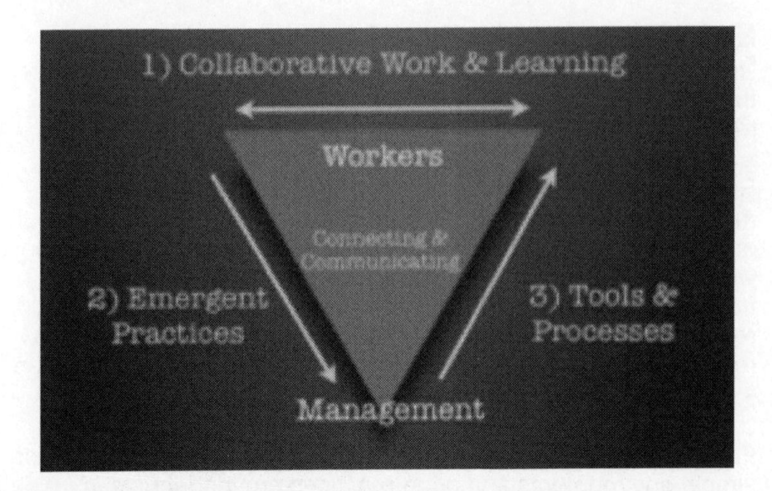

Inverting the Pyramid

So what models will work for our complex environments? The hierarchical organizational pyramid is a model that has worked for centuries. It's premised on the beliefs that management has access to the necessary strategic information and knowledge. Because knowledge is thought to be power, management best understands the outside world and can clearly tell the workers what needs to be done and how.

In a complex, networked environment the lines of communication are no longer clear and the walls between the workers and the outside world are porous. Many workers know more about the outside environment than management does. Today, the relationship between workers and management is not as clear as it once may have been. Effective organizations are starting to look more like inverted pyramids.

As The Cluetrain Manifesto succinctly stated almost a decade ago, "Hyperlinks subvert hierarchies". Hierarchies may not die in the future but they may have to co-exist with a new form of workplace organization, the Wirearchy.

Researcher and analyst Jon Husband says that wirearchy is, "a dynamic two-way flow of power and authority based on information, knowledge, trust and credibility, enabled by interconnected people and technology". The Internet has created interconnectedness on a massive scale. Power and authority must now flow two ways for any organization to be effective. This requires information, knowledge, trust and credibility. Wirearchy in action is evident in open source software development projects, with minimal command and control, yet able to compete directly with large hierarchical corporations.

A New Model for Training

Workers at the bottom of the traditional organizational pyramid are those who interact closest with their environment (market, customers, information). To be effective today they need to be constantly probing and trying out better ways of work. Management's job is to assist this dynamic flow of sense-making and to respond to workers' needs, within a trusted network of information and knowledge sharing.

The main objective of the new training department is to enable knowledge to flow in the organization. The primary function of learning professionals within this new work model is connecting and communicating, based on three core processes:

* **Facilitating collaborative work** and learning amongst workers, especially as peers.

* **Sensing patterns** and helping to develop emergent work and learning practices.

* **Working with management** to fund and develop appropriate tools and processes for workers.

The only certainty about the future from here on out is that it won't resemble the past. For example, instructional designers no longer have time to develop formal courses. Survival requires people who can navigate a rapidly-changing maze at high speed. They need to find their own curriculum, figure out an appropriate way to learn it, and get on with it. It's cliché to say that people have to learn how to learn. Management needs to support self-learning, not direct it.

Workers will also have to be their own instructional designers, selecting the best methods of learning. Furthermore, given the increasingly reciprocal nature of knowledge work, they will have to know how to teach. Each one-teach-one is at the heart of invent-as-you-go learning. The training department should be encouraging and supporting these activities.

Next?
Will training departments survive to address these issues? The cards are still out. After all, we are in a global economic depression, and training is the perennial first sacrifice.

What would happen if you called for closing your training department in favor of a new function?

Imagine telling senior management that you were shuttering the classrooms in favor of peer-to-peer learning. You're redeploying training staff as mentors, coaches, and facilitators who work on improving core business processes, strengthening relationships with customers, and cutting costs. You're going to shift the focus to creativity, innovation, and helping people perform better, faster, cheaper. You might want to give it a try.

Perhaps the time has come.

Become a Chief Meta-Learning Officer

Today's organizational turmoil is more than just a temporary downturn. The implications will be long-term and significant, calling on CLOs to rethink how they approach their work.

The scope of the chief learning officer's job is mushrooming. CLOs will neither prosper, nor even survive, if they fail to take responsibility for the overall learning process in their organizations. Here's why, and what to do about it.

If you're looking for a way to weather the economic downturn, be aware that this is a permanent climate change, not a passing storm. Most of the time, the global economy is cyclical. It has its ups and downs, but the underlying pattern remains the same. A swing in one direction is balanced by a swing in the other. But what we are experiencing today is fundamental. Things are not going to return to where they were, for we are witnessing the birth of a new world order. We're moving toward continuous change.

Everything is rooted in a life cycle. It's young or old, evolving or dying.

Three hundred years ago, the steam engine replaced manual labor, and industrialists built factories for manufacturing and canals to open up trade. People migrated from farms to cities. Clock-watching replaced working to the rhythm of the sun. Repetitive, mindless factory labor replaced working with farm animals and fields. Taking orders replaced thinking for oneself. Times were chaotic, but eventually, people harnessed electricity, laid rails, rationalized production and created the unprecedented material wealth we enjoy today.

As we move from the industrial age to the era of networks, once again humanity is in turmoil. Yesterday's bedrock is today's soup. Businesses, governments and citizens are becoming densely interconnected. The denser the connections, the faster the cycle time of the networks. Everything is relative because we all depend upon one another. The past no longer mirrors the future. Survivors will be those who learn to deal with surprises as they arrive. The industrial age ended with what we call the "Golden Age of Training." Training was born in the early 20th century and is likely on its last legs.

Companies are focused on sustainability. Staying alive is more important than quarterly earnings. This is a wonderful opportunity for experimentation on a grand scale. For the moment, companies can invest in longer-term projects without being penalized by financial markets that overemphasize the short term.

Organizations must seize the opportunity to change while things are in flux. It's time for them to leap from current conditions to the brave new world of the future. Crossing a chasm takes a bold leap; baby steps won't get you to the other side. Getting to the future will require innovation, luck and perseverance, but that's the price of staying alive.

This big-picture, longer-term viewpoint is meta-learning, and we CLOs need to become chief meta-learning officers.

The View From the Balcony

Your charter as chief meta-learning officer is to optimize learning throughout the organization, not just in the pockets that once belonged to HR. This takes a broader perspective than what you deal with day-to-day. You've got to rise above the noise to see the underlying patterns and then optimize them.

Take a deep breath, clear your head and join us in walking up the steps to a metaphorical balcony. In the plaza below, people are working, talking, gossiping, bragging, coaching, bargaining, learning, competing and playing, as people who get together are wont to do.

No matter what's happening in the plaza, you can always go up to the balcony for a look at the bigger picture.

Among the crowd you can spot colleagues, employees, customers, stakeholders, partners and prospects, as well as total strangers. Groups form and dissipate. News sweeps through the throng. Some people enter the plaza; others depart. All the while, people in and outside of your organization are talking with one another and learning: problem solving, collaborating, innovating. Of course, most learning happens outside the classroom.

On a table alongside your vantage point lies an array of spyglasses, lenses, prisms, telescopes, X-ray glasses, infrared scopes, night-vision goggles, lorgnettes, 4-D glasses and wide-angle binoculars. Each lens provides a selective view of what's going on in the organization's learning plaza below.

Pick up the anthropologist's spyglass to examine the behavior in your workplace. Are people sharing information or hoarding it? Are they learning as part of their work, or is learning a separate activity unto itself? Are people treating one another with respect and honesty, or are they playing politics and posturing? Are they taking time for reflection, or are they so busy they only live in the moment? Are they experimenting and taking risks or are they doggedly following the rules? Are people working collaboratively, or are they doing things in isolation?

Now let's look through the "network connection-sniffing" scope at the quality of learning connections. Is conversation across departments free and easy or hampered by artificial boundaries? Is it easy for people to connect with people in the know? Can people instantly get their hands on the information required to do their jobs? Do our networks route around failure? Are mistakes tolerated and even encouraged? Does everyone have opportunities to learn, or just people new to their jobs? Do all stakeholders have high-quality connections to the organization?

All too often, new hires encounter locked-down, crippled, old-school technology at work that's nowhere near as effective as what they are accustomed to at home.

Take a look through the Web 2.0 lens to focus on the use of collaborative technology. Are people using instant messaging, background profiles, locator systems, social networks, news sources, search engines and multimedia resources that are as good as or superior to what they are accustomed to in their homes? Can workers interact directly with customers? Are discoveries recorded and shared with one another and documented for future use? Do workers have blogs or other means to express themselves? Are workers trusted to view YouTube videos, speak for the organization and access the entire Web?

Now pick up the informal learning magnifier. Are there comfortable places for people to talk? Is informal collaboration encouraged? Are workers intrinsically motivated to learn and increase their professionalism, or are they waiting for the next class or workshop? Are people learning from observing others, generating or grasping nifty graphics, and reflecting on experience? Are people with common professional interests hanging out together, helping each other get better at their thing? Is any of this activity nurtured by the chief meta-learning officer, or is informal learning left to happenstance? Do you see coaches, mentors, scribes, stewards, gardeners and learning ecosystem architects from the organization improving the learning process?

Put on the learning skills spectacles and look at your people. Are they efficient in their learning? Are they wasting time on poorly structured searches? Do they mistakenly trust the information they find instead of analyzing it? Are they connecting to the right people, or whoever is closest? Are they communicating clearly and interpreting data effectively? Do they re-represent problems, and are they applying useful problem-solving approaches?

Feel free to grab any lens from the table. Look at your organization from the big-picture level. Are people helping one another learn? Are they fulfilled in their work? Are they smiling? Are they having a good time? Are they committed? Are they bringing innovation to the organization? Are they "being all they can be?" Is this sufficient to get your company across the chasm?

Before you descend the steps back into the fray of business as usual, take a moment to ponder whether you're doing all you can to create a great environment for learning for the people down in the plaza. Visualize what the view of an effective organization would look like. Taking a meta-learning viewpoint will increase your organization's odds of sustainability in tough times and of prosperity in great ones.

Participatory culture

ACTIVE	PASSIVE
Web 2.0 culture: Pull	**School culture: Push**
learner-driven	instructor-driven
Process focus	Event focus
Content defined by learner	Content mandated by others
Relationships, conversation	Courses, workshops

Close the Training Department

Let's begin thinking about the role of the chief meta-learning officer by clearing the slate. Imagine the training department didn't exist. Tear up the org chart and rethink what needs to be done.

If you were starting from scratch, what functions would you create? Be careful here, for the ever-faster pace of change and the inherent unpredictability of our complex world render old-style training, which focused on past practice, obsolete. "Execution" isn't the operative word; "innovation" is. You need to concentrate on learning as problem-solving, collaborating to take advantage of new situations and having the connections to deal with novel situations. These are the tools needed to survive and thrive.

Paint a scenario of what the new world will look like, and work backward to discover what it takes to get there. Involve stakeholders because breaking through to the other side is a group effort. You've got to go through the scenario planning with your people to co-create a vision you believe in. Here are some of the characteristics we see.

In business, networks supplement, surround and challenge hierarchies. Sound vision and leadership will inspire, not control, workers. Managers, workers, customers and partners will recognize we're all in this together. Organizations are going to have to be more flexible, more nimble, be able to adapt and move faster. That requires faster and more effective problem solving. We know innovation isn't the product of one person, but of collaboration and ongoing work by people who are motivated and supported.

In work itself, rote tasks are being automated, and knowledge work is what creates value. According to Dan Pink in his book *A Whole New Mind*, the greatest value is born of contributions that integrate left- and right-brain skills to be creative and capable. Furthermore, most knowledge work is boss-less, challenging the worker to make decisions on the spot. This takes knowing how to learn and who to turn to rather than trying to figure out things in advance. In essence, it requires learning on demand.

Corporate culture is becoming participatory. Authenticity, transparency, sharing, experimentation, peer power and togetherness are what it takes to succeed in a networked environment. As the tendrils of communications networks slither through silos and corporate boundaries, network values become the default organizational values. Cisco, which lives and breathes networks, is an example of baking network values into a corporate culture.

Instructional designers will become rangers who nurture learning ecologies instead of planters who live for one crop but disappear after the first harvest. Learning design will shift its gaze from events to processes; from helping people acquire skills to helping them participate in ongoing inquiry; and from focusing on explicit, top-down lessons to helping people gain the tacit knowledge to learn on their feet.

Free range learners

Free-range learners choose how and what they learn. Self-service is less expensive and more timely than the alternative. Informal learning has no need for the busywork, chrome, and bureaucracy that accompany typical corporate training. Less is more.

Technology enables networks, but the major changes in store are not about the technology. Our challenge, according to Yochai Benkler in his article "Complexity and Humanity," is "to build systems that will allow us to be largely free to inquire, experiment, learn and communicate, that will encourage us to cooperate, and that will avoid the worst of what human beings are capable of, and elicit what is best."

Here's a test: In your organization, can individuals admit mistakes? If they can't, they keep making the same ones. Yet, you can't celebrate mistakes, so what do you do? It's OK to lose, if you don't lose the lesson.

The chief meta-learning officer needs to know where the organization is headed before deciding how to get there. Does this picture ring true for your organization? Is this where you're headed? If not, we encourage you to shape up a scenario that does.

Assess Opportunities for Process Improvement

Is your organization's approach to learning sustainable? Are your people learning enough to work in concert and create the future company you want to be associated with? How do your efforts stack up against those of your peers in major corporations?

These are not easy questions to answer. That's the way it is when civilization makes tectonic changes. Ask yourself if your organization looks at learning as an opportunity or a cost. How far ahead do you look when making decisions about corporate learning? Do you invest in helping your workers learn to learn? Learn to teach?

Have you taken charge of learning for your organization, or just training?

Network Era Productivity: Not Your Father's ROI

Today's networked era requires a new way to make investment decisions that incorporates intangible assets and more accurately depicts how value is created.

The industrial age has run out of steam. Look at General Motors. Look at Chrysler. We are witnessing the death throes of management models that have outlived their usefulness.

The network era now replacing the industrial age holds great promise. Networked organizations are reaping rewards for connecting people, know-how and ideas at an ever-faster pace. Value creation has migrated from what we can see (physical assets) to intangibles (ideas). Look at Google and Cisco.

Understandably, seasoned executives, chief learning officers among them, are having a devil of a time shifting from the industrial age mindset of logic, certainty and bounded constraints to the network gestalt of interaction, self-organization, unpredictability and fewer limits to potential. The pressure is constantly on to meet quarter-to-quarter revenue and earnings targets that in turn accentuate the need to take decisions that support achieving those targets. At the same time, we are shifting into an era in which knowledge work and learning occur where re-engineered business processes collide with a participative and interactive ecology of information flows.

How can a chief learning officer hope to make informed judgments in this continually expanding networked environment that's flowing ever faster, spreading power among its members and producing outsized impacts in unpredictable ways? What to do?

One cherished industrial age concept that is proving particularly difficult to let go of is return on investment (ROI). But like Pontiacs and Oldsmobiles, old-school ROI's day in the sun is waning. In an environment of continuous flow and interaction, there's a need to consider an emerging metric: return on investment in interaction (ROII). The working definition of ROII is the observable development of capacity and capability to create economic values out of intangibles.

Consultants and smart-aleck MBAs will tell you if you want to sell a big project internally, you've got to talk ROI. It's the language senior managers understand. Being fluent in ROI talk addresses the "hard" tangible returns stemming from an investment in a specific project or capacity. It is supposedly the secret handshake that gets you to the inner circle of those who control budget dollars.

Let's look at what ROI was, how it needs to be changed and how to recapture its original intent in the network era, in which continuous learning and knowledge work are becoming inseparable. As Steven Forth of the LeveragePoint division of the Monitor Group puts it, "Too many people who talk about the ROI of learning are focused on being precisely wrong rather than directionally correct."

Traditional ROI

ROI is an accounting and financial management concept businesses use to decide where to make investments and to assess the success of investment decisions after the fact. ROI reduces both return — R, what you expect back — and investment — I, what you expect to put in to numbers — making it possible to compare one investment opportunity to another. The numbers tie back to categories on the balance sheet and income statement, (i.e. tangible assets and hard-dollar returns).

ROI is what you get for your money, divided by what you spent to get it. It's R/I expressed as a percentage. In a business culture that is skeptical of nonnumerical reasoning, ROI implies disciplined, mathematical rigor. It ties actions to intended results. It shows the logic of how results will be achieved.

Companies set up ROI hurdle rates to gauge whether there will be sufficient payback over a reasonable and defined period of time to justify the capital invested to acquire additional capacity or produce a defined result. Companies also use ROI to evaluate past performance. In retrospect, what was spent and what benefits were received? This simplifies making the case for similar projects in the future.

What You Can't See

In the network era, things you can't see are more valuable than things you can. Thomas Stewart sounded a clarion call in his book *The Wealth of Knowledge* with his exhortation that building the capacity to create economic value through things such as innovating and enhancing brand reputation is as important, or more important, than generating specific results from a specific initiative. Twenty-five years ago, intangibles accounted for less than a third of the value of the S&P 500. Today, intangibles can make up more than 80 percent of that value.

On paper, Google's net worth was about $30 billion at the end of 2008. That's what it paid for computers, buildings and stuff you can see, minus debts and the expense of wear and tear. Stock market investors value Google at $125 billion. Where does the extra $95 billion come from? Intangibles.

"Intangible assets — a skilled workforce, patents and know-how, software, strong customer relationships, brands, unique organizational designs and processes, and the like — generate most of corporate growth and shareholder value," wrote NYU Professor Baruch Lev in *Harvard Business Review* in June 2004.

Corporate decision makers say their goal is to increase shareholder value. In a networked, information-based environment, shareholders value brand, reputation, ideas, relationships and know-how. These assets don't appear on the balance sheet, but more and more often they provide a corporation's competitive edge. These most important aspects of the business aren't recognized by old-school accounting and therefore aren't factored into ROI calculations.

Organizations that make decisions based solely on things that are sufficiently tangible to be counted directly might as well consult a Ouija board to set their goals. Leaving the most important sources of value out of the ROI equation is not conservative — it's foolish.

Measuring intangibles involves making judgment calls, so managers often exclude intangibles from their ROI calculations. Several purported authorities on calculating ROI suggest taking intangibles into account by putting them on a list but refusing to estimate their value. This leads you to comparing numbers to words, apples to oranges.

You Must Manage What You Can't Measure
"You can't manage what you can't measure" was a mantra of industrial age management. Adopting F.W. Taylor's brilliant research and models, generations of managers have carried stopwatches and pored over measurements in a continual quest to make things work better. Efficiency was the road to riches in the slower-moving, predictable industrial age, and measurement was the proof of the pudding.

While the measurement meme works when your goal is to tweak the way you've been doing things and other operational decisions, it doesn't apply to making judgment calls, strategic choices or disruptive innovations.

Executives manage immeasurable things all the time. The more powerful the executive, the more likely he or she is involved in effectiveness — doing the right things rather than doing things right. Intuition, judgment and gut feelings guide these more important decisions. Qualitative assessment often can make up for a concrete numeric result.

Make a hypothesis of cause and effect. Interview a statistically significant sample of the workforce to see if the hypothesis holds up. Often, results obtained from social science research methods will produce more meaningful feedback than solid counts of the wrong thing.

The old "can't measure, can't manage" dodge doesn't free businesspeople from making decisions under conditions of uncertainty, and the network era ushers in uncertainty in spades.

Making Decisions in the Network Era

A business network is a group of individuals or organizations that are linked together by factors such as values, visions, ideas, financial exchange and collaboration to further the ends of the corporation. Business networks share common characteristics with all networks:

• They multiply like rabbits because the value of a network increases exponentially with each additional connection.

• They naturally become faster and faster because the denser the interconnections, the faster its cycle time.

• They subvert hierarchy because previously scarce resources such as information are available to all.

• Network interactions yield volatile results because echo effects amplify signals.

• Networks connect with other networks to form complex adaptive systems whose outcomes are inherently unpredictable.

Intangibles travel via networks, and networks are the infrastructure for doing business in the future. An overarching caveat here: Strategist and practitioner Stuart Henshall said trust is critical. "It's the one qualitative factor all networks depend upon."

ROI, the tool we once used to evaluate projects in stable times, clearly is not up to the task. The impacts of collaboration-based knowledge work are accelerating. However, the Western world is lurching from crisis to crisis, and executives are under constant pressure to perform. It's difficult for them to give up models they understand well.

In the future, organizational effectiveness will be defined by the interaction of workers in a networked environment. Exchanges of information and knowledge are what make peoples' brains work on a purpose and what gets the imagination going to formulate pertinent responses. However, the return on networked collaboration is less tangible than the results generated from stable and ordered sequential tasks that dominate the efficiency-oriented industrial era.

So we face the problem of convincing managers to adopt new mental models that incorporate the intangibles generated by a whole system, the organization and its interconnected networks. Making a business decision to invest in new ways of working is a complex process involving many factors and intricate tradeoffs, such as:

• Risks must be weighed against rewards.

• Short-term vs. long-term aims.

• Alignment with strategic initiatives.

• Scarce resources call for shrewd horse trading.

Identifying and Measuring ROII

The focus in this new world of work is to do what's important and involve those who know what's important, why it's important and what they know (or know how to find out) about a problem or issue. To begin measuring increases in productivity and value in a networked social computing environment, we propose return on investment in interaction (ROII), derived from the principles of Metcalfe's law of networks.

Some core assumptions about ROII :

• Continuous flows of information are the raw material of an organization's value creation and overall performance.

• Information flows are carried by links, alerts, RSS feeds, search engines, aggregatlon and filtering of content.

• All leading vendors' productivity platforms now feature collaborative social networking and computing.

• These platforms' architectures facilitate purposeful cross-silo communications and exchange.

In a June 2008 "The Network Thinker" blog post, social networking pioneer Valdis Krebs outlined four generic metrics that are becoming widely accepted as leading to observable, tangible measurable outputs:

• Increase in size of network.

• Increase in internal network connectivity.

• Increase in connection to valuable third parties.

• Increase in number of projects formed from all three factors above.

It's important to note here that we are not proposing a definitive answer, but rather the need to debate and clarify the issues. Each of the principles outlined above proposed by Krebs addresses the productivity of network activity. Unpacking them can help us understand how to begin to assess ROII.

Increase in Network Size

If we follow the logic of two heads are better than one, and therefore X heads are better than two, in social- and knowledge-building networks, we can expect to find:

• More engagement with an issue.

• More analysis by more people.

• More input from more people.

• More possibilities that may have been overlooked.

• Quicker and more comprehensive analysis.

CapGemini's relaunch of its knowledge management initiatives offers a great example. Its initial program wasn't working: 20 percent year-on-year usage decline, three and a half year average document age and an average of seven years to refresh current knowledge. It relaunched informally via word of mouth and within six months had 27,000 of 83,000 employees using it, involved in 900 communities exchanging information and pertinent knowledge on a daily basis. All that activity came without spending a single dollar on formal internal communications or training.

Increase in Internal Network Connectivity

Increases in network connectivity involve the degree, frequency, density and concentration of information flows between nodes in a social network. The organization is able to define better business and market intelligence, more frequent and tangible customer centricity and responsiveness, and clear instances in which cross-silo knowledge exchanges lead to tangible results.

At CapGemini, six months after the informal launch, the 900 communities of practice were using 500 forums, 500 wikis and more than 250 expertise- or project-focused blogs. Business results as defined in the previous paragraph are not long behind.

Increase in Connection to Valuable Third Parties

In today's increasingly interconnected environment, ignoring external parties that have an interest in products or services is a guarantee for trouble. These interested parties talk about brands or offer up opportunities, and organizations that respond rapidly and effectively to issues gain competitive advantage.

Ford Motor Co. opened up its launch of the new Sync service to customer input and conversation. With 1 million page views in less than 12 months, the company experienced a significant reduction in customer-service support costs as 10,000 customers began to offer each other tips, pointers and answers. Further, it began to receive significant tangible market intelligence as engaged users began to share product integration and compatibility experiences, tips and tricks.

Increase in Number of Projects

ROII is obvious when the scope, degree and intensity of interaction increase due to implementation of the three above principles. An increase in the number of projects creates value as people learn to work together effectively in networks, putting informal learning to work on resolving issues, creating opportunities and generating activity that enhances an organization's reputation for listening and responding effectively.

Fast Company recently published an article on Cisco Systems' large-scale adoption of social computing as the main means of working with information and knowledge. CEO John Chambers said that as a result, Cisco has gone from being able to focus on three to five strategic initiatives at a time, to now working on 26-27 strategic initiatives in parallel.

Informed Judgment

The heart of the matter is providing decision makers with an informed business case that ties investment to the results that it brings. A solid case describes results in business terms, such as increased revenue, better customer service, reduced cost or speedier time to performance.

Network returns are asymmetric, so simplistic count-'em-up approaches are no longer viable. But how can one make a solid network-era case to an executive who is still playing by yesterday's rules?

The answer is to improve the corporate network as a continuous process, not as a project with a hurdle rate. Improving network performance need not be all-or-nothing. It can be implemented in small stages. Break major decisions into numerous low-risk incremental decisions. Instead of making one major decision a year, CLOs might look at boosting network results as a series of monthly decisions. Continuous monitoring of the statistics of ROII would guide mid-course corrections.

Life was simpler when you could measure performance by counting the number of widgets produced, shipped or sold. Given that the networked workplace and markets are here to stay, how can managers begin to adapt and refocus long-standing mental models about what and where to invest precious energy and time? An effective response to this conundrum is qualitative assessment.

Create a hypothesis and use existing techniques — surveys, focus groups, facilitated brainstorming — to find out what employees and customers are doing and how they want to work together. Then, check it out with a wider sample of the workforce to see if it holds up. It's clear we are moving rapidly into a networked world in which responsiveness, innovation, gaining competitive advantage through learning faster and embedding knowledge into products and services are all important.

In a world of intangibles, we need to contribute to the productivity, viability and profitability of any given enterprise. We should rethink and expand our methods for making judgments about where, when and how we invest in the ongoing interaction between our employees and customers. That is the return on investment in interaction.

Develop Your Elevator Pitch for a Learning Initiative

Imagine you are riding the elevator to your office on the sixth floor. Just before the doors close, a senior executive from your organization hops in for the ride. "What are you working on?" she asks. You have thirty seconds to a minute to sell your concept for a project to boost organizational intelligence. That's your **elevator pitch.**

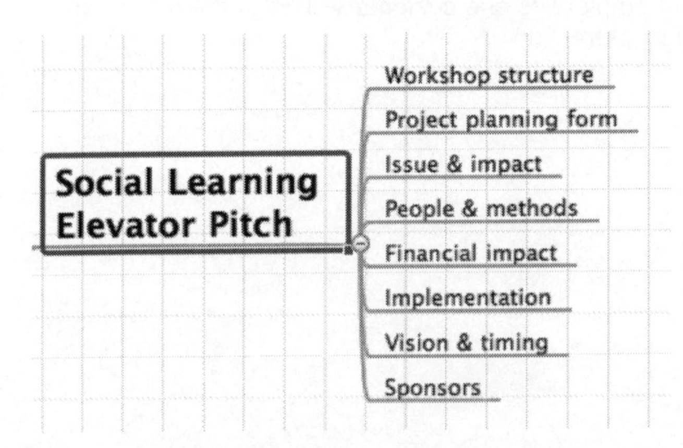

Your pitch needs to explain what you are proposing to do, how it will help the organization, who will be involved, and why you will be successful. To sell your idea, you must answer the question that's top of mind for every skeptical executive, "What's in it for me?"

Frequently organizations invite me to spend a day or two with a group of managers, showing them how to spot opportunities for improvement, flesh out action plans, and convince their people to get on board.

Our objective is for each person to leave the session with an elevator pitch for a proposed project for increasing organizational effectiveness.

I'm a realist. I recognize that many of the managers attending the workshop will never give their elevator pitch. Or they'll deliver it poorly or to the wrong person. But if the overall group plants the seeds for a dozen different game-changing projects, the odds are that several of them will make a huge improvement in the organization's collaborative intelligence.

Workshop structure

Every organization is different, so before delivering a workshop I take time to talk with staff, managers, and sometimes customers, too. I may conduct a survey of workers or managers, easy to do in these days of automated data collection and email. I try to gauge what is top on the organizational agenda, what the culture is like, where the corporate arteries are clogged, and what keeps managers awake at night. This enables me to configure a targeted, custom workshop.

Before the workshop, I tell participants "You must identify a performance gap you would like to help close with informal or social learning before attending our workshop. It's the price of admission."

While every workshop is unique, most follow a common pattern. First, I tell stories about how other organizations have harnessed their brainpower. Then, small groups of participants discuss the material in light of their own organization. Next, each person homes in on their own situation, jotting down a few lines on a planning form.

We repeat this cycle of presentation, discussion, and planning for each of a set of questions, for example:

Issue: What do you want to help the organization do better?

Impact: What is the potential impact?

People: Who will be involved and what roles will they play?

Methods: How do you propose to make the improvements?

Financial impact: Quantify the outcomes of the change.

Implementation: What are the barriers to success? What's the process?

Vision: What does the project look like?

Timing: What is your timeframe?

Sponsors: Whom do you need to get on board?

Name: Give your project a one- or two-word name.

Throughout the session, participants are thinking through and deciding upon the elements of their proposals. At each stage, they take notes or draw diagrams on a planning form.

What makes a good pitch

At the conclusion of the session, everyone writes their 30-second elevator pitch and presents it to others in their group. Sometimes everyone pitches the entire group, and we award prizes to the most compelling.[28]

You should be able to jot down the main points of your change project on the back of an envelope. In fact, I sometimes distribute envelopes to people in the workshop for just this purpose.

---

[28] You can see workshop participants doing their elevator pitches at a workshop Clark Quinn and I conducted at DevLearn 09 in San Jose at http://www.youtube.com/user/jakeross1#p/u/9/py37gZWrqNw

If the rationale for your project won't fit on the envelope, you need to distill it to essence. Take your logic up a level. What's the big picture? What's the final outcome?

The envelope's an interim step to delivering your pitch orally. Once you've presented the essence of your proposal succinctly to someone else, you'll no longer need the envelope as a crutch.

The next three pages show a sample planning form.

Project Planning Form

Issue: What do you want to help the organization do better? Choose an important challenge that might be solved with informal or social learning.	
Impact: What is the potential impact? ☒ Increase revenue ☒ Lower cost ☒ Time to performance ☒ Improve service ☒ Boost efficiency ☒ Flexibility ☒ Innovation	
People: Who will be involved and what roles will they play? ☒ Workers/ learners ☒ Mentors/ coaches ☒ Elders/experts ☒ Facilitators ☒ Sponsor ☒ Stakeholders	

Vision: What does the project look like? What's your sales pitch?	
Timing: What is your timeframe? What are the major steps?	
Sponsors: Whom do you need to get on board? Who do you want to join you in the elevator?	
Name: Give your project a one- or two-word name. Choose a "brand name.	

Hints for developing your plan

The Issue

The issue must address a significant upside opportunity for the organization, something a reasonable sponsor will find compelling.

Describe outcomes, not steps to getting to them. "Increasing the amount of informal learning" is not a viable issue; it's but the means to an end. The underlying issue could be something like "reduce customer service errors by 20%" or "bring new reps up to speed two months faster."

Look for issues that save time, increase revenue, cut costs, or improve efficiency.

	Save time	Increase Revenue	Cut Costs	Improve Efficiency
Make sales force productive sooner	•	•		•
Educate customers online		•	•	
Increase reach	•	•		•
Eliminate travel and delivery costs	•	•	•	•
Reduce staff turnover	•		•	•
Reduce cycle time	•		•	•
Keep up with a gusher of new products	•	•		•
Enriching the value chain	•		•	•
Launch products virtually	•	•		•
Improving the productivity of channel partners	•	•		•
Manage the people value chain			•	•
Bringing e-process to cottage industries	•		•	•
Build customer communities		•		•
Transform business model	•	•		•
Enriching the value chain	•			•

Organizations have used informal, networked approaches to solve challenges like these. Use the list as a catalyst to your thinking.

Substandard revenue

☒ Sales are declining, customers are postponing decisions
☒ Sales force cannot express benefits of new products
☒ Sellers unaware of industry conditions and competition
☒ Friction in relationships with distributors
☒ Partners are not well informed

☒ Arms-length relationships with customers

Deficient service
☒ Response time to customers is substandard
☒ After-sales inquiries are bogging down call centers
☒ 800 numbers and phone trees are driving customers away
☒ Service is inconvenient for customers, not 24/7
☒ Not building customer loyalty
☒ Customer and prospects are confused, frustrated

Inefficiency and bureaucracy
☒ People don't know who knows what
☒ Can't the right information when you need it
☒ Project coordination is tedious and things fall through the cracks
☒ Re-creating the same documents over and over again
☒ Don't learn from people who join us from competitors
☒ Documentation is dated, versions confusing

Unenthusiastic, sluggish staff
☒ People are not innovators and don't keep up
☒ Our know-how is walking out the door due to retirement and turnover
☒ Turnover is too high
☒ When people leave, we never hear from them again

Underdeveloped organization
☒ Difficult to collaborate
☒ Takes too long for new hires to become productive
☒ Analysis paralysis
☒ "Wait and see" attitude = missed opportunities

Suboptimal execution
☒ Not everyone is on the same page
☒ Our people don't know our history, values, culture
☒ Set in our ways, reluctant to change

- [x] Not moving fast enough to stay ahead of competitors
- [x] Functional silos thwart process improvement
- [x] Acting like separate companies long after the merger
- [x] Teams don't discuss the trends that drive our business
- [x] Don't reflect on our successes and failures
- [x] Don't take advantage of our collective intelligence

Not learning

- [x] We are falling behind
- [x] Not prepared for onslaught of digital natives
- [x] Training can't keep pace with the business
- [x] Training administration and delivery cost too much
- [x] Managers hoard information

Impact

What's in it for the organization? Explain this to your sponsor.

People

An organization that is committed to working smarter needs to assess the impact of helping employees learn at every step in their career cycle with the company. What's it worth, for example, to offer learning opportunities to potential recruits before they come on board? These "pre-hires" can become familiar with the company before signing on. This can cut hiring mistakes that hurt both the organization and the new hire.

Seasoned employees are not going to flock to classes and workshops; they have work to do. But making it easier for them to learn through collaboration, self-service learning, and skill bites helps sharp people become sharper. Making a producer just a little bit more productive returns giant rewards at the bottom line, more than anything you could do to beef up what the novices are doing.

Increasingly, the people who work for an organization are not on the payroll. They are contract workers and people called in for a particular project. They work for an outsource provider. They are temps, specialists, consultants, and service providers.

As companies focus on core and delegate overhead activities to others, more people are paid on company invoices and fewer individuals receive paychecks. This does not mean the workers who don't receive paychecks are exempt from needing to know what is going on and to continuously get better at what they do. It's the logic of the supply chain: the inefficiencies of bad links get passed along to the customer eventually; companies must optimize the performance of the chain. That means considering the merits of improving the brainpower of everyone who works for the company, not just those who receive paychecks drawn on the company's bank.

Markets are relationships. Value has moved from the nodes to the connections. No business can survive without good ties to a healthy ecosystem. Learning together builds strong relationships. And if your product is worthy, an informed customer is a better customer.

Methods

Our focus in the workshop is on building platforms to increase brainpower over time, not programs that run in a single point in time.

You might think of it as constructing virtual meeting places and stores of wisdom instead of developing curriculum and specific lessons.

The challenge is to come up with activities and on-going processes that foster communities of practice, collaboration, story-telling, information feeds, self-service learning, and finding what you need, when you need it.

To maintain your focus on processes, not programs, consider what comes before your proposed activity and what comes after:

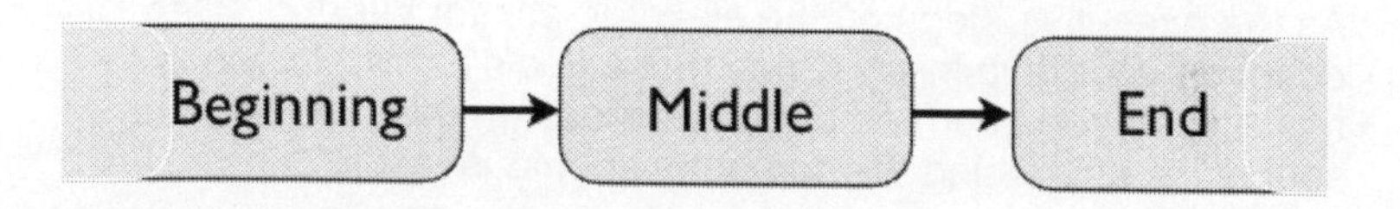

Financial Impact

Quantify the impact of your proposed activity in dollars and cents.

Informal/social network learning initiatives have outsized returns. If your project is not going to bring in at least $1,000,000, find another project.

When you bring in millions of dollars worth of benefits at a cost of only thousands, you don't need three-place accuracy to make your case. Plus or minus 50% will suffice.

That said, the only legitimate metrics of learning are business metrics, i.e. the value of changed behavior to the organization. In order to be heard, you *must* express yourself in these terms.

Implementation

What are the major barriers to success? Consider the likely pitfalls. Then describe how you plan to overcome them.

Vision
Put the pieces together. What are you proposing to do?

Timing
Specify half a dozen milestones. What is the timeframe for each?

Sponsor
Who has to sign off on your project to make it happen? Who do you need to convince? How do you plan to buttonhole this individual in the elevator?

Name
Pick a shorthand name for your project. Brand it. Make it sound like something exciting and desirable.

Commitment
As the executive steps off the elevator, ask for support. "Can I count on your help in achieving these goals?" "Would you like me to keep you informed of our progress on this?" "Does this sound like something the company should invest in?"

Jane Hart and Charles Jennings

Cheat sheets

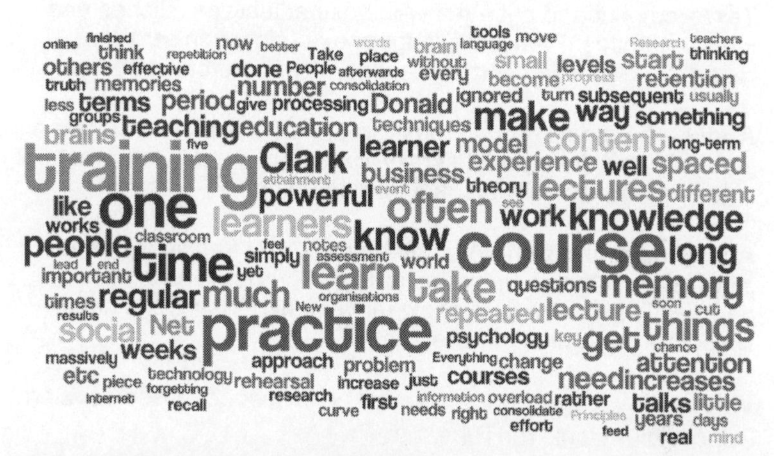

Donald Clark: 10 ways to shorten courses

Donald Clark[29] has blogged that cognitive overload is the norm in education and training. New teachers present too much too soon, to bewildered learners. Lecturers hammer out dense, hour-long lectures. Trainers construct overlong, padded-out courses. Whether it's classroom, lecture, conference talk, workshop or eLearning, it's usually too long. Don't take a scalpel to your courses, take an axe - aim for 30% reduction on first pass.

Learning objectives – if your course has these up front –ditch them. They're boring and irrelevant. You need to interest learners not turn them off.

'Introduction' – if this appears as your first module, chapter, slide etc – cut it. I don't mean make it shorter; I mean massacre it. 'The history of…' is particularly irrelevant.

---

29 Donald Clark is the wittiest person I know. He founded what became the largest eLearning firm in the UK and then sold it. Donald has made his money, so he can say whatever he feels like. And he does. He pillories blowhards and calls BS for what it is when he sees it. The lists of ten items are priceless. http://donaldclarkplanb.blogspot.com The USA has a Donald Clark, too. Different fellow. Nowhere near as funny.

Pretty but useless graphics – all those graphics that simply illustrate and don't instruct –stock photos of over eager people in offices. Don't insert graphics that simply match key nouns in the text.

Text – cut, cut and cut again. All those adjectives, clichés and long sentences. Forget the language of print such as 'With regard to ' etc. Use short sentences. Use more bullet points.

Audio – if it's background music get rid of it. Annoying beeps on input will also drive people crazy. Extraneous audio is a waste of time and may actually distract from learning.

Annoying animation - Animated words and transitions, that are all whiz-bang but serve no instructional purpose. Animation is only useful if you have to show movement. Flash is the usual suspect – reign those flashers in.

Video – anything longer than a TV ad is suspect. Keep as short as possible. Think YouTube, not TV.

Glossary – only in very technical courses. If you're using words the learner doesn't understand, rewrite, don't rely on a glossary.

Donald Clark

Abandon fixed times – don't do the '1 hour' of learning or 1 hour lecture or full day course. Make it only as long as it needs to be.

Happy sheets – they don't tell you anything about learning, so abandon them altogether.

Lessons Learned from a 12 social learning implementations

- **Platform choice** – choosing the most appropriate platform is important for your SLE – whether it be Facebook, Ning or Elgg. Each has their pros and cons – consider these carefully, See this comparison chart[30] of three platforms according to different criteria.
- **Terminology** – the name of the site and its description is important. Do you call it a "social network", "social environment" or "collaboration platform"? or even use the term social? Naming of terms like friends is key – OK for Facebook, but not for business; I've changed this to Contacts and Colleagues in different sites
- **Piloting** – make sure the size is right; community projects require numbers; group projects can be smaller
- **Growth** - let the site grow naturally and organically - tend it and nurture it but don't force it. Slow steady growth is better than fast use and then tail-off. Evolution is better than revolution!
- **Promotion** – when promoting the site, viral marketing techniques work well – ie don't force everyone on it as a user – work with groups that are enthusiastic– let them talk about it; sooner or later others will want to join in,
- **Usability -** bear in mind that when people that have used other social networking systems will be influenced by them; new users seem to adapt faster – they have no preconceived ideas of what it should look like.
- **Success measures -** don't worry about stats – number of users, number of posts, number of discussion. Focus on the value that it is bringing to the different groups. Get groups to say how they will determine whether their own group space has been successful. This will probably be in terms of better communication, easier collaboration, increase in productivity or performance etc – rather than how many times X or Y made a blog posting.

Cybernetics with Paul Pangaro

An interview with cybernetician Paul Pangaro begins,

---

30 http://www.c4lpt.co.uk/handbook/comparison.html

Cybernetics comes from the Greek word for steering, specifically the art of steering. As you steer, you have an objective. You have an idea of where you want to go, but as you set out to get there, you're blown off course. You don't go straight; you have some backs and forths. So cybernetics involves the notion of using feedback to get from your action to your goal.

In fact, the word feedback comes from this activity in the middle of the twentieth century by a bunch of extraordinary people, Gregory Bateson, Margaret Mead, John von Neumann, Nobert Wiener, Heinz von Forrester, and others who said, 'There's this thing that systems do. They have a goal and use information to get to that goal. Let's call that *feedback*.'

The reason we should care is that intelligent systems, human beings, have goals, and they use feedback to get to those goals. Cybernetics, the science of feedback, information, and goals, is incredibly valuable in a number of different disciplines.

You can see the two-part interview on YouTube. Here's a diagram of how feedback works:

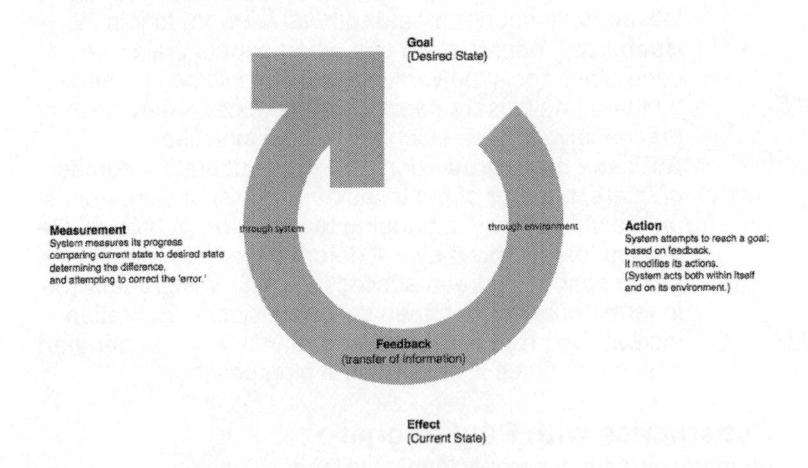

Paul uses the principles of cybernetics as a framework for improving conversations:

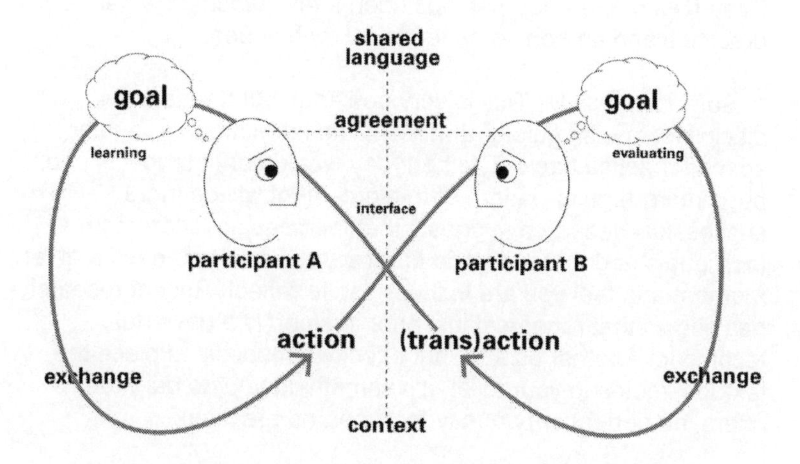

Donald Clark: 10 techniques to massively increase retention

This is the classic 'forgetting curve' by Ebbinghaus, a fundamental truth in memory theory, totally ignored by most educators and trainers. Most fixed 'courses' or 'lectures' take no notice of the phenomenon, condemning much of their effort to the world of lost memories. Most educational and training pedagogies are hopelessly inefficient because they fail to recognise this basic truth. Smart learners get it. They revise over a period, with regular doses to consolidate their memories.

Little and often
The real solution, to this massive problem of forgetfulness, is spaced practice, little and often, the regular rehearsal and practice of the knowledge/skill over a period of time to elaborate and allow deep processing to fix long-term memories. If we get this right, increases on the productivity of learning can be enormous. We are not talking small increase in knowledge and retention but increases of 200-700%. It has the potential to radically alter the attainment levels in schools, colleges, universities and organisations. OK, that's the theory, what about the practice?

What strategies enable spaced practice?

I'll start with a few 'learner' tips, then a few 'teacher/trainer' practices and end on some technical techniques.

1. Self- rehearsal – This is very powerful, but needs self-discipline. You sit quietly, and recall the learning on a regular, spaced practice basis. The hour/day/week/month model is one, but a more regular pattern of reinforcement will be more successful. Research suggests that the spacing different for individuals and that it is good to rehearse when you have a quiet moment and feel you are in the mood to reflect. Recent research has shown that rehearsal just prior to sleep is a powerful technique. Another bizarre, but effective, model is to place the textbook/notes in your toilet. It's something you do daily, and offers the perfect opportunity for repeated practice!

2. Take notes – write up your learning experience, in your own words, diagrams, analogies. This can result in dramatic increases in learning (20-30%). Then re-read a few times afterwards or type up as a more coherent piece. It is important to summarize and re-read your notes as soon as possible after the learning experience.

3. Blogging – if the learner blogs his/her learning experience after the course, then responds to the tutors', and others' comments for a few weeks afterwards, we have repeated consolidation, and the content has a much higher chance of being retained.

4. Repetition – within the course, but also at the start of every subsequent period, lesson or lecture, repeat (not in parrot fashion) the ground that was covered previously. Take five or ten minutes at the start to ask key questions about the previous content.

5. Delayed assessment – give learners exercises to do after the course and explain that you will assess them a few weeks, months after the course has finished. This prevents reliance on short-term memory and gives them a chance to consolidate their knowledge/skills.

6. Record – it is education and training' great act of stupidity, not to record talks, lectures and presentations. They give the learner subsequent access to the content and therefore spaced practice.

7. Games pedagogy – Games have powerful pedagogies. They have to as they are hard. It works through repeated attempts and failure. You only progress as your acquired competence allows. Most games involve huge amounts of repetition and failure with levels of attainment that take days, weeks and months to complete.

8. Spaced e-learning – schedule a pattern in your online learning, so that learners do less in one sitting and spread their learning over a longer period of time, with shorter episodes. Free your learners from the tyranny of time and location, allowing them to do little and often. In education this is homework and assignments, in training subsequent talks that need to be emailed back to the trainer/tutor.

9. Mobile technology – the drip feed of assessment over a number of weeks after the course or redesign the whole course as a drip-feed experience. We have the ideal device in our pockets – mobiles. They're powerful, portable and personal. Push out small chunks or banks of questions, structured so that repetition and consolidation happens. This usually involves the repeated testing of the individual until you feel that the learning has succeeded.

10. Less long holidays – it terms of public policy, increasing school results would be betters served by avoiding the long summer holiday and restructuring the school, college and University years around more regular terms and less long vacations.

Benefits
The retention benefit works like compound interest as you're building on previous learning, deepening the processing and consolidating long-term memory. It is, in my opinion, the single most effective strategic change we could make to our learning interventions.

Eric Davidov:

Five Easy Steps to an Instant Infrastructure for Social Learning

Step 1 - Strategize: There is no one "right" Social Learning strategy, and there is no one right way to develop one. The approach to strategy development depends on several factors such as your organizational structure, existing learning programs, organizational learning culture, and the value executives place on informal learning. The most powerful approach to strategy development, from my experience, is to develop one that is business-driven. In other words, aligned to larger company goals like increased innovation, increased collaboration across traditional organizational silos, reducing reliance on the aging workforce, compressing time to performance, etc. The strategy should paint a compelling picture of the future state of social learning, clearly articulate the business case for change, and outline the roadmap for how you will get from "here" to "there" (including what must change, stop, and continue).

Deliverables:

- Social Learning strategy and approach document.
- User Stories for selected networking, collaboration, knowledge management, and learning technologies.
- List of expected challenges, uncertainties and risks with a supporting mitigation plan.
- Defined methods and tools to monitor and evaluate Social Learning behaviors and benefits realised.
- An end-to-end High Level Approach and Process Definition for "Implementation and Support."
- Benchmarking data (in order to validate the overall strategy and approach).
- A list of critical success factors and key planning assumptions.

Step 2 - Implement: Select, procure, install, develop, prepare and test the 'Social Learning' ecosystem' (technology, sites, policies, procedures, governance, and team members). I advise you to conduct a proof of concept and pilot test before committing to an enterprise wide implementation.

Deliverables:

- A mobilised Social Learning eco-system (technologies, governance, policies, procedures, services, and roles). Initially you might consider focusing on the most important communities of practices or workforce roles – where the business has the greatest need.
- One trained and capable community manager for each selected community of practice or workforce roles. The community manager is critical to the success of the Social Learning system. The people in this role will provide oversight on usage and policy compliance, manage content, manage community engagement, track and report trends-needs-benefits-impact, and help resolve issues.
- Basic training for "users" on the administration, policies, and use of the Social Learning system.
- Change management plan to increase awareness, understanding, commitment, and buy in. See step 4.

<u>Step 3 - Source and Develop Content</u>: Develop, source, and repurpose "content", and place it on the Social Learning system prior to the go live date. The "targeted users" will need a reason to use the new Social Learning system on day one. Front loading the system with "content" will help create some attraction and persuade many of the "targeted users" to log on – and then come back again and again.

Deliverables:

- Select and "train" 5 to 10 subject matter experts (SME), from each of the targeted communities of practice or workforce roles.

- Training course and guidelines for the selected SMEs to help them front load the Social Learning system with "content". The content will be presented in the form of blogs, wikis, discussion threads, podcasts, documents, etc.
- Training course and guidelines for the selected SMEs to help them monitor discussion forums, connect people to people and people to content, and promote "good" content via ratings, add the content to their favourite's page, and provide special mention of the content on their blogs.

Step 4 - Engage the Business: Engage with the business to build stakeholder sponsorship, leadership support, and to understand the cultural challenges and work environment realities in order to drive the desired 'Social Learning' behaviors and outcomes.

Deliverables:

- Stakeholder Map for each of the targeted communities of practice and workforce roles, as well as for IT, HR, Communications, and Knowledge Management teams.
- Documented concerns, uncertainties and expectations of stakeholders and community members, and an associated communication plan and engagement approach.
- Creation and delivery of communications and engagement deliverables and activities (including the change management plan from step 3).
- Service description for supporting the targeted communities of practice or workforce roles, and a dedicated point-of-contact for each.

Step 5 - Monitor and Evaluate: Monitor use of technology, networking patterns, knowledge sharing and consumption, and discussion threads in order to evaluate the business case, identify best practices, unblock challenges, and improve the 'Social Learning" approach and outcomes.

Deliverables:

- A list of required 'data', proposed 'data' sources, developed tools, and a data collection plan with clear timeframes and responsibilities.
- Report(s) of key findings, conclusions, results, and recommendations.

Jennings/Reid-Dodick "C" Curve for L&D

The Jennings/Reid-Dodick 'C' Curve for L&D

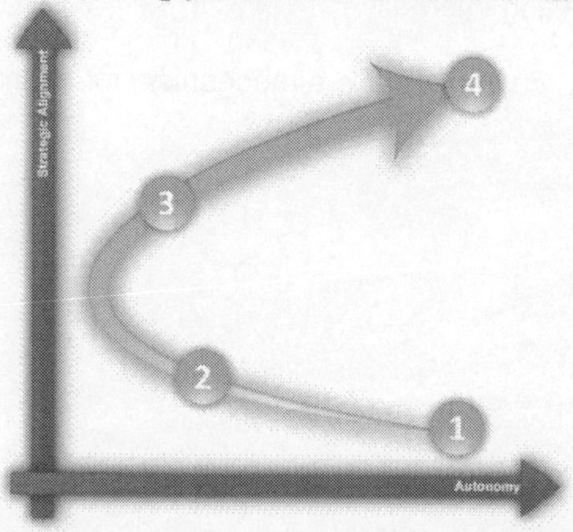

Migration to an Accountability Oriented Framework

We used the 'C' curve model to define the journey needed to build an L&D function that was accountable for business results, whose operation was closely aligned with the company's overall strategy, that embedded the 'efficiency & effectiveness' mantra but - at the same time - where the component parts of L&D could have some autonomy to operate and make decisions locally.

This ultimately resulted in a **federated organisational structure** – a small core L&D team sitting in the corporate HR centre managing the overall strategy, alignment, standards, infrastructure etc. while the majority of L&D resources (and their budgets) sat in the various business lines delivering operational L&D services to their stakeholders. L&D was held together by a central governance board (mostly senior business managers, but chaired by the HR Director), and functional reporting lines for each of the Heads of Learning (every major business unit had one) into the CLO (my role).

The ‘C’ curve shows the steps that were taken to move to an accountability oriented structure that worked for us.

Ideally organisations want to move from [1], where pieces of the L&D puzzle are operating autonomously without being strategically aligned, to [4] where they still have a level of autonomy, but <u>are</u> strategically aligned.

Many organisations are still living with [1] and don’t really know how to move away from having a gaggle of un-coordinated L&D/ Training groups who are all doing their own ‘thing’ and often competing internally.

The ‘C curve model is a mechanism for making that move.

Five Ingredients of Making eLearning Work

http://c4lpt.co.uk/articles/cipd.html

Some of the problems ...

- Online courses
  - take too much time and money to create; and
  - employees (often) don't like or fully use them
- Blended solutions
  - provide limited interaction (communication and collaboration) between learners
- Systems and tools
  - are costly; and
  - are not paying off or living up to expectations

1 Re-think your definition of "e-learning"

"Information, instruction, education, training, communication, collaboration and knowledge sharing"

Tom Kelly, Cisco Systems, 2000

REMEMBER
the 80%-20% rule

Focus more on the informal
Place efforts on formal only where essential

(compliance, regulatory training)

2 Think about productivity / performance improvement / support as well as training

REMEMBER
Learning is a means to an end; not the end itself

It's about improving the productivity and performance of individuals, teams and the business

Measure success in these terms
NOT
course completions or test results

Think JIT not JIC
Think on-the-job
Think on-demand, workflow-embedded solutions

3 Think PEOPLE not just CONTENT

Encourage people to:
Communicate
Collaborate
Connect
(Co-)Create
Share

Help people to help themselves i.e. self-organise
(= support a bottom up culture)

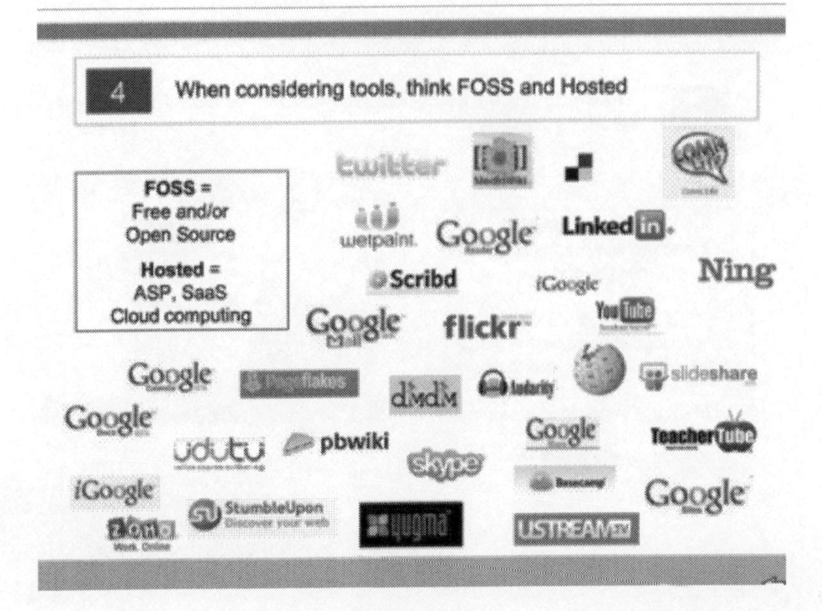

5 Think quick, easy, short and disposable solutions BUT don't re-invent the wheel!

Solutions need to be relevant to their needs and fit with their way of working
Working and learning need to merge

Dimensions of Clark Quinn's Learning Environment

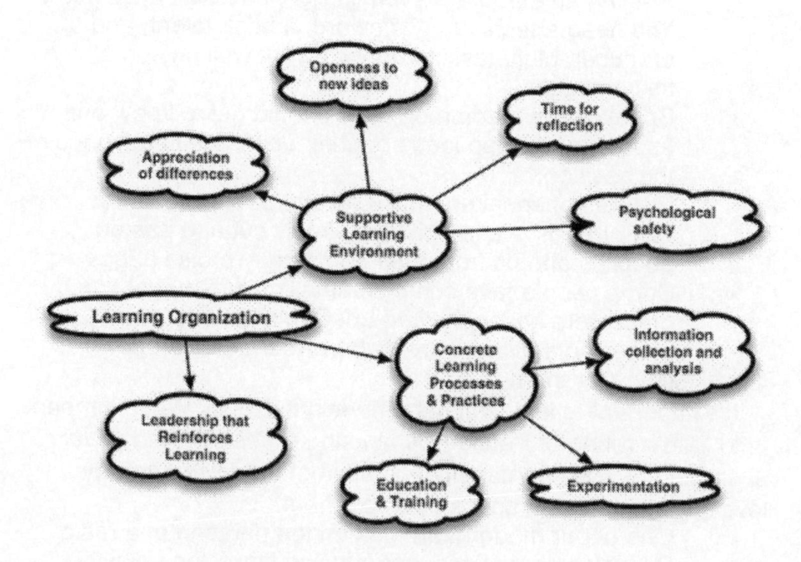

Lessons from the 24-hour Marathon of LearnTrends

I learned a lot in the course of putting this together.

- Staging an elaborate event is like putting on a t.v. show. You need a technology steward, a host, talent, and a producer. Multi-tasking doesn't work well on something this ambitious.
- Speakers on a common topic should get to know one another and swap ideas on their approach in advance of the session.
- Pictures of speakers make an event more real. For Learntrends, we could have simply cut and pasted people's photos from their community profile pages.
- Some people take commitments lightly. Several presenters never showed up. Some volunteer moderators disappeared when we tried to pin down times for them to cover.

It's important to inject fun into the event. Nancy White jumped in to lead a round of Pecha Kucha using slides she had never seen before. The spontaneity and spirit of fun raised energy levels. Need fun stuff sprinkled throughout.

- One of our moderators took on the persona of a radio DJ, asking questions, announcing times, and playing music during lulls. This was great. In the wee hours of the morning, another moderator conversed easily with anyone who dropped in, the talk-show therapist.
- We encountered numerous issues with sound. No matter how much prompting we provided, people showed up throughout without headphones, not having done an audio check, or with mediocre net connections. I want a system that's as easy as tuning in a telephone conference call.
- We recorded the sessions directly off the web, i.e. outside of Elluminate. Recordings are going up now.
- Expanding the event from 3 hours to 24 only a dozen days before we went live was a stretch. I was hoping to catch the spirit and activism that pulled the first BarCamp together in less than a week. We didn't make it. Our community bonds are not that strong. Except for the planning team on the Skype Chat, people didn't get enthusiastic about the concept.

Five Big Factors of Personality - OCEAN

In contemporary psychology, the **"Big Five" factors** of personality are five broad domains or dimensions of personality which are used to describe human personality.

- Openness
- Conscientiousness
- Extraversion
- Agreeableness
- Neuroticism

Four-factor Mobile Learning Framework

- *Content*: the provision of media (e.g. documents, audio, video, etc) to the learner/performer
- *Compute*: taking in data from the learner and processing it
- *Capture*: taking in data from sensors including camera, GPS, etc, and saving for sharing or reflection
- *Communicate*: connecting learners/performers with others

from Clark Quinn

Four Predictions for 2010

eLearn magazine, an astute online publication from the ACM conducts an annual predictions round-up. Here is what appeared in our crystal balls this year.[31]

Wave Crests

Google Wave is already set to become a very popular tool this year, and I think it represents the way that tools are going to evolve in the near future, that is that the social functionality found in standalone tools is going to merge and become amalgamated into more integrated "learning" tools. Also I think (and hope) we will see learning systems moving away from managing or controlling users and instead providing open learning environments that enable both formal and informal personal and group learning to take place.
—Jane Hart, social learning consultant at Centre for Learning & Performance Technologies

Move It or Lose It

This is the decade of *time*. Time-to-performance will become the dominant metric for learning. Businesses in 2010 will become faster-paced and more unpredictable. Quick and agile companies will overtake hide-bound traditional organizations. Speedy change requires rapid learning, workers will increasingly set the pace. Mobile, geo-aware, smart phones will provide performance support. We'll focus more on nurturing learning ecosystems ("learnscapes") than on finger-in-the-dike point solutions. As Elbert Hubbard warned, "The world is moving so fast these days that the man who says it can't be done is generally interrupted by someone doing it."
—Jay Cross, chairman of Internet Time Alliance

Break Out!

I'm hoping this will be the "year of the breakthrough." Several technologies are poised to cross the chasm: social tools, mobile technologies, and virtual worlds. Each has reached critical mass in being realistically deployable and offers real benefits. And each complements a desired organizational breakthrough,

---

[31] http://elearnmag.org/subpage.cfm?section=articles&article=106-1

recognizing the broader role of learning not just in execution, but in problem-solving, innovation, and more. I expect to see more inspired uses of technology to break out of the "course" mentality and start facilitating performance more broadly, as organizational structures move learning from "nice to have" to core infrastructure.

—Clark Quinn, executive director of Quinnovation

New Mode for 'Learning'
The increasing awareness that learning is the result of experiences, practice, conversations, and reflection rather than a demonstration of acquisition of information will mean focus and effort moves away from the development of structured learning content and towards the implementation of new approaches for facilitating interaction and experiences through learning in the workplace. This will challenge training and L&D departments to the limit, who will realize they need to change their modus operandi, get closer to their stakeholders and become more responsive or cease to be relevant. Speed-to-competence will become the key driver.
—Charles Jennings, CEO of the Internet Time Alliance and Duntroon Associates

10 General Principles for Leading and Managing in the Interconnected Knowledge Workplace

Jon Husband

1. Customers, employees and other stakeholders are all interconnected, and have access to most, if not all the information that everyone else has

2. The organization chart usually reflects power and politics in the organization ... more often than not, customers and employees find work-arounds to create the experiences that delight.

3. People interconnected by the Internet and software have ways of speaking to each other – and so they do that – all day long.

4. Champion-Channel-Coordinate replaces Command-and-Control.

5. Conversations are where information is shared, knowledge is created and are the basis for getting the right things done

6. Trust, Transparency and Authenticity are the glue that holds it all together.

7. The Workplace of the Future will be more diverse – in terms of demographics, values, gender, race and language.

8. New, integrated and sophisticated technologies are being developed and implemented – and the knowledge workers of tomorrow will be more interconnected than ever.

9. We're All In This Together.

10. There's No Going Back to "Normal" – Permanent Whitewater is the New Normal.

It's almost trite to say this – the only constant is change.

John Medina's Brain Rules

Exercise. Exercise boosts brain power.
Survival. The human brain evolved, too.
Wiring. Every brain is wired differently.
Attention. We don't pay attention to boring things.
Short-term memory. Repeat to remember.
Long-term memory. Remember to repeat.
Sleep. Sleep well, think well.
Stress. Stressed brains don't learn the same way.
Sensory integration. Stimulate more of the senses.
Vision. Vision trumps all other senses.
Gender. Male and female brains are different.
Exploration. We are powerful and natural explorers.

The human brain is the product of 10 million years of evolution, 99.8% of it in caves, on the savannah, hunting and gathering.

Hard-wired cave brains

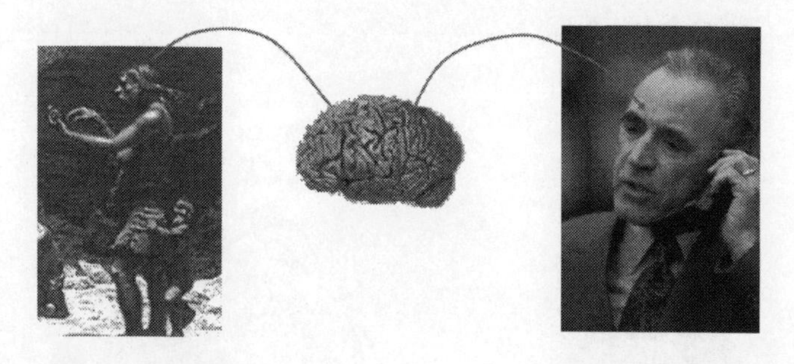

Sight mammals
- Short-term focus
- Fight or flight
- Take world as it is

Brain wants:
- Sense of control
- Known context
- Safety

The World Café

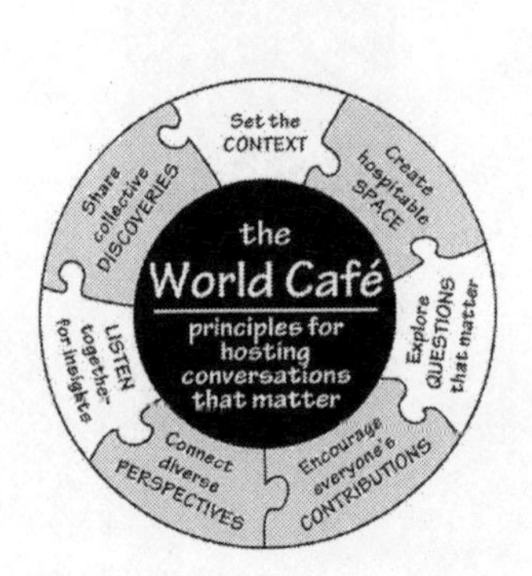

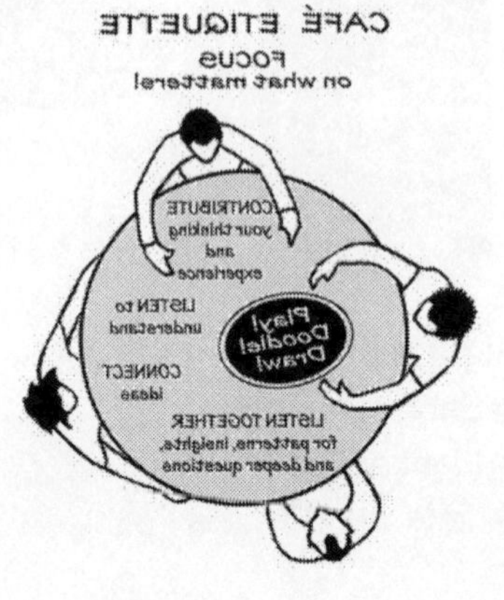

Buy the book!

Concepts from the Net

Here are some pearls of wisdom gleaned from the development of the internet:

Time trumps perfection. In the old days, training wasn't released until it passed through a gauntlet of editors, proofreaders, packagers, double-checkers and worrywarts. (Lots of training was obsolete before it hit the street.) The Net has taught us to value timeliness over relentless typo searching.

Everything is a work in progress. If it's not finished, label it "draft" or "beta," but don't hold it up. Think of a blog: Part of its charm is its informality, the idiosyncrasies of its author and its status as an opinion, not a law. People learn more when presented with material that is controversial because uncertainty engages the mind.

The user chooses the package. Few learners are totally ignorant of the area they seek to learn more about. "Testing out" is absurdly time-consuming compared to simply learning the little bit one needs to know. The Net enables the learner to get "just enough" and no more. Why take a course if you can get things done with a nugget gleaned from Books 24x7 or About.com?

Online networks facilitate personal connections. The Net enables one to rely on the kindness of strangers. Hundreds of people I didn't know before have helped me learn; I keep my karma account in balance by helping others learn. The Net even enables you to talk with your heroes if you're daring enough.

To learn something, teach it. The Net empowers each of us to express ourselves publicly. Sharing ideas is both selfish and generous. Explaining something online clarifies your thinking and reinforces your own learning.

It's a small world after all. Around the world in 80 milliseconds. Wow! With Skype, you can talk with people all over the globe through Voice over IP (VoIP). For free. The world is my oyster. Why not? Fewer than one in five internet users is based in the United States.

Me-learning. Dr. Google and Professor Amazon have taught me a lot more than four years of honors studies at an Ivy League college. Why? For one thing, I've forgotten more calculus, Wittgenstein, physics, Nietzsche and French than I'll ever know because I was driven by someone else's agenda rather than my own.

Outboard brain. You don't need to memorize something if you know where to find it. For the past 30 years, I've been collecting tidbits of knowledge, frameworks for thinking and useful algorithms, at first on paper and now in bits. Most of this is on the Net. It helps me avoid reinventing the wheel. Haven't you started building your self-help portfolio? Never mind, soon we'll have the Library of Congress on our PDAs.

Self-organization. The internet is magical. It takes care of itself. From a few standards and protocols, the Net has woven itself without a weaver. It's a tribute to the wisdom of gaining control by giving control. The lesson? Let it be. Trust the Force, Luke. Some things are destined to happen on their own. Let them.

Jane Hart's

SMARTER Approach to Workplace Learning

S - **Social** and collaborative approaches underpin the SMARTER approach to workplace learning. This does not simply mean throwing social media tools at a problem to create a social solution, but more importantly means ...

M - shifting your thinking towards a Knowledge Economy **mindset** that includes encouraging ...

A - **autonomous** learners/workers to solve their own learning/ business problems in their own way, which means and will lead to ...

R - a **reduction** in the amount of formal training provided - since training is certainly not the answer to every learning or business problem.

T - All of the above will be underpinned by **technology** ...

E - BUT by a technology**-enabled** approach (e.g. using a collaboration platform) rather than a technology-managed approach (e.g. a LMS).

R - This will lead to a more **responsive** and agile organisation, and one where "learning=working and working=learning".

Jay's First Principles: People

Perception is reality.

- Placebos work.
- Hawthorne effect.
- Halo effect.
- There need be no commodities.
- Reality is relative: we each have our own.
-

Mental expectations set real limits.

- Learned helplessness.
- "They are able because they think they are able." Virgil
- Optimism works better than pessimism.
- Logic = blinders to intuitive exploration.
-

Modern people have cro magnon brains.

- The human brain is the product of 10 million years of evolution, 99.8% of it in caves, on the savennah, hunting and gathering.
- Our relatively modern "thinking" brains are in perpetual contact and conflict with our ancient "feeling" brains.
- Pre-agricultural troglodytes lived entirely in the now. Our brains didn't need to plan very far ahead, so looking longterm is not in our natural repertoire.
- Our brains seek patterns, often finding one when it's not intentionally there. As we retell a dream, our brains invent the context to make sense of nonsense. We do this in waking life as well, but are not conscious of it.
-

People are warm-blooded, omnivorous, sight-mammals.

- We are creatures.
- Circadian rhythms control our thinking.
- If it full empty it; if it's empty, fill it; if it itches, scratch it.
- Fight or flight response is the root of stress in the office as well as the jungle.
-

People like what they know; they don't know what they like.

- In marketing, position services for maximum halo effect.
- First we make our habits, then our habits make us.
- Personal comfort zone = blinders, rut.
- Change threatens stability.
-

Be alert. Keep an open mind. Follow your heart.

- Mindfulness matters.
- Be here now.
- Walk in other people's shoes.
- Get out of your comfort zone.
- Learning is an *active* process.
-

To every thing there is a cycle.

- You're born, you live, you die.
- You live on through your children, your start-ups.
- Epigensis = born at the right time.

Jay's First Principles: Things

Everything flows.

- Time flies.
- Nothing alive is ever finished.
- Worthwhile documents, policies, reports, and relationships live.
-

All things are connected.

- Connections often as important as the things they connect.
- Value of a network increases exponentially to the number of nodes.
-

Less is more.

- Simplicity is the ultimate sophistication
- When confronted with two explanations, choose the simplest.
-

Everything exists on numerous levels.

- Level of abstraction/detail. Meta-.
- No matter what's happening in the plaza, you can always go up to the balcony for a look at the bigger picture.
- Laterality, everything/idea has neighbors, related by concept, co-location, timing, etc.
- Everything is rooted in a life cycle. It's young or old, evolving or dying.
-

Process is power.

- Give a man a fish and you feed him for a day. Teach a man to fish and you feed him for a lifetime. --Chinese Proverb
- One person's process is another person's content.
-

Virtually everything is on a continuum. It's shades of gray rather than black or white.

- There is no absolute truth. There is no meaning without context.
-

Most things in life are beyond our control.

- Better to think things through than to thrash and force-fit.
- The mind and body are one.
-

In diversity is strength.

- Diversification decreases risk.

- All of us are smarter than one of us.
-

Shit happens.
- Entropy.
- Moorphy's Law (On Internet time, shit happens exponentially.)
- Chaos.

Jay's First Principles: Technique

In business, take Jack Welch's advice...
- focus on customers
- resist bureaucracy
- think imaginatively
- invigorate others.
-

How to behave
- Live as if this is all there is.
- Look for the best in others. Other esteem.
- Share my thoughts and feelings. Be authentic.
- Open the door to feedback.
- Smile. Learn. Laugh. Pay attention.
- Practice optimism. Be here now.
- Live with intention.
- Think out of the box.
- Do what I love. Do it with gusto.
- Maintain balance.
- Don't obsess.

Seek patterns
- Homeostasis -- central tendency, self-correction, standard deviation.
- Pareto's law: 20% of the resources yield 80% of the results.
- Self-organization
- Organize by product or area or function

I don't ask him "What's the problem?" I say, "Tell me the story." That way, I find out what the problem really is. --Avram Goldberg

Structure follows strategy. (Strategy = plans and policies by which a company aims to gain advantages over its competitors.)

Clark Quinn: Performance Environment

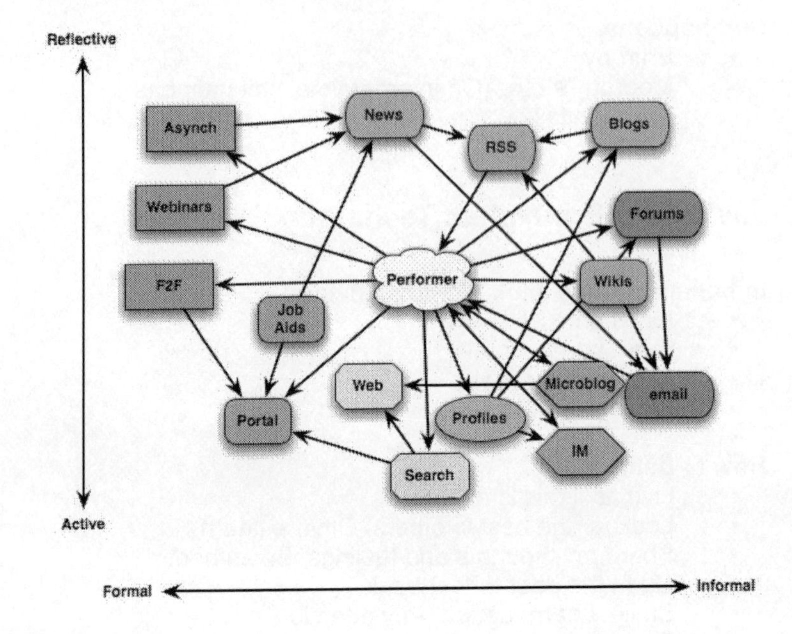

Dave Snowden's Cynevin Framework

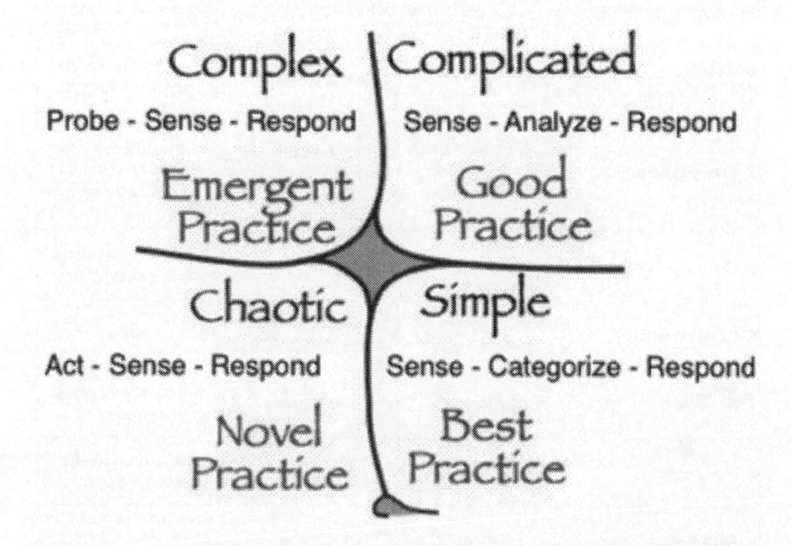

Centre for Learning & Performance Technologies

September 2010 Edition

	Free public tools	Google tools	Elgg
1: Social Networking	Facebook, LinkedIn Ning	Orkut, Google Groups	profiling, relationship building, open/closed groups
2: Tagging content	within each of the tools		across the site
3: Social bookmarking	Delicious, Diigo	Google Bookmarks	personal, group and site bookmarking
4: File-sharing	YouTube, Vimeo, Flickr, Photobucket, Slideshare, Prezi, Screencast.com, Screentoaster	Google Video, YouTube Picasa, Google Docs Google Calendar Google Maps	upload/share files embed resources in web/blog pages
5: Communication	Skype Dimdim YahooMail	Gmail, Google Talk	internal messaging chat, group forums
6. Collaboration	Bubble.us, Wetpaint, Etherpad, Udutu	Google Sites Google SideWiki	wikis
7: Blogging	Wordpress	Blogger	personal and group blogs
8: Podcasting	iTunes, Audacity	Google Base	upload podcasts audio player
9: RSS Feeds	Bloglines	Google Reader	store and read internal and external RSS feeds
10: Micro-blogging	Twitter	Jaiku	internal updates can be sent to Twitter
Integration	Netvibes Netvibes for Enterprises	iGoogle Google Apps Google Wave.	seamless interface dashboard menu bar

Dan Pink's Evolution to the Conceptual Age

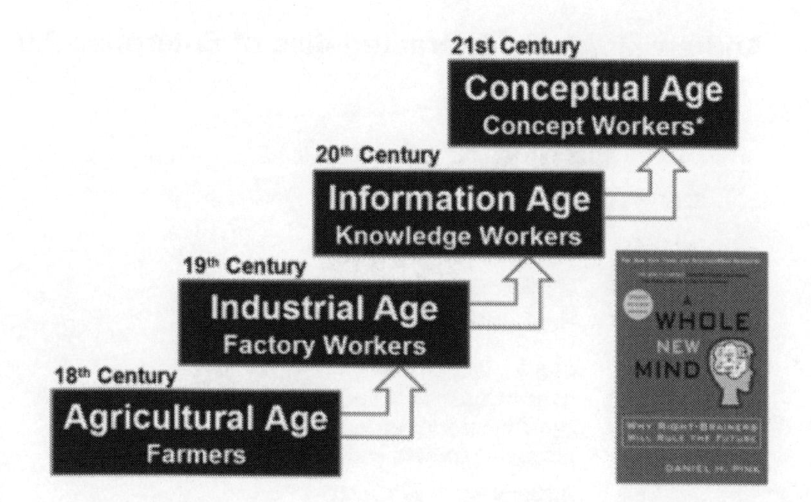
21st Century
Conceptual Age
Concept Workers*
20th Century
Information Age
Knowledge Workers
19th Century
Industrial Age
Factory Workers
18th Century
Agricultural Age
Farmers
A
WHOLE
NEW
MIND
WHY RIGHT-BRAINERS
WILL RULE THE FUTURE
DANIEL H. PINK

Andrew McAfee's Characteristics of Enterprise 2.0

Early View of Enterprise 2.0 Elements

Search – Discoverability of information drives reuse, leverage, and ROI.

Links – Using URIs to forge thousands of deep interconnections between enterprise content 24/7.

Authorship – Ensuring every worker has easy access to Enterprise 2.0 platforms.

Tags – Allowing natural, organic, on-the-fly organization of data from every point of view.

Extensions – Extend knowledge by mining patterns and user activity.

Signals – Make information consumption efficient by pushing out changes.

Dion Hinchcliffe's Update of McAfee's SLATES

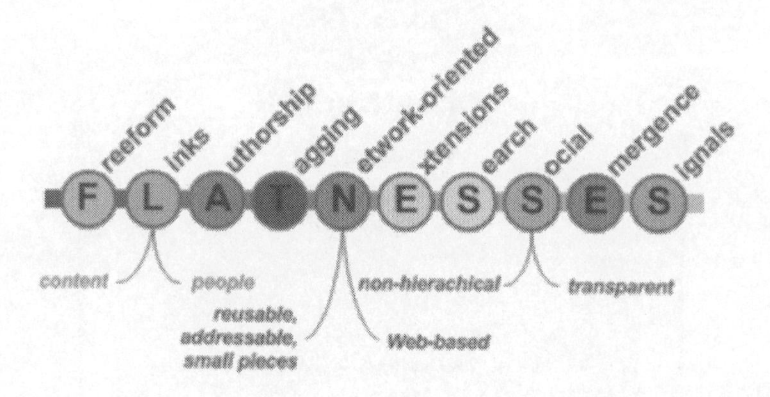

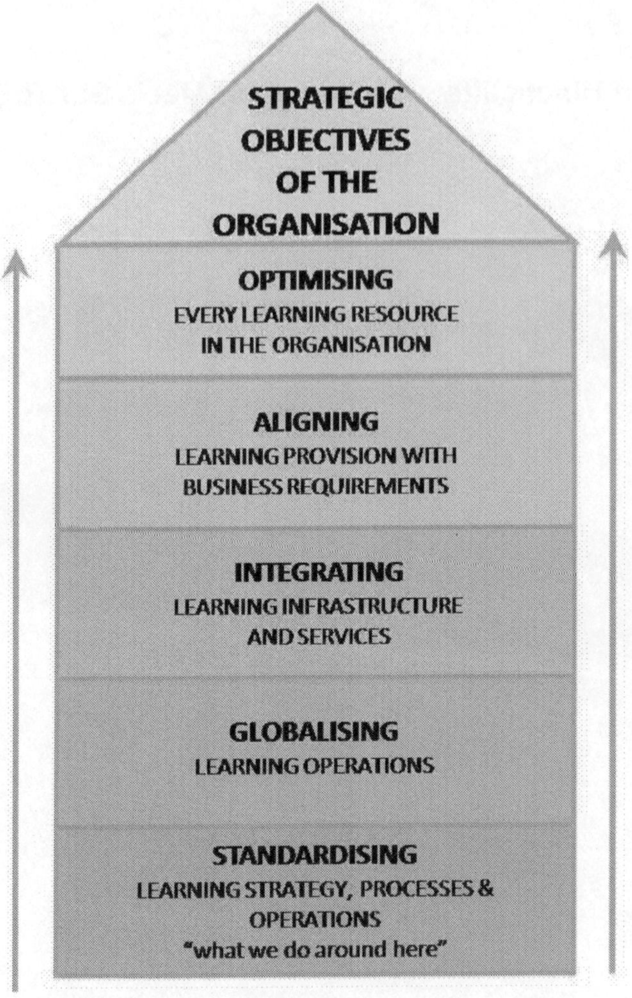

STRATEGIC OBJECTIVES OF THE ORGANISATION

OPTIMISING
EVERY LEARNING RESOURCE IN THE ORGANISATION

ALIGNING
LEARNING PROVISION WITH BUSINESS REQUIREMENTS

INTEGRATING
LEARNING INFRASTRUCTURE AND SERVICES

GLOBALISING
LEARNING OPERATIONS

STANDARDISING
LEARNING STRATEGY, PROCESSES & OPERATIONS
"what we do around here"

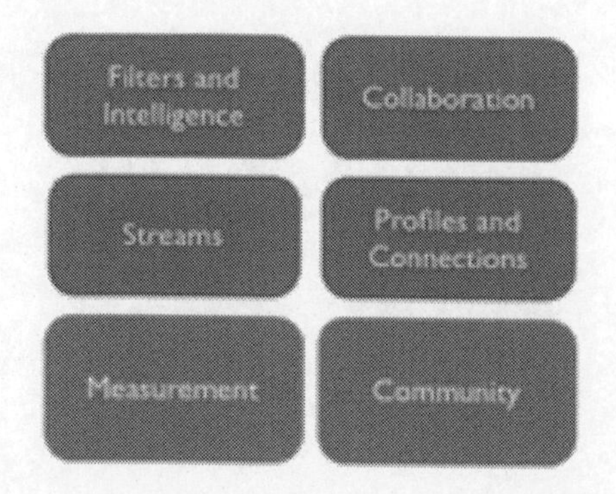
Filters and Intelligence
Collaboration
Streams
Profiles and Connections
Measurement
Community

sample learning principles of operation

Business Driven
- Ensure all learning and development is aligned to the strategic priorities of the business

Agility
- Build an agile and flexible workforce able to take on increasingly changing demands in the workplace

Involvement
- Involve leaders as coaches, learning facilitators and subject matter experts

Scalability
- Design learning that is scalable, sustainable and can leverage across the enterprise and across continents

Design and Development
- Leverage the latest design principles so learning is personalised and embedded into employees' work

Innovation
- Adopt an innovative mindset where learning is accessible on multiple channels of delivery including Web 2.0/Web 3.0 and on collaborative platforms

Partnerships
- Build a network of best-of-breed University and professional body partnerships to offer programs customised to our business needs

Metrics
- Measure and report the business impact of investment in learning & development at enterprise and business unit level.

Communications & Branding
- Use learning & development as a vehicle to increase the ability of the organisation to attract, recruit and retain talent

Dion Hinchcliffe: Social Business Models

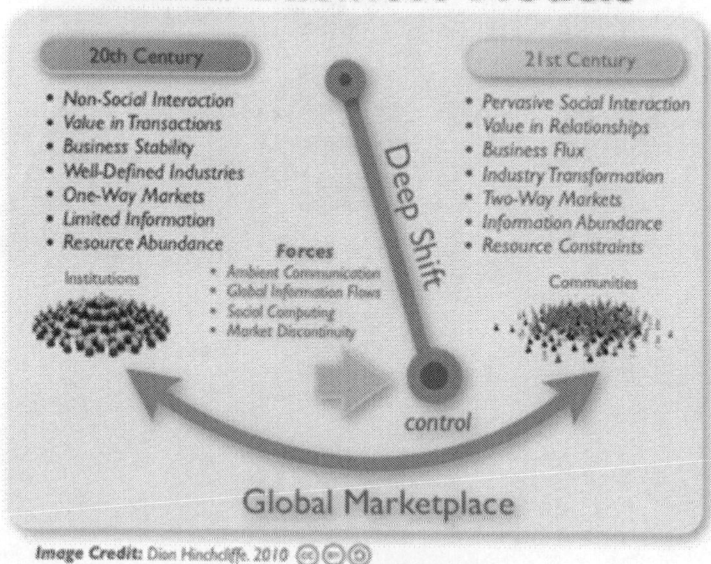

Charles Jennings on Governance

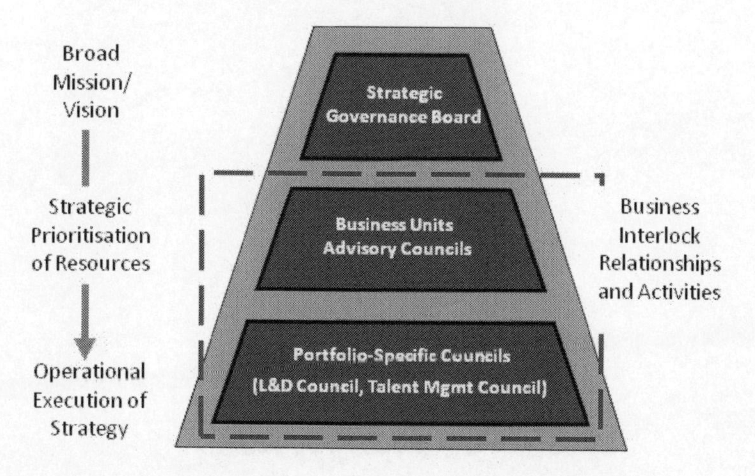

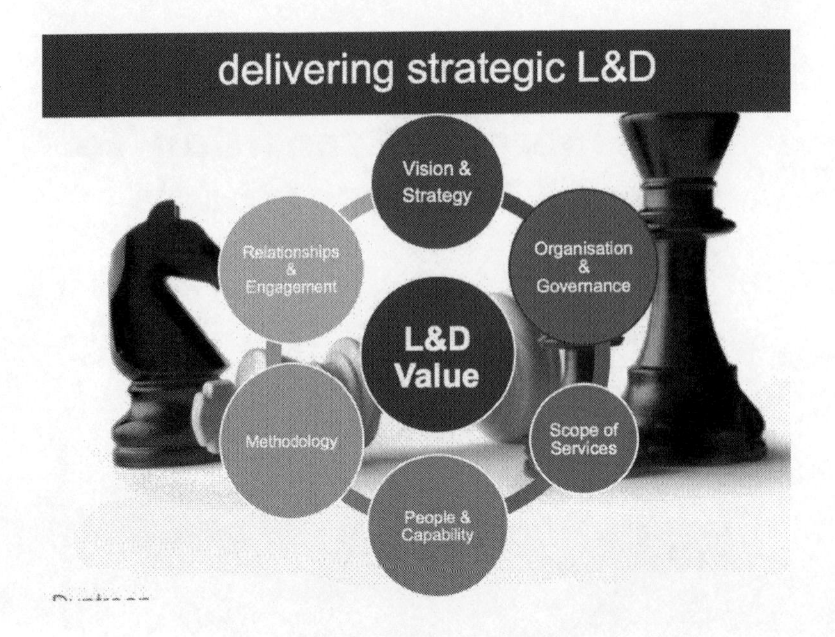
delivering strategic L&D
Vision & Strategy
Organisation & Governance
Scope of Services
People & Capability
Methodology
Relationships & Engagement
L&D Value

Don't Take Jay's Advice

For several years, I advised clients to "leap the chasm" to balance their investments in informal and format learning. Follow the prescriptions in this unbook.

Now I counsel them to cross the chasm when they are ready. If the leadership of the organization isn't ready to leap, win their support through a governance structure. Otherwise, you probably won't complete the jump.

Clark Quinn's 7 C's of Natural Learning

- Choose
- Commit
- Crash
- Create
- Copy
- Converse
- Collaborate

CLO Responsibilities

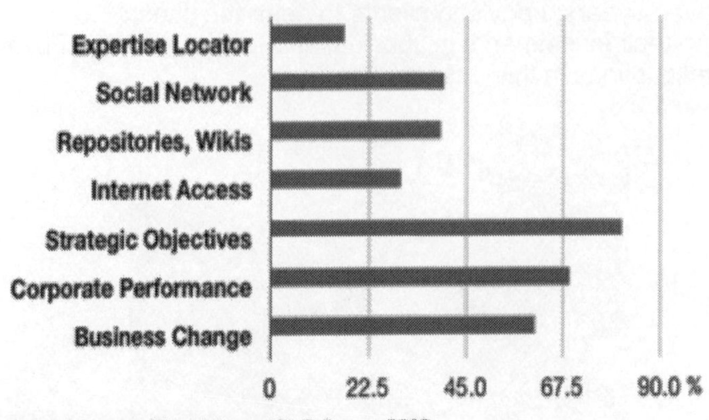

Donald Clark: 10 techniques to massively increase retention

This is the classic 'forgetting curve' by Ebbinghaus, a fundamental truth in memory theory, totally ignored by most educators and trainers. Most fixed 'courses' or 'lectures' take no notice of the phenomenon, condemning much of their effort to the world of lost memories. Most educational and training pedagogies are hopelessly inefficient because they fail to recognise this basic truth. Smart learners get it. They revise over a period, with regular doses to consolidate their memories.

Little and often

The real solution, to this massive problem of forgetfulness, is spaced practice, little and often, the regular rehearsal and practice of the knowledge/skill over a period of time to elaborate and allow deep processing to fix long-term memories. If we get this right, increases on the productivity of learning can be enormous. We are not talking small increase in knowledge and retention but increases of 200-700%. It has the potential to radically alter the attainment levels in schools, colleges, universities and organisations. OK, that's the theory, what about the practice?

What strategies enable spaced practice?

I'll start with a few 'learner' tips, then a few 'teacher/trainer' practices and end on some technical techniques.

1. Self- rehearsal – This is very powerful, but needs self-discipline. You sit quietly, and recall the learning on a regular, spaced practice basis. The hour/day/week/month model is one, but a more regular pattern of reinforcement will be more successful. Research suggests that the spacing different for individuals and that it is good to rehearse when you have a quiet moment and feel you are in the mood to reflect. Recent research has shown that rehearsal just prior to sleep is a powerful technique. Another bizarre, but effective, model is to place the textbook/notes in your toilet. It's something you do daily, and offers the perfect opportunity for repeated practice!

2. Take notes – write up your learning experience, in your own words, diagrams, analogies. This can result in dramatic increases in learning (20-30%). Then re-read a few times afterwards or type up as a more coherent piece. It is important to summarise and re-read your notes as soon as possible after the learning experience.

3. Blogging – if the learner blogs his/her learning experience after the course, then responds to the tutors', and others' comments for a few weeks afterwards, we have repeated consolidation, and the content has a much higher chance of being retained.

4. Repetition – within the course, but also at the start of every subsequent period, lesson or lecture, repeat (not in parrot fashion) the ground that was covered previously. Take five or ten minutes at the start to ask key questions about the previous content.

5. Delayed assessment – give learners exercises to do after the course and explain that you will assess them a few weeks, months after the course has finished. This prevents reliance on short-term memory and gives them a chance to consolidate their knowledge/skills.

6. Record – it is education and training' great act of stupidity, not to record talks, lectures and presentations. They give the learner subsequent access to the content and therefore spaced practice.

7. Games pedagogy – Games have powerful pedagogies. They have to as they are hard. It works through repeated attempts and failure. You only progress as your acquired competence allows. Most games involve huge amounts of repetition and failure with levels of attainment that take days, weeks and months to complete.

8. Spaced e-learning – schedule a pattern in your online learning, so that learners do less in one sitting and spread their learning over a longer period of time, with shorter episodes. Free your learners from the tyranny of time and location, allowing them to do little and often. In education this is homework and assignments, In training subsequent talks that need to be emailed back to the trainer/tutor.

9. Mobile technology – the drip feed of assessment over a number of weeks after the course or redesign the whole course as a drip-feed experience. We have the ideal device in our pockets – mobiles. They're powerful, portable and personal. Push out small chunks or banks of questions, structured so that repetition and consolidation happens. This usually involves the repeated testing of the individual until you feel that the learning has succeeded.

10. Less long holidays – it terms of public policy, increasing school results would be betters served by avoiding the long summer holiday and restructuring the school, college and University years around more regular terms and less long vacations.

Benefits

The retention benefit works like compound interest as you're building on previous learning, deepening the processing and consolidating long-term memory. It is, in my opinion, the single most effective strategic change we could make to our learning interventions.

Donald Clark: Do happy sheets work?

Ask Traci Sitzman[32] who has done the research. Her work on meta-studies, on 68,245 trainees over 354 research reports, attempt to answer two questions:

Do satisfied students learn more than dissatisfied students?

After controlling for pre-training knowledge, reactions accounted for:

•2% of the variance in factual knowledge

•5% of the variance in skill-based knowledge

•0% of the variance in training transfer

The answer is clearly no!

Are self-assessments of knowledge accurate?

- Self-assessment is only moderately related to learning
- Self-assessment capture motivation and satisfaction, not actual knowledge levels

Self-assessments should **NOT** be included in course evaluations

Should **NOT** be used as a substitute for objective learning measures

Additional problems

Ever been asked at a conference or end of a training course to fill in a happy sheet? Don't bother. It breaks the first rule in stats

---

[32] http://donaldclarkplanb.blogspot.com/2010/05/traci-sitzman-happy-sheet-killer.html

– randomized sampling. It's usually a self-selecting sample, namely those who are bored, liked the trainer or simply had a pen handy. Students can be 'Happy but stupid' as the data tells you nothing about what they have learnt, and their self-perceptions are deceiving (see Traci's research).

Donald Clark: 10 reasons to dump lectures

I give a lot of talks at conferences but always make it clear that this no way to deliver learning. Unfortunately people are addicted to the format. Why? It's easy just to turn up and listen. It's a lazy format for lazy learners. Also, I'm astonished at the number of people who turn up for conferences talks and take no notes. It is like turning up for a tennis match with no racquet.

This brings me to the one-hour format. Conference talks, lectures in universities, periods in schools and the 'one-hour' of e-learning pricing model, all of these fall foul of the deep addiction to the 'hour of learning' delivered as a lecture.

Babylonian hour: we only have hours because of the Babylonian base-60 number system. It has nothing to do with the psychology of learning.

Passive observers: lectures turn students into passive observers. Research shows that participation increases learning, yet few lecturers do this (Brophy & Good, 1986; Fisher & Berliner, 1985; Greenwood, Delquadri, & Hall, 1984).

Attention fall-off: our ability to retain information falls off badly after 10-20 minutes. The simple insertion of three 'two-minute pauses' led to a difference of two letter grades in a short and long-term recall test (1987, Winter).

Note-taking: lectures rely on note taking, yet note-taking is seldom taught, massively reducing their effectiveness (Saski, Swicegood, & Carter, 1983).

Disabilities: even slight disabilities in listening, language or motor skills make lectures ineffective, as it is difficult to focus, discriminate and note-take quickly enough in a lecture (Hughes & Suritsky, 1994).

One bite at cherry: if something is not understood on first exposure there's no opportunity to pause, reflect of get clarification. This 'one bite of the cherry' approach to learning is against all that we know in the psychology of learning.

Cognitive overload: lecturers load up talks with too much detail leading to cognitive overload. In addition they often go 'off on one', with tangential material.

Tyranny of location: you have to go to a specific place to hear a lecture. This wastes huge amounts of time.

Tyranny of time: you have to turn up at a specific time to hear a lecture.

Poor presentation: many lecturers have neither the personality nor skills to hold the audience's attention.

'Lectures were once useful; but now, when all can read, and books are so numerous, lectures are unnecessary. If your attention fails, and you miss a part of a lecture, it is lost; you cannot go back as you do upon a book." Samuel Johnson

Donald Clark: 10 proven facts about learning

1. Spaced practice

Perhaps the most significant fact we know about learning, yet it is almost completely ignored by the 'curse of the course and classroom'. We learn through practice, little and often. Ebbinghaus proved it in 1885, and almost everyone in the learning profession has studiously ignored it for well over a century. Demster reported this sad state of affairs in American Psychologist (The Spacing Effect: A Case Study in the Failure to Apply the Results of Psychological Research, 1988). We forget things quickly and that the most effective way to prevent this forgetting is to practice at spaced intervals over time. Knowledge is easy to learn but hard to retain. Forget this and you condemn yourself to, at best to unnecessary effort in learning, at worst failing to learn much at all – the true story behind most learning effort.

2. Cognitive overload

This well know phenomenon is extremely common in teaching and training. A lack of understanding about how memory works leads to a lack of preparation of material in terms of size, order and engagement, leading to weak encoding, a lack of deep processing then poor retention and recall. Almost all courses are too long, present material in the wrong way and lead to unnecessary forgetting. Simplify to prevent cognitive overload.

3. Chunking

Perhaps the easiest and simplest piece of learning theory to put into practice. Chunking means being sensitive to the limitation of working memory. Less is more in learning and distilling, rather than enhancing, elaborating and creating lots of distracting noise, is a virtue in teaching. Unfortunately the ‘song and dance’ act in the classroom is often cacophonous.

4. Order

The order you learn things is critical to how they will be stored and recalled, yet education and training continues to jumble and confuse content. This is critical in language learning, science, maths and indeed, every subject. Learn things in the wrong order and you’ll end up having to unlearn.

5. Episodic and semantic memory

Once you understand that the things we learn are stored differently, i.e. we have different types of memory, then you'll be more sensitive to the necessary differences in teaching. We still have far too much reliance on text (semantic) for subjects that need a visual (episodic) approach. You see this everywhere, from text heavy PowerPoints to whiteboards, manuals and hand-outs.

6. Psychological attention

Learning does not take place without psychological attention, so setting up classrooms and scenarios that inhibit attention, or distract from learning, is massively counter-productive. I fear that much so called 'collaborative learning' falls into this trap. Cramming 30 plus teenagers into a small, airless classroom is no way to encourage attention. There are at least 30 other human distractions, the windows and daydreaming to content with. The bottom line is that most learning is best done on your own or one-to-one.

7. Context

We know that recall is enhanced by learning in the physical context in which one is expected to perform. Yet most teaching is done in alien environments – classrooms ad training centres. We have plenty of proof that work-placed learning needs to be massively increased and non-contextual classroom teaching decreased.

8. Learn by doing

From William James and John Dewey through to Kolb and Schank, we've had a torrent of theory showing that we learn lots by doing, yet much teaching and training is locked into a over-theoretical, knowledge and not skills, model. There is a barely a subject around in schools ad training that wouldn't benefit from a boost in experiential learning.

9. Understand 'peer' groups

The work of Judith Harris (*The Nurture Assumption*) will change the whole way you look at parenting and teaching. Her

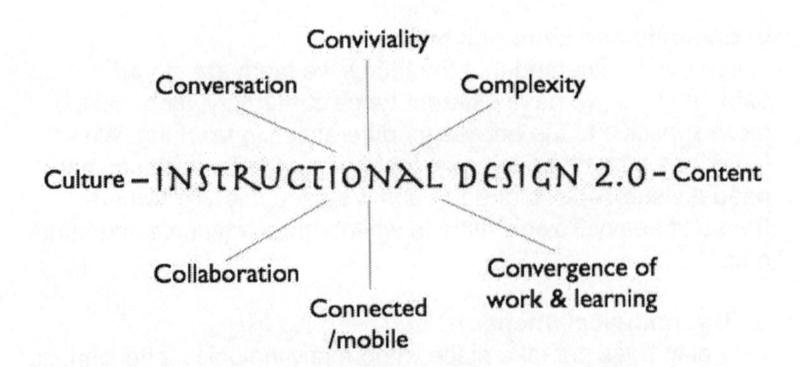

revolutionary scientific work showed that most books on parenting and teaching overestimate the influence of parents and teachers, and under-estimate the role of genetics and peer pressure. There are some real and practical steps one can take to avoid the obvious traps. These are largely ignored in education and training. Read the book.

10. Murder the myths

This is perhaps the most useful piece of scientific advice for teachers and trainers – dump the snake oil techniques. These include learning styles, playing music while you learn, Brain Gym, left-right brain theories, NLP, stating the objectives at the start of a course…the list goes on.

Conclusion

Many teaching practices are in direct opposition to the psychology of learning. When it comes to education and training, the professions have doggedly chosen unproven pedagogy over prove psychology. This is why so little progress has been made, and why huge amounts of extra funding leads to such razor thin, marginal improvement. There are literally dozes of proven findings in the science of experimental psychology that are largely ignored. This is why the Bristol study I referred to in my Paxman piece is so worrying.

Jane and Charles in Salisbury with new company car.

Instructional Design 2.0

Our new world calls for fresh thinking about instructional design. If we'd done the graphic above, summarizing concepts of instructional design, we would have found it chock full of "analysis" and "development" and "assessment." Now that the focus has shifted from push to pull, these words have fallen off the chart.

The role of the instructional designer has diverged into many roles. Each of us is responsible for maintaining our personal learning environment. More people connect to the net with smart phones than computers. The modern designer's toolkit contains a plethora of new, powerful techniques: storytelling, information architecture, wikis, and unmeetings, to name a few.

After assessing what's wrong and right with using traditional instructional design methods in present time, we'll highlight specifics on collaboration, content, and community.

Designing for an uncertain world

Clark Quinn

My problem with the formal models of instructional design (e.g. ADDIE for process) is that most are based upon a flawed premise. The premise is that the world is predictable and understandable, so that we can capture the 'right' behavior and train it. Which, I think, is a naive assumption, at least in this day and age. So why do I think so, and what do I think we can (and should) do about it? (Note: I let my argument lead where it must, and find I go quite beyond my intended suggestion of a broader learning design. Fair warning!)

The world is inherently chaotic. At a finite granularity, it is reasonably predictable, but overall it's chaotic. Dave Snowden's Cynefin model, recommending various approaches depending on the relative complexity of the situation, provides a top-level strategy for action, but doesn't provide predictions about how to support learning, and I think we need more. However, most of our design models are predicated on knowing what we need people to do, and developing learning to deliver that capability. Which is wrong; if we can define it at that fine a granularity, we bloody well ought to automate it. Why have people do rote things?

It's a bad idea to have people do rote things, because they don't, *can't* do them well. It's in the nature of our cognitive architecture to have some randomness. And it's beneath us to be trained to do something repetitive, to do something that doesn't respect and take advantage of the great capacity of our brains. Instead, we should be doing pattern-matching and decision-making. Now, there are levels of this, and we should match the performer to the task, but as I heard Barry Schwartz eloquently say recently, even the most mundane seeming jobs require some real decision making, and in many cases that's not within the purview of training.

And, top-down rigid structures with one person doing the thinking for many will no longer work. Businesses increasingly complexify things but that eventually fails, as Clay Shirky has noted, and adaptive approaches are likely to be more fruitful, as Harold Jarche has pointed out. People are going to be far better equipped to deal with unpredictable change if they have internalized a set of organizational values and a powerful set of models to apply than by any possible amount of rote training.

Now think about learning design. Starting with the objectives, the notion of Mager, where you define the context and performance, is getting more difficult. Increasingly you have more complicated nuances that you can't anticipate. Our products and services are more complex, and yet we need a more seamless execution. For example trying to debug problems between hardware device and network service provider, and if you're trying to provide a total customer experience, the old "it's the other guy's fault" just isn't going to cut it. Yes, we could make our objectives higher and higher, e.g. "recognize and solve the customer's problem in a contextually appropriate way", but I think we're getting out of the realms of training.

We *are* seeing richer design models. Van Merrienboer's 4 Component ID, for instance, breaks learning up into the knowledge we need, and the complex problems we need to apply that knowledge to. David Metcalf talks about learning theory mashups as ways to incorporate new technologies, which is, at least, a good interim step and possibly the necessary approach. Still, I'm looking for something deeper. I want to find a curriculum that focuses on dealing with ambiguity, helping us bring models and an iterative and collaborative approach. A pedagogy that looks at slow development over time and rich and engaging experience. And a design process that recognizes how we use tools and work with others in the world as a part of a larger vision of cognition, problem-solving, and design.

We have to look at the entire performance ecosystem as the context, including the technology affordances, learning culture, organizational goals, and the immediate context. We have to look at the learner, not stopping at their knowledge and experience, but also including their passions, who they can connect to, their current context (including technology, location, current activity), and goals. And then we need to find a way to suggest, as Wayne Hodgins would have it, the *right stuff*, e.g. the right content or capability, at the right time, in the right way, …

An appropriate approach has to integrate theories as disparate as distributed cognition, the appropriateness of spaced practice, minimalism, and more. We probably need to start iteratively, with the long term development of learning, and similarly opportunistic performance support, and then see how we intermingle those together.

Overall, however, this is how we go beyond intervention to augmentation. Clive Thompson, in a recent Wired column, draws from a recent "man+computer" chess competition to conclude "serious cognitive advantages accrue to those who are best at thinking alongside machines". We can accessorize our brains, but I'm wanting to look at the other side, *how* can we systematically support people to be effectively supported by machines? That's a different twist on technology support for performance, and one that requires thinking about what the technology can do, but also how we develop people to be able to take advantage. A mutual accommodation will happen, but just as with learning to learn, we shouldn't assume 'ability to perform with technology augmentation'. We need to design the technology/human system to work together, and develop both so that the overall system is equipped to work in an uncertain world.

I realize I've gone quite beyond just instructional design. At this point, I don't even have a label for what I'm talking about, but I do think that the argument that has emerged (admittedly, flowing out from somewhere that wasn't consciously accessible until it appeared on the page!) is food for thought. I welcome your reactions, as I contemplate mine.

The diagram below attempts to capture the layers of systems that support tools, both formal and informal.

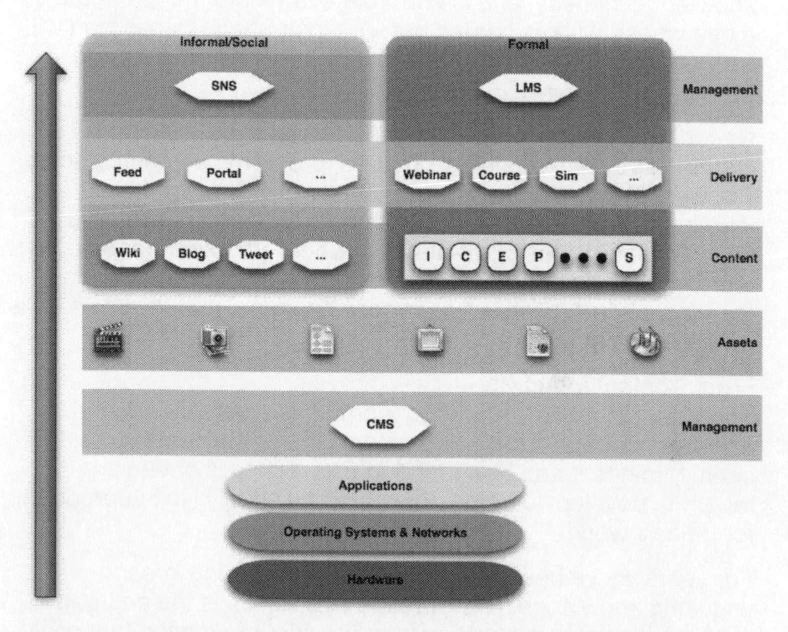

On top of the hardware and systems are applications. There are assets (with media tools) you create that can (and should) be managed, and then they're aggregated into content whether courses or resources, that are accessible through synchronous or asynchronous courses or games, portals or feeds, and managed whether through an LMS or a Social Networking System.

Instructional Design or Interactivity Design in an interconnected world?

Instructional design is not only seen as a core competency for learning and development/training specialists, but it's a huge industry, too. Most learning vendors tout their 'expertise in instructional design' as a key reason as to why we should engage them to produce learning content. If we do so, then almost invariably their approach is around developing content in an 'instructionally-sound way' to produce a set of 'learning interventions'.

I have a real problem with this approach and the thinking behind it.

It simply isn't appropriate for the needs of the 21st century knowledge industry, and is arguable even more inappropriate for those whose work is carried out with their hands rather than with their minds.

Let's Forget About Events
Undoubtedly instructional design is crucial if the mindset is learning **events** – modules, courses, programmes and curricula. However, if the mindset has stretched beyond event-based learning to where most learning occurs for workers, which is in the workplace at the point-of-need, where **process-based learning** serves best – and where *learning through doing* and *learning as part of the work process* happens, then ID takes on a whole new dimension.

From Content to Activity
The vast majority of structured learning is ***content-rich*** and ***interaction-poor***. That's understandable in the context of a 20th century mindset and how learning professionals have been taught to develop 'learning' events. But it simply isn't appropriate for today's world.

For years we've been led to believe that 'learning' meant acquiring knowledge. If knowledge acquisition is the end-game, then the logical conclusion was to provide information that could be turned, whatever the magic employed, into knowledge in the recipient's head. Believe me, the old idea that data becomes information which in turn becomes knowledge and finally transmogrifies into wisdom has been debunked years ago. We use our knowledge and experience to interpret data and information. Wisdom comes to a few only after years of experience.

These days we're a little better informed about what constitutes learning. It's not that there have been fundamental discoveries in the field. There have been a few, but we've also spent more time observing learning in action. And 'action' is the key word. It's become clear that **learning is about action and behaviours**, not about how much information you hold in your head. If we train our dog, or our goldfish, we can observe learning by the fact that the animal can do something it couldn't do before the training started. If their behaviour isn't modified then we can only conclude that they haven't learned. We have no idea of knowing, of course, but it may be that the dog 'knows' what it should do ("sit, now!') but, for reasons known only to itself, can't (or won't) execute the action.

Ebbinghaus and All That
Knowing something doesn't necessarily mean that you've learned it. Challenging?

Let's test this hypothesis. I attend a course on how to use my company's new CRM system. The instructor (or virtual instructor delegated into an eLearning course) steps me through the various processes and delivers the learning content in an engaging way. I even have an opportunity to try things out on a 'training system'. At the end of the course, I take an assessment. I pass with flying colours.

The training has been successful and I've learned. Right?

Not necessarily. What I've done is managed to retain information in short-term memory. Even if I'm successful in transferring this to long-term memory - and it's likely that most won't transfer. Dr Ebbinghaus' experiment revealed we suffer an exponential 'forgetting curve' and that about 50% of context-free information is lost in the first hour after acquisition if there is no opportunity to reinforce it with practice.

I've only learned (or learned successfully – I don't know what unsuccessful learning is – can someone please help me out with that?) when I can use the CRM system without constantly asking for help or referring to some documentation. And it's almost impossible to achieve this without having the experience of using the system/tool. And I have no hope of learning without plenty of practice. Experience and practice are two of the main ways we change our behaviours and learn.

The Value of Real ID
If experience and practice, rather than knowledge acquisition and content, are the drivers of the learning process, what do

Instructional Designers need to do to be effective?

The need to become **Interactivity Designers**. That's what they need to do.

My colleague, Clark Quinn (www.quinnovation.com) knows a thing or two about designing learning experiences, having been a leading expert in the field in both academia and the business world for some years. Clark talks about *learning experience design*. He provides good explanations of his thoughts and approach here and here.

I find both Clark's *learning experience designer* and also the term *interactivity designer* helpful because they move us beyond *instruction* to where the real meat of learning is, to actions and interactions, experiences and conversations.

Unlocking the Power of Experience

Each of us holds hundreds of experiences inside our heads that can be used to improve our own performance and the performance of those around us In both formal and informal learning environments. We just need to figure out how to tap into those experiences – that's where the skills in interactivity design come in.

Good ID will result in the design of experiences that can build capability and learning far more quickly and effectively than by filling heads with information and 'knowledge' and then hoping that will lead to behavioural change.

We need designers who understand that learning comes from experience, practice, conversations and reflection, and are prepared to move away from massaging content into what they see as good instructional design. Designers need to get off the content bus and start thinking about, using, designing and exploiting learning environments full of experiences and interactivity.

As they do this they'll realise that most of the experiences and interactivity they can draw on will occur outside formal learning environments.

Mobilizing your organization

Increasingly, your concept workers are carrying smartphones, and using these devices to augment their intelligence. For personal use, they're using not just using calendars and address books, but increasingly they are tapping into applications like email and IM or Twitter to communicate, Facebook and/or LinkedIn to stay in touch, Maps to locate themselves, search to make themselves more effective in meetings, phones to snap pictures of their hotel room number or their parking spot, and others to find food or other necessities nearby, etc. They're accessorizing their brains to make themselves more effective.

Recognize that this isn't going to slow down; as demands are increased, workers will increasingly look for tools that make their lives easier, wherever and whenever they are. Workers want to be effective and not waste time, and these tools offload capability to what the devices do well. Increasingly we see that those who best augment themselves are the most successful.

The patterns of use are indicative. As the Zen of Palm indicated years ago, computers are used only several times a day, but for long periods, but mobile devices are more typically used many times a day for quick access. And quick access is increasingly characterizing the types of needs we have 'in the moment'. We want quick solutions to problems, whether it's information ('content') we want immediately, an answer to a question; or the ability to capture some information for review or access later, or to have the device do some work for us such as a computation, or to communicate with others. We have a need, and we want the capability *now*!

And as our learning theories are beginning to tell us, it's not about know-what, it's about know-who. Whether it's George Siemen's *connectivism*, social constructivist theory, or the recognition that innovation isn't individual, we're smarter when we're connected.

The implications are clear. Mobile is a key component in effective performance. Increasingly, most of our access to information resources will likely come from mobile devices. As the workflow moves from desktop to meeting rooms, conversations in the hall, and elsewhere, our access will need to be independent of device. And we're much more effective with these devices in hand than not.

So we need two things: we don't want devices to be barrier to access, and we don't want to limit the use of these devices.

As it is, the social media break is replacing the cigarette break as employees duck outside to connect to their social networks to check in on what's going on. This is because they're not allowed these tools in the workplace. Which is crazy: why do you want to limit people's access to part of their distributed brain? It's like cutting off the flow of blood to the brain before engaging in business (they're called "ties" because they tie off your thinking)!

And, as content becomes interoperable, as we take advantage of standards and tools that let us separate out the form it appears in from the actual message (read: XML), I suggest that mobile delivery may be the initial target. Face it, the minimalism we use in mobile design actually works better for web and other delivery! When we look across the continuum from the periphery of the community of practice to the center, increasingly the resources are not courses, but content (job aids, podcasts) and connection to others.

Mobile is increasingly the vehicle for business, and consequently mobile is a component of a full workscape or performance ecosystem. When work = learning = work, mobile is increasingly the access mechanism for the quick answer to support ongoing learning in the workflow. Sure, there are issues to be addressed, but the answers exist. Mobile is doable now, and it's time to embrace it before your competitors do. It's way past time to get as mobile as your workforce already is.

Collaboration

Six heads are better than one. That's why half a dozen seasoned professionals put together the brain trust known as Internet Time Alliance.

Trust

Trust is very important in our lives. As children we put our trust in our parents. As we grew we learned to make decisions regarding when we should trust and when we should be more circumspect. When we start a new job or project we spend time figuring out whom we can turn to for advice, who we can trust, and whose advice we need to double-check.

With the rise of the networked society and the increasing use of social networking tools, trust is probably on our minds every day. Who doesn't hesitate before clicking on that shortened URL from a friend on Facebook or someone we follow on Twitter and wonder whether it's genuine or whether the account has been hijacked and the link is about to initiate some malware infection from an unknown server in some unknown location that just may not be caught by our spam/malware protection software?

So, trust is probably at the forefront of our thinking most days.

Trust and Getting Things Done in Organisations

Trust relationships are powerful allies in getting things done in organisations. I think we're all aware of that.

If we're working in L&D strong trust relationships with senior leaders and middle managers are vital. Without a high level of trust anyL&D manager will find it almost impossible to embed a culture of learning in their organisation.

Trust and 'A Seat at the Table'

Like HR, many training and learning departments have been trying for years to gain *a seat at the top table* in their organisation. To a large extent these attempts have failed and it's worth asking why this is the case.

Although the age-old management credo that 'our people are our greatest asset' has now moved beyond lip-service in many organisations (despite the fact that the value of this 'greatest asset' still isn't explicitly shown on a balance sheet), the leadership of the part of the organisation that's directly responsible for working, advising and helping extract maximum performance from this asset is still not welcome as an equal member of the senior management team. Sure, CLOs and senior L&D managers may regularly be invited to present new initiatives or 'state of play' reports to senior management meetings, but that's different from being inside the tent or having a 'seat at the table' and contributing to ongoing strategy development.

This situation raises a couple of questions for me - and they're both tied to trust and trust relationships.

The first question is: "Do most senior managers actually believe that L&D managers play an important role in keeping the organisation running and on-track"?

Associated with this is a second question: "Do most managers think that L&D can add value"?

I think both of these questions come back to *competence trust* and to *relevance*. They beg the question as to whether business managers have confidence that their L&D department can make a difference, impact organisational performance and the balance sheet. In other words, is L&D relevant in business terms? If it isn't, then why include passengers on the senior leadership team.

So, what can CLOs and L&D managers do to address this?

Different Types of Trust

Firstly it's worth understanding about the some of the different types of trust and then developing a plan to build trust with your senior business colleagues.

Trust is qualified In a number of ways. For some there are two types - *competence trust* and *benevolent trust*. The difference is this. The first is the 'I believe you know what you're talking about, so I'll trust your opinion' type of trust. In other words,' I believe that you're *competent* so I'll trust you'. The second is the 'I believe that you won't tell me anything that will harm me, so I'll trust your opinion' type of trust.

Another view of how we come to trust someone or not is defined as being based on our assessment of their *benevolence*, *integrity* and *ability*.

Now, no matter how we define it, it's important that L&D managers address trust in its many forms in building solid relationships with senior business managers. And trust is a two-way thing. I'll trust you if you trust me...

Moving L&D up the Agenda

If you want to move L&D up the agenda and have the opportunity to be involved in strategic decision-making, you need to demonstrate that the L&D managers and their teams are trustworthy.

You do this by building trust relationships. By demonstrating that you understand the problems business managers are facing, and then by working with them to deliver solutions to resolve those problems demonstrably, quickly, efficiently. By doing this you will start to build competence trust and benevolent trust relationships. You'll also go a long way towards engendering your managers' trust in your ability and competence to deliver business solutions, and a feeling that you are a trusted partner, someone who can be relied on.

If you work on this basis – get close to your business managers, analyse their problems with them, advise them of the options open to them from your professional L&D standpoint, take their input, and then develop effective solutions, and demonstrate the efficacy and impact in the most straightforward way possible – in business terms – you will find that a trust relationship will develop.

That's the way to get a seat at the top table. It's not magic. You'll just find yourself being invited to provide advice and suggestions at early stages in the strategy-setting process. You'll find people calling you up because the CEO or CFO has recommended you as someone who can help managers with their problems.

You may even find HR colleagues asking how you have managed to become a trusted consultant and advisor to the CEO and CFO and other senior leaders.

Come Together

Organizations have woken up to the power of people working together. Collaboration gets things done and is the most powerful learning tool in the CLO's playbook.

Twenty years ago, colleagues at far-flung enterprises communicated by phone, mail and fax. The world moved at a slower pace. FedEx slashed the time required to receive a document, but we were still stuck with a one-way medium. Expensive conferencing equipment enabled remote meetings if audio was all you needed. Proprietary videoconferencing packages transmitted video back and forth, but most people stopped watching the pictures once the novelty wore off.

Then, along came the Internet. Today's organizations are learning the power of people working together in real time. The use of instant messaging migrated from high school to corporate life. Cheap, simple conferencing tools let workers meet wherever there's an online connection. Presence-awareness systems route calls to people wherever they are now, not where they used to be. Expertise locators connect workers to people with answers; social software connects them with friends and colleagues. Online team rooms keep the lights on as projects move around the world, passed from one team to the next. Skype gives people the ability to place free video calls over the Net. Software such as Second Life allows executives — in avatar form — to give presentations to one another in virtual boardrooms.

The social learning revolution has only just begun. Corporations that understand the value of knowledge sharing, teamwork, informal learning and joint problem solving are investing heavily in collaboration technology and are reaping the early rewards.

The problem? Most corporate collaboration infrastructure is a haphazard collection of point solutions rather than what one would put together given the opportunity to start with a blank slate. And what's wrong with that?

- It wastes people's time.
- Unmanaged technologies introduce security risks.
- Communications from one medium are often incompatible with another.
- Each technology comes with its own logins and conventions.
- Information is not captured for reuse or the building of peer-rated FAQs.
- Maintenance becomes a nightmare for central staff.
- Coordination breaks down. For example, bloggers may not communicate well with IM users.
- Overlapping technologies are subject to breakdown.
-

This is not atypical when companies adopt new technologies. As people begin to rely on these solutions, however, they seek out a more solid, coordinated approach. Now's the time.

Furthermore, far too many CLOs take no responsibility for the social media that makes collaboration work.

In recent surveys, Dr. Clark Quinn and I found that less than 40 percent of CLOs are involved in corporate decisions about communities of practice, social networks, content repositories, wikis and Internet access. Fewer still are involved with learning for customers, partners, distributors and the supply chain.

A quarter of the CLOs admitted that their corporate cultures do not value or encourage collaboration and teamwork. A similar proportion reported that their people did not learn new developments via in-house discussion forums.

At the Fall 2009 Chief Learning Officer Symposium, Rebecca Ray, senior vice president of global talent management and development for MasterCard, shared information from yet another survey. She revealed that 40 percent of CLOs do not tie metrics to business performance; 40 percent or less allocate their budget to support business initiatives; and 70 percent could not provide an example of a great CLO in action, driving performance.

Counterbalancing these tales of woe, Ted Hoff, vice president of the Center for Learning and Development at IBM, described his company's dedication to work-based collaborative learning. The goal is to create constant teaching moments. Every participant in the career advisor program has at least one mentor. IBM is linking partners and clients into its collaborative infrastructure. Hoff has successfully shifted funding from formal learning to informal collaborative learning.

Still, 77 percent of the CLOs that Quinn and I surveyed said their people are not growing fast enough to keep up with the needs of the business. I fear that the picture for many CLOs is yet another example of corporate dyslexia: the inability to see the writing on the wall.

Collaborate or Die

Traditional learning is bursting at the seams because there is always more to learn and unlearn. More knowledge was created in 2009 than in all of previous history. New discoveries invalidate former truths.

What *is* learning when information is liquid and any curriculum dies in infancy? We used to learn in order to get along in the environments we take part in. Familiarity with how things worked enabled us to adapt, and adapting to one's surroundings is still the goal of learning.

Collaboration rules

When people work together instead of individually, they produce greater results and derive more pleasure from their work. Until quite recently, collaboration was not easy, especially when distance was involved or people couldn't access the same information or a worker couldn't figure out who was the right person to contact. Those barriers are fading fast. Software and networks that support collaboration are in place and inexpensive. Everyone complains about departmental silos; social networks bore through silo walls.

I asked Harvard Business School's Andrew McAfee, who coined the term Enterprise 2.0, why he thinks social software will transform the business world. He told me that today's collaborative technologies can knit together an enterprise and facilitate knowledge work in ways that were simply not possible previously. They have the potential to usher in a new era by making both the practices of knowledge work and its outputs more visible.

Many Happy Returns

Business has already squeezed the big process improvements out of its physical systems, but for many companies, collaboration and networking processes are virgin territory. The upside potential is staggering: people innovating, sharing, supporting one another, all naturally and without barriers. The traditional approach has been to automate routine tasks in order to reduce cost; the new vision is to empower people to take advantage of their innate desire to share, learn together and innovate.

Web 2.0, the "collaborative web," renders overstuffed file cabinets and hard drives overflowing with email obsolete. Members of a group can share information and make improvements to one copy that's virtually available to everyone. Workers learn to remix rather than re-invent, and having everyone read from the same page reduces the odds of mistaking obsolete information for current. Distance no longer keeps workers apart. As we remove obstacles, the time required to do anything shrivels up.

Why bother?

Collaboration that does not increase revenue, improve relationships with customers, cut costs, grow employees, expand innovation, communicate values, streamline the work process, or help execute strategy should not be funded.

Companies are using social software to:

- Speed up the flow of information through the organization
- Improve customer service

- Streamline workflow and slash bureaucracy
- Unleash the power of collective intelligence
- Create nerve centers for corporate news and market intelligence
- Make all corporate know-how accessible 24/7
- Recruit the best candidates for new positions and make them productive quickly
- Replace training classes with informal, hands-on learning
- Open the process of innovation to all employees
- Help workers build strong, supportive relationships
- Enable managers to assess the status and direction of projects
- Empower all employees to contribute ideas and feel part of the team
- Develop more productive relationships with customers, prospects, recruits, partners, supply chain, and other employees

Compared to old-style groupware such as Lotus Notes, today's social software is simple, unstructured, emergent, inherently transparent, and it scales.

Social media for collaboration

Social media tools support:

• social interactions and connections with people.

• collaboration and sharing and the creation of user-generated content.

• the building of a new phase of eLearning, often referred to as E-Learning 2.0 or Social Learning.

In the first part of this article I discussed three types of social media tools: social bookmarking, social file sharing and social networking services. In part two I considered micro-blogging services, like Twitter, and their use for personal and informal learning, professional networking and as an alternative learning channel.

In this final part I am going to take a broad look at collaborative working and learning.

The term collaboration has a variety of meanings and as there are a number of ways that people can collaborate to work and learn together, it is important to decide what type of collaboration you want before you select a tool.

Here are 12 types of collaborative activities/scenarios and some suggestions of tools to support them.

1. Collaborative brainstorming and mindmapping.

Scenario: A number of individuals want to work together for group problem solving, requirements gathering, action planning, note-taking, idea visualisation or perhaps to structure a collaborative document.

Tools: Mindmapping tools let you create a visual representation of a collection of ideas in a tree-like structure. The different contributions are often colour-coded so that you can see who added what. Mind maps can then be stored and shared online. Mindmapping tools include:

• Mind42 from *www.mind42.com* MindMeister from *www.mindmeister.com*

• Comapping.com from *www.comapping.com*

2. Collaborative diagramming

Scenario: A group of individuals want to build collaborative diagrams like flowcharts, organisation charts, SWOT diagrams, wireframes, and so on.

Tools: Collaborative diagramming and graphic tools include:

• Gliffy from *www.gliffy.com*

• LucidChart from www.lucidchart.com

• Dabbleboard from www.dabbleboard.com

3. Collaborative authoring

Scenario: A number of individuals want to work on a common document and have an equal ability to add, edit, or delete items in it. They also want to be able to keep track of everyone's individual contributions.

Tools: Collaborative authoring tools ensure there is only one version of the document rather than multiple copies showing different edits. Co-authoring might, however, take place in real-time (i.e. a number can work on the document simultaneously) or where contributors are locked out until a contributor has completed his input and the document has been updated. There are a couple of different types of tools that can be used for collaborative authoring.

Wiki tools are essentially editable web pages. The most well-known example of a wiki is of course, Wikipedia, the collaborative encyclopaedia. Wiki tools that support the creation of group wikisites are now becoming serious business and can be employed for many different purposes such as education. Although a wiki site can be public or private, editing a wiki generally requires a contributor to log in, so that all changes to the page are tracked. A log of activity is maintained, and contributors can be notified of changes via email or RSS. There are now a huge number of free and commercial wiki tools available. These include:

• Wetpaint from www.wetpaint.com is a free platform that includes social networking functionality so that individuals can connect with one another.

• Google Sites from www.google.com/sites is Google's web authoring tool for both personal and group websites.

• Confluence from *www.atlassian.com/software/confluence/* is a popular enterprise system that offers MS Office and SharePoint integration.

Online office suites have a combination of productivity and collaboration functionality which support collaborative content authoring, but may also include other tools. Suites include:

• Google Docs from *www.google.com/docs* includes word processing, spreadsheet and presentation elements. You can create documents or upload from MS Office or Open Office. You can choose who can view or edit the documents as a web page. Documents can also be saved on your computer in a number of formats such as PDF.

• Zoho Suite from *www.zoho.com* includes Writer (word processing), Sheet (spreadsheet) and Show (presentation) tools as well as other tools including a wiki.There is compatibility with MS Office tools, and you need to use your Google account to sign into Zoho.• Microsoft Office Live Workspace from *www.officelive.com/* allows users to save Word, Excel and PowerPoint documents online, and lets you control who views and edits the files

There are also a number of other stand alone tools that focus on specific types of documentation collaboration, e.g.

• Editgrid from *www.editgrid.com* is an online collaborative spreadsheet service.

• Sliderocket from *www.sliderocket.com* is used to work in sync with others on presentations.

4. Collaborative reviewing

Scenario: An individual has created a document and now seeks feedback from others in order to revise it. The individual wants to make the final decision about which suggested changes are incorporated in the document.

Tools: Most people would use Microsoft Word's Track Changes or Comments functionality to edit and comment on a document, but this means that the author has to review a number of versions of the document with different changes. If a wikitype solution were to be used, then all the reviewers would have the ability to change the original documentation which is also not wanted here. In this case, a co-reviewing tool is required, for example:

• PleaseReview from *www.pleasetech.com/pleasereview.htm* provides a secure, browser-based review environment. Reviewers can see each other's comments and changes and can reply, and authors can decide which comments and changes to accept. Authors

get a single document with consolidated comments and changes.

5. Collaborative reflection

Scenario: A group of individuals want to share their ongoing thoughts, ideas and reflections with the public or a private group of colleagues, and encourage comments.

Tools: The best way to do this would be to set up a multi-author blog and ensure that the commenting functionality is enabled. Commenting can be set to open or subject to moderation by the blog owner, as required. There are now many blogging tools in the marketplace, here are a few that support multi authors.

• Blogger from www.blogger.com is Google's free blogging tool.

• Wordpress from www.wordpress.com is another popular free blogging tool.

• TypePad from www.typepad.com is a commercial, hosted blogging platform (Multi-authoring available in Pro account only).

6. Collaborative commenting

Scenario: An individual has produced a resource, e.g. a document, presentation or video and wants to share it with others and encourage feedback on it.

Tools: There are many websites that allow users to host and share their content in different formats either publically or privately, and for registered users to rate or comment on the content. A few of these include:

• Scribd from www.scribd.com for documents.

• Flickr from www.flickr.com for images.

• YouTube from www.youtube.com for videos.

• Slideshare from www.slideshare.com for presentation slidesets.

7. Collaborative annotation

Scenario: An individual wants to share a web page they have found with their colleagues or other team members. In addition they also wish to annotate it.

Tools: There are a number of tools that allow users to mark and make notes about webpages, by adding, for instance, sticky-like memos to bookmarks, or by bookmarking articles with relevant text highlighted. Examples of tools include:

• Diigo from www.diigo.com lets you add notes and in-page highlights

• iLighter from www.i-lighter.com lets you highlight, collect and share the web

• Trailfire from www.trailfire.com lets you add notes (aka trail marks) and save annotated webpages

8. Collaborative Productivity

Scenario: A group of individuals want to improve their collective productivity in a variety of different ways.Tools: There are a multitude of tools that support group productivity:

• Google Calendar from www.google.com/calendar is suitable for collaborative meeting scheduling.

• Remember the Milk from www.rememberthemilk.com/ is a task management tool that you can share with others.

• skrbl from www.skrbl.com is a free online whiteboard.

9. Collaborative Working (Spaces)

Scenario: A team of employees want to have access to a shared workspace where they can work together by uploading files (documents, spreadsheets, etc) and share them with one another, either as reference material or perhaps to work on a collaborative task or document.

Tools: Collaborative workspace tools are sometimes referred to as groupware. Some have basic functionality, others, particularly those intended for enterprise use, often include a variety of other tools like blogs and wikis as real-time communication tools. Here are three examples:

• Google Groups from http://groups.google.com is a free, hosted service that lets members have discussions as well share files.

• Central Desktop from www.centraldesktop.com/ is a tool for team, group or enterprise collaboration in a wiki-enabled platform.

• Microsoft SharePoint from www.microsoft.com/sharepoint/ is an enterprise workspace platform for sharing information and working together in teams, communities and people-driven processes.

10. Collaborative Project Management

Scenario: A project manager wants to manage the internal or external projects of a team of people.

Tools: Some of the collaborative workspace tools (above) focus on supporting project management, e.g. task management, time tracking, reporting, etc, as well as team communication. Tools include:

• 5pm – *www.5pmweb.com/*,

• Basecamp - *basecamphq.com/*

• Easyprojects – *easyprojects.net/*

11. Collaborative Course Design and Development

Scenario: A group of learning designers and subject matter experts want to work together on creating an e-learning course.

Tools: Collaborative course design and development tools let users collaboratively capture, storyboard, develop, review, test, and publish courses quickly and easily. Tools include:

Atlantic Link's Content Point - *www.atlantic-link.co.uk/home_content* point.htm

• Unison - *rapidintake.com/unison/index.htm*

• Mohive's E-Learning Publishing Suite – *www.mohive.com*

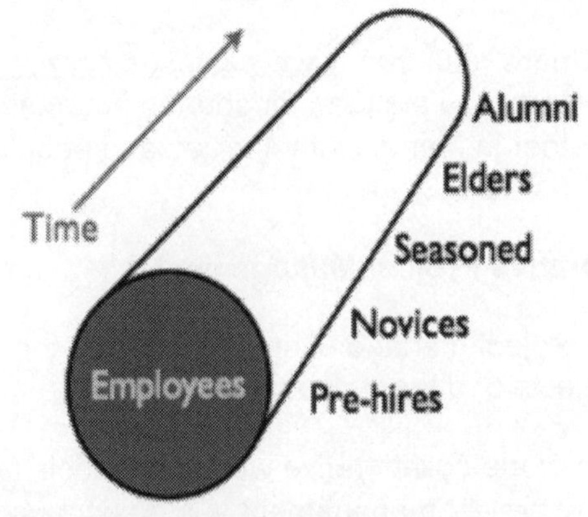

12. Collaborative Learning (spaces)

Scenario: A group of individuals want to have access to a shared space where they can learn together either formally or informally e.g. to work on a collaborative learning project or to improve the performance of the whole group by sharing experiences and ideas as well as resources.

Tools: Most corporate learning management systems have limited, if any, collaboration functionality and only focus on the delivery and management of formal course content. Educational course management systems (aka virtual learning environments in the UK), on the other hand, generally have more communication and collaboration features like wikis and blogging tools, e.g.

• Moodle from www.moodle.org is an open source VLE that has several collaborative tools that can be incorporated into a formal course learning space. This rich learning platform is now making its way into the business world.

There are also several other open source systems that can be installed and configured to create collaborative, informal work/ learn spaces for organisations, that include a range of other social activities like user profiling, social bookmarking as well as blogging and file sharing. Tools in this category include:

• Drupal – www.drupal.org

• Elgg – www.elgg.org

This article has provided examples of only a small number of tools that support collaboration and sharing in the workplace. For over 2.500 tools that can be used for learning and performance support, take a look at the Directory of Learning Tools I maintain at the Centre's website - c4lpt.co.uk/Directory/

And, if you are looking for help with building an informal collaborative work/learn space in your organisation, then Internet Time Alliance from www.Internet*TimeAlliance.com* can provide guidance on establishing and nurturing an online community.

Whose Learning?

Last month I conducted several workshops to inject informal and social learning practices into hidebound organizations that were anxious to ramp up to the future. I encouraged them to address the needs of people who had traditionally been left out of the corporate training agenda.

In the old days, corporate training departments focused solely on workers on the payroll. Most of the effort went into getting novices up to speed and grooming fast-trackers as future leaders. Training departments largely overlooked improving the skills of seasoned employees, despite the fact that these were the people whose efforts were paying the bills.This myopia is the result of looking at training as a cure for cluelessness rather than the route to ever-greater levels of performance. The logic went, "If it's broken, fix it," but don't waste time converting adequate performers into stars. The world's become too competitive to let this neglect continue.

Any organization that is committed to working smarter needs to assess the impact of helping employees learn at every step in their career cycle. What's it worth, for example, to offer learning opportunities to potential recruits before they come on board? These "pre-hires" can become familiar with the company before signing on. This cuts costly hiring mistakes that hurt both the organization and the new hire.

Seasoned employees are not going to flock to classes and workshops; they have work to do. But making it easier through collaboration, self-service learning and skill bites helps sharp people become sharper. Making a producer just a little bit more productive yields greater rewards than anything you can do with novices.

Old hands may have known it all in yesterday's world, but they can only remain productive by keeping up with changes. Furthermore, a company that doesn't tap its community elders as coaches, mentors and guides is missing an important trick. IBM and other corporations generate leads and harvest insider knowledge by keeping former employees in the community — and, therefore, in the loop.

Increasingly, organizations are sustained by people who are not on the payroll. These are contract workers and individuals called in for a particular project. They are temps, specialists, consultants and service providers. Perhaps they work for an outsource provider.

However, these workers are not exempt from needing to know what's going on and continuously getting better at what they do. It's the logic of the supply chain: Since inefficient links get passed along to the customer, companies must optimize the performance of the chain. That means improving the brainpower of everyone who works for the company — not just those who receive paychecks.

The Cluetrain Manifesto, a set of 95 principles for businesses operating in the newly connected workplace, just turned 10 years old. Here's the clue: Markets are conversations. Doc Searls, co-author of the manifesto, amended that to "markets are relationships." Exactly. Companies can't exist in isolation. Value has moved from the nodes to the connections. No business can survive without good ties to a healthy ecosystem.

And that applies to customer relationships as well. Take me, for example. I recently purchased a snazzy video camera. The manual appears to have been written for rocket scientists. The companion Web site is simply a PDF of the manual. Ugh.

Developing an amazing piece of machinery like this camera must cost millions. For just $100,000 more, the company could have set up a discussion site for customers to swap information, opened a customer hot line, hired an English grad student to write a coherent self-study manual, gotten feedback for new product development and provided a list of links to useful sites for new HD video camera owners. And to attract prospective buyers, they could have opened up lessons for all would-be videographers.

If I were greeted with useful resources such as those, I would be much more likely to buy from the same supplier again. As it is now, I have learned nothing from the camera makers, they have learned nothing from me, and we have no relationship at all.

Shouldn't chief learning officers shoulder the responsibility for learning by everyone in the extended enterprise?

How to Kick Off Collaborative Project Groups

It is never easy to change the way people relate to one another at work. People and corporate cultures have different views on being open, taking risks, trying new things, realigning responsibilities, learning new technologies, and trusting one another. What works in one organization may fail in the next.

Some communities self-organize. Give them a place to meet, get out of the way, and watch the community grow. That's great for purely social communities like Facebook, but it's not sufficient when you need a team to work collaboratively on an important project.

Here is the advice from seasoned project managers who have set up dozens of collaborative teams. Your mileage may vary, but most managers agree that initial projects have a better chance of thriving if:

- Participants have a shared need.
- It's easy for participants to see what's in it for them.
- The information involved is not controversial.
- A sound business case can be made.
- Stand-alone implementation is feasible (i.e., not requiring connection with other systems)
- The project yields a good example to use when getting support for other projects.
- You can open in New Haven.

New Haven? Sixty years ago, producers staged new plays at the Shubert Theater in New Haven, Connecticut, before taking them to Broadway. No critics were in the audience, so if a major overhaul was required before the official release, no one was the wiser. Similarly, if your first prototype bombs, it's nice to be able to sweep it under the carpet and begin anew.

There is nothing more difficult to take in hand, more perilous to conduct, or more uncertain in its success, than to take the lead in the introduction of a new order of things.

Machiavelli

To maintain focus, the owner of a project should prepare a document in response to these questions:

- What is the goal of the collaboration?
- What's the current situation?
- What do expect it to be after the project?
- How will this be accomplished?
- What is the business benefit? (In business terms.)
- Who's going to take part?
- What might go wrong?
- Is this a one-time project or an on-going process?
- Do we have sponsorship higher up?
- Who will participate on the team?
- If it's a one-timer, when will it be completed? What is the kill date?
- Who is the project champion?

Display your answers prominently on the wiki, blog, or whatever tool is involved. Collaboration demands transparency.

New recruits are refusing to work with organizations that don't permit them to post a personal profile, use instant messenger, and connect to friends when they encounter a question. Assign them to collaborative teams. Elliott Masie tells of his disappointment with a new hire who had the continual distraction of six friends always a click away on her desktop. How could she concentrate? Then he realized that instead of having one new person working for The Masie Center, he had seven!

Gain team member commitment

It's great to begin a long-term collaboration with a face-to-face meeting. Either in person or virtual, social bonding comes before business, for that's the platform on which the work will be built. Begin with games and getting-to-know-you exercises. Give people time to talk and become familiar with one another.

Social connections remain vital throughout the collaboration. People work best with people they know. Encourage people to share information about themselves. Post photographs of participants. Pinpoint their locations on a map..

It's important that collaborators work under the same set of assumptions. Discuss each of these areas and ask for individual commitment to them.

- Respect the team, and do what is best to accomplish the objective. Be selfless, not selfish.
- Members will be active. If a member spots something to improve the collaboration, she volunteers to do it.
- Members freely share ideas and suggestions. They do not hoard information or keep secrets.
- Members treat each other with respect. The team is committed to continuous improvement.
- Members care for one another emotionally, helping one another over rough spots and fears.
- Use whatever tools are appropriate to advance the project: phone calls, on-line meetings.
- Members trust one another. They "make this marriage work."

Be prepared for push-back. Workers who see collaboration as hindering their work rather than supporting it will be reluctant to join the effort. Organizations that are accustomed to a single viewpoint (usually top management's) can become rattled as other voices begin to speak. It's useful to recruit a band of early supporters to help sell the value of the project.

Learning is woven into the fabric of every modern business. It's the way we adapt to change. We've got to rid ourselves of the notion that learning is just the chief learning officer's business. Learning is so much more than that. Learning is the lifeblood of commerce, and it's every corporate citizen's job to make it better. It's time to invite customers to join the party.

Learning and social networks and customer communications and partner relations and marketing and sales aren't islands. They're all facets of the same thing: the corporate commons of work and learning. Some astute companies are exploring how a social learning community can remove barriers separating customer and corporation. It's all about learning conversations.

The Cluetrain Manifesto is one of the most important business books of the late 20th century. Its primary message is that markets are conversations. That conversation must be authentic; you can't fake it. Its language is "natural, open, direct, funny and often shocking." Honest conversation builds lasting customer relationships.

Never, never, never, never give up.

Winston Churchill

Conversations also are the most effective learning technology ever invented. Learning is social. Most of what you learn, you learn from and with other people. You do so in the give-and-take of conversation. While it's a book about business, not learning, *The Cluetrain Manifesto* presciently challenges its readers to "imagine a world where everyone was constantly learning, a world where what you wondered was more interesting than what you know, and curiosity counted for more than certain knowledge."

Making a lesson stick takes more than a talking-head video, no matter how compelling the speaker. That's why this community site challenges participants to specify their goals, set up milestones and receive reminders. There's a personal learning journal for keeping track of progress, there's a forum for asking questions and sharing opinions, and there's a community that enables members to learn with one another. The entire site was designed with learning in mind.

When thousands of people join a community, its conveners need metrics to assess progress and chart their next steps. Web-based analytics are easily baked into online communities such as this, and Google now provides a service that enables a Web site to compare itself to its peers.

Most people who visit a social networking site never go beyond the opening page. People hate to be taught, but they love to learn.

Combining learning and marketing is win-win. Here's why:

1. Informed customers are better customers. They know the goods. They trust the brand. They buy more.

2. Learning relationships are two-way. Customer-learners keep coming back. Familiarity breeds loyalty. Participants bring in their friends.

3. Analytics inform marketing decisions. Administrators monitor changes in customer interests and behavior. They have a channel for direct feedback and suggestions from the marketplace.

You can set up an online social learning community without waiting in line for IT to help. Many communities run on turnkey platforms. Cut it on, and you're good to go. Isn't it time to include customers in your organization's learning plans

Who Knows

What would you think of an assembly line where workers didn't know where to find the parts they were supposed to attach? Absurd, you say. Heads would roll. Yet for knowledge workers, this is routine. Consider a knowledge worker stymied by a lack of information, hardly an uncommon situation. In fact, in many professions, knowledge workers spend a third of their time looking for answers and helping their colleagues do the same.

How does our knowledge worker respond? She is five times more likely to turn to another person than to an impersonal source, such as a database or a file cabinet. Often she asks whoever happens to be close by, the denizen of the next cube or someone getting a cup of coffee. Half the time, this person doesn't have a clue.

If I had six hours to chop down a tree, I'd spend the first four sharpening the axe.

Abraham Lincoln

Only one in five knowledge workers consistently finds the

information needed to do their jobs. This happens to knowledge customers, too, half of whom bail before completing online orders. Other studies have found that knowledge workers spend more time re-creating existing information they were unaware of than creating original material.

All this slows the pace of the enterprise, burns out the workforce with scut work, reduces responsiveness to customers and increases job dissatisfaction. Reinventing the wheel, looking for information in the wrong places and answering questions from peers consumes two-thirds of the average knowledge workers time. Slashing this waste time provides a lot more time to devote to improving the business, reducing payroll or, more likely, a bit of both.

This knowledge productivity problem is destined to get worse before it gets better. The haystack is getting bigger exponentially. Corporate information doubles in volume every 18 months. Half of the recorded information in the entire world has been created in the past five years!

Specialists used to keep their heads above the flood tide of incoming knowledge by knowing more and more about less and less. In today's interconnected world, boundaries between disciplines are becoming porous. Everything is multidisciplinary. We have to know more and more about more and more.

Successful organizations will connect people. Learning is social. We learn from, by and with other people. Conversation, storytelling and observation are great ways to learn, but they aren't things you do by yourself.

Job one is to help knowledge workers find the answers they need. Rob Cross and others describe many ways to go about this in a marvelous book, *Creating Value With Knowledge*, edited by IBMs Eric Lesser and Laurence Prusak (Oxford University Press, 2003).

If people are going to go to other people for answers, make it easy for them to get to people in the know. (Get them to look for their keys where they're likely to find them, not where the lights better.) Set up help desks to support new product rollouts and organizational initiatives. Have the help desk apply the 80/20 rule and document the common queries in a mercifully short FAQ. Then, tier responses by triage. First query the FAQ, then ask the help desk, and if those don't work, contact the prime subject-matter expert.

Learning a new software release is a special case. Since a

release generally builds on an existing foundation, workers more often need answers to specific questions than the sort of overview that workshops and courses provide. Trial-and-error is a great way to learn so long as there is a way to deal with roadblocks. Since the release is new, learners wont find answers in-house. In this case, outsource mentoring to a firm that does have the answers.

Emotions Trump Logic

> *No problem can be solved from the same level of thinking that created it.*
> Einstein

Michael Allen shocked his audience at the eLearning Guild's Annual Gathering in early 2007, when he announced that ADDIE was dead. ADDIE (analyse-design-develop-implement-evaluate) had been the mantra of orthodox instructional designers for half a century. Developed by the military in an era when behaviorism was king of the psychology mountain, ADDIE rested on the assumption that learners are completely logical.

Michael developed an authoring system named, of all things, Authorware. The software locked in analytical instructional design. Of all people, he's telling us to pay more attention to emotions than to logic, for that's the way people operate.

"We didn't know it was wrong at the time," he said. eLearning doesn't deliver the goods: it does not change behavior. Psychotherapy does change behavior, so Michael opened the door to working with heart and mind.

When Allen Interactions develops a program these days, they begin by soaking up the learners' context by living in the potential learning community. They then create a few rapid prototypes. They sleep on it. And that's the usual starting point for a kick-ass program.

Meta-learning

My designs for learning are less systematic than Michael's. I inevitably begin with a metaphorical trip up to the balcony. Looking down from the balcony affords a broader perspective on what's going on. Climb high enough, and you begin to see processes at work.

Examining learning itself rather than what is learned is an example of meta-learning. Despite the folklore, "learning to learn" is but a small slice of the meta-learning pie. Michael's recognition that ADDIE-based eLearning didn't work is an example. I plan to take you into another aspect of meta-learning.

From afar, learning resembles a value chain. Each have inputs, processing, and outputs. Some processes work well, some not so well. Acting as if emotion plays no role in learning is akin to suggesting that clocks have nothing to do with efficient manufacturing.

For the past dozen years, my view from the balcony has led me to explore learning+web ("eLearning"), learning+job environment ("Workflow Learning"), and learning without restraints ("Informal Learning").

Come with me to a higher balcony. From this vantage point, we see that learning is but one of many processes employed to attain business results. If something improves the overall value of the ecosystem and/or the welfare of the individual worker, I'm in favor of it. (Assuming it's legal.) This includes helping the individual worker build personal strengths and overcome personal obstacles.

My traditionalist critics take a more narrow view. They don't think it appropriate to interfere in the worker's personal life. You can deal with outside indicators like dress codes, zany behavior, and funky odors, but you are not allowed to even consider what goes on inside a worker's head.

I don't understand how a Chief Learning Officer can say "It's not my department" when it's obvious that a worker's mental health, physical fitness, emotional balance, outlook on life, authenticity, and social skills have a tremendous impact on work quality, not to mention personal satisfaction. What part of the value chain do they not understand?

Steve Jobs, at Stanford graduation, said "You've got to find what you love. And that is as true for your work as it is for your lovers. Your work is going to fill a large part of your life, and the only way to be truly satisfied is to do what you believe is great work. And the only way to do great work is to love what you do. If you haven't found it yet, keep looking. Don't settle. As with all matters of the heart, you'll know when you find it. And, like any great relationship, it just gets better and better as the years roll on. So keep looking until you find it. Don't settle."

Let's go up one more level to look at the changing culture of business. The Industrial Age is over. Brains are replacing machines. Front-line workers are taking responsibility for making decisions, among them what and how they learn.

All learning is co-creation. It's participatory. You learn by playing the game. But to get out on the field, you must be able to kick the ball, jump the hurdle, or toss the Frisbee. Winners in the game played in most organizations know how to speak, write, convince, know their goals, appreciate their disabilities, give a presentation, learn from experience, and find happiness and fulfillment in their work. Health, technical savvy, a good network of contacts, and other things are vital, too, but we don't have space to cover them here.

In sum, individual learners need to participate in the new business ecosystem to keep up and to create value. Shouldn't chief learning officers do what they can to help?

New Roles for Instructional Professionals

Ellen Wagner, Curt Bonk and Charles spent 30 minutes facilitating a discussion on the topic of 'New Roles for Learning Professionals'. Going back through notes and the archive of the (very animated) chat/discussion that took place, some clear threads emerged on the types of capabilities that a 21st century L&D department need to have.

Here are some of the core capabilities identified:

1. consulting / coaching acumen (as well as learning acumen) that is focused on performance problems and outcomes. The ability to engage with senior (and not-so-senior) line managers to identify the root cause of performance problems, and not simply focus on learning.

2. the ability to 'speak business'. An understanding of business goals is the 'so what' in learning. Everyone in L&D should be able to read and draw conclusions from a balance sheet and P&L account and understand the business drivers that line managers are focused on.

3. a good grasp of technology – across-the-board - but especially emerging technologies, and how they can fit into learning solutions

4. adult learning – an understanding of how adults learn in the

workplace, and 'what works' in organisational learning.

Along with these, another set of attributes such as: 'empathy, ' listening', 'tolerance for ambiguity', 'basic communication ability' were identified as essential by participants.

Harold Jarche also made the important point that 'attitude trumps skills' for a learning professional. We've known that in a more general sense for years – many of us have used the axiom 'hire for attitude' when we're recruiting. I certainly have found it has served me well. I can't think of any situation where I've hired on the basis of attitude where I would have done otherwise in retrospect.

Personal Intellectual Capital Management

> *you are the most important person in the universe.*
> *so is everyone else.*
>
> *—e. e. cummings*

Ultimately, you're responsible for the life you lead. It's up to you to learn what you need to succeed. That makes you responsible for your own knowledge management, learning architecture, instructional design and evaluation.

Professionally, we design learning experiences to meet concrete objectives. We plan ahead to prepare for the future. We try to avoid reinventing the wheel. We build systems to leverage the knowledge we already possess. We gather feedback so we can do better next time.

Personally, we should do no less. Intellectual capital is what separates winners from losers, and I want the best I can get. My personal learning and knowledge management are too important to leave to chance. So are yours.

Analysis

Choose your goals. For next month, the next year, the next decade and before you die. Think about what you must learn to achieve them.

Become aware of how you learn. Your brain hosts a continuous, internal conversation. If you don't like what you hear, change it.

Design

You don't need to know something if you know where to find it. Set up your own knowledge repository. For 20 years, I've saved factoids, quotations and reference information on my computer. It's searchable. I couldn't do without it.

You are what you learn. List your inputs—magazines, Web sites, courses and colleagues. Will these inputs enable you to learn what you need to know? If not, change them.

Life is not a true-or-false test. Everything is relative. Recognizing that what once appeared black or white is actually a continuum of grays is healthy unlearning.

Implementation

Be your own sports psychologist. Visualize achieving your goals. Then go for it!

The process of change sees to it that lots of what you've learned is obsolete, inappropriate or simply dead wrong. The world is riddled with complexity. Admitting that some of what you know is wrong makes room to learn new things.

To deepen understanding and plant something in memory, teach it to someone else.

Human nature values urgency over importance. If the phone rings while you're working on an important project, you answer it. You defer the important to tend to the trivial. Dumb move. Dedicate time each day for long-term thinking. Take time to learn. Remember the 80/20 rule! And don't forget to cut off the phone.

Evaluation

Level 1. Are you happy? Do you lead the life you want to lead?

Level 2. Can you demonstrate what you're learning? Is your learning sound?

Level 3. Are you progressing in ways that increase your economic value? Are you deepening relationships with family and friends? Are you growing spiritually?

Level 4. Are you doing your part to make the world a better place?

Storytelling

Slide after slide of bulleted sentence fragments is an awful thing to sit through. If the speaker giving the presentation reads them to you word for word, it makes a bad spectacle even worse. Regardless of these unpleasantries, PowerPoint has become the language of business.

PowerPoint also happens to be learning's most popular authoring tool. Many software packages enable learning and development leaders to narrate a PowerPoint presentation and upload it to the Web. The problem is that if live lectures are ineffective, prerecorded ones online are going to be even more ineffective. Unfortunately, being a subject-matter expert doesn't necessarily make someone an expert public speaker. Sadly, many experts think the purpose of a PowerPoint presentation is to expose the audience to content and pure information—as if emotion plays no part in getting a message across.

However, it makes no more sense to blame PowerPoint for boring presentations than to blame fountain pens for forgery.

Steve Denning, the author of several books on storytelling, recalls not being able to get fully engaged into someone's PowerPoint presentation. He recognized that PowerPoint can be too concrete, and therefore, he abandoned PowerPoint in his own presentations in favor of telling stories. No one missed it. When you hear a powerful story, you internalize it. Your imagination makes it your story, and that's something that will stick with you.

Cliff Atkinson's book *Beyond Bullet Points: Using Microsoft PowerPoint to Create Presentations That Inform, Motivate and Inspire* shows how to use Hollywood's script-writing techniques to focus your ideas, how to use storyboards to establish clarity and how to properly produce the script so that it best engages the audience.

Atkinson recently told me the story of a presentation that made a $250 million difference. Attorney Mark Lanier pled the case against Merck in the first Vioxx-related death trial, brought by the widow of a man who died of a heart attack that she believed was caused by the painkiller. Before preparing his presentation, he read "Beyond Bullet Points," and invited Atkinson to Houston to lend a hand in putting his presentation together.

"We used the three-step approach from the book," Atkinson said. "Then (Lanier's) flawless delivery took the experience beyond what I imagined possible. He masterfully framed his argument with an even flow of projected images and blended it with personal stories, physical props, a flip chart, a tablet PC, a document projector and a deeply personal connection with his audience."

Fortune magazine's coverage of the trial describing Lanier's presentation said, "The attorney for the plaintiff presented simple and emotional stories that strongly contrasted with Merck's appeals to colorless reason." Fortune reported that Lanier "gave a frighteningly powerful and skillful opening statement. Speaking…without notes and in gloriously plain English, and accompanying nearly every point with imaginative, easily understood (if often hokey) slides and overhead projections, Lanier, a part-time Baptist preacher, took on Merck and its former CEO Ray Gilmartin with merciless, spellbinding savagery."

Lanier's technique was persuasive and aimed to get the jurors to believe in his "simple, alluring and emotionally cathartic stories, versus Merck's appeals to colorless, heavy-going, soporific reason. Lanier is inviting the jurors to join him on a bracing mission to catch a wrongdoer and bring him to justice." The Texas jury awarded the widow $253.4 million.

You may be thinking, "I don't have time to do something that elaborate." Put that in perspective: If you spend months on a complex project, isn't it worth a few days to wrap up the results into an effective presentation? If you're using PowerPoint as an authoring system, remember this: A presentation and self-directed learning are two totally different experiences, and the fact that they both may be in PowerPoint doesn't change that. For compelling presentations, follow the advice in "Beyond Bullet Points." And for training that works, follow the tenets of sound instructional design.

The Value of Not Re-inventing the Wheel

Founded in 1976, Canada's CGI provides billions of dollars worth of sophisticated IT and business process services from 100 offices serving clients in 16 countries. CGI has members, not employees, because it treats its staff as if they were investors — and indeed, 80 percent of them are.

Three years ago, knowledge management at CGI was the proverbial black hole that sucked in information and energy but never let it out. The staff who fed the beast meant well, but it wasn't equipped to provide CGI's professionals the up-to-the-moment technical savvy they needed. In a firm that relies on its wits to outperform competitors in a fast-moving global field, this situation was not sustainable.

CGI executives tapped Ross Button as vice president of technology leadership with a mission of heading a project to raise collective intelligence. Button and his staff of two, with in-sourced assistance from specialist groups within the firm, assembled what came to be known as Internet Inside. Imagine having your own, custom version of the internet running behind your firewall.

Internet Inside is more complicated than that, but not much. Most of the software is open-source: Drupal, SourceForge, MediaWiki, WordPress, some crawling utilities, browsers and RSS, coupled with a typical intranet infrastructure and the Microsoft Office/ Exchange suite.

Because few people will willingly change the basic way they send and receive information, participants send and receive information via their Microsoft Outlook accounts. The other software is free or cheap — not a trivial matter. A typical proprietary application that goes for $50 a seat is a million-dollar expense for a company the size of CGI. Also, the open-source community continuously improves the software's design, making incremental improvements instead of disruptive installations of new versions.

Most important of all, the Web software provides a social layer that connects people with one another and with information. CGI employees are geographically dispersed, but their collective intelligence system connects the dots.

Internet software travels with an invisible companion, the memes and processes I call internet culture. The Net is an environment for sharing. The Net values pragmatism and immediacy. On the Net, people speak conversationally, absent the officiousness of the traditional business memo.

Button said he will never cease putting tools into CGI's agile infrastructure. There will always be new requirements and better ways to support the business. For the foreseeable future, Web 2.0 and rich-internet application techniques will influence not only CGI, but its customers and the business world at-large. By cultivating Web 2.0 inside, CGI incubates lessons it will later share with outsiders.

People who study networks use shorthand for a persistent phenomenon: the 100:10:1 rule. In a group of a hundred people, only one person is likely to initiate dialogue. Ten people will comment, argue, question, provide examples and stoke discussion around the one individual's seed. A hundred people learn from observing and applying what they silently learn from the others. When social networking theory was immature, silent partners were denigrated as lurkers and losers. But without silent observers, everyone would be talking at once and chaos would ensue.

CGI has dozens of communities of a hundred or so like-minded professionals. Groups have formed around topics such as Java, enterprise architecture, banking, insurance, dot-net and business intelligence. For a group to be successful, Button makes sure each community has at least one person planting seeds.

Admission is by invitation only, limiting participation to like-minded individuals and keeping the groups to workable size. Participation in a community is based on need and qualifications.

About 4,000 CGI people belong to one or more communities. Every item that is shared as news is screened by a knowledgeable person before distribution to the group. Removing the noise of mediocre or erroneous outputs increases the fidelity of results. Applying one person's time at the front end saves the time of hundreds at the receiving end.

CGI has begun tagging all dialogues, not just by topic, but also by roles of the participants. A few years hence, CGI will have sufficient information to identify in-house experts based on past discussion. Beyond that, collective filtering may be able to point to people who are the best bets for pioneering future technologies.

Internet Inside at CGI is proof positive that simplicity is the ultimate sophistication.

Unmeetings

Admission and travel to conferences claim a significant amount of many corporations' investment in learning. That's why CLOs need to be aware of a fresh alternative that costs less and works better.

Professionals attend conferences to learn things, yet conference participants often say they learn more in the hallway than in formal sessions. Unconferences bring the hallway conversations back into the main tent by handing control to participants instead of experts on stage.

According to Wikipedia, An unconference is a conference where the content of the sessions is driven and created by the participants, generally day-by-day during the course of the event, rather than by organizers.

Software guru Dave Winer began promoting the unconference format after sitting in the audience at a conference, waiting for someone to say something intelligent. The idea came while listening to a speaker drone through PowerPoint slides, nodding off or in later years checking e-mail or posting something to his blog.

An unconference begins with participants suggesting topics they want to present or hear about. The hosts post an attendance list for all to see. All this generally is coordinated on a wiki.

Unconferences have a general theme but no set agenda and scant organization. Instead, the group collaboratively determines the direction of the gathering, creating an ad hoc agenda.

They don't have attendees and presenters; everyone is a participant. The assumption is that the people in the room know more than the people on the stage.

In lieu of a speaker talking to an audience, a discussion leader or reporter weaves together a story that the participants tell. Helpers hold microphones to the mouths of participants who have something to say. The result is more Oprah than a lecture.

The discussion leader cuts short speakers who are repetitious, confusing or self-promotional. PowerPoint presentations are not allowed.

Everyone is encouraged to instant message, blog, and e-mail to assist the flow of ideas. Participants document what's going on with blogs, podcasts, video streams and photos posted to Flickr.

A good unconference also is punctuated with multiple opportunities to schmooze and reflect.

Last fall several people were talking about the exclusivity of a private unconference in the Bay Area, so they decided to start their own. That evening a notice on the Web announced an open, welcoming, once-a-year event for geeks to camp out for a couple days with WiFi and smash their brains together. It's about having a focal point for great ideas.

Six days later several hundred of us rallied in Palo Alto, Calif., for a free, full-blown, two-day event complete with great content, pizza, beer, WiFi, sponsors, T-shirts, buttons and press coverage. Imagine setting up a conference in six days instead of six months!

The co-leader of the Palo Alto unconference said in his blog, "When we embarked on this strange and fantastic journey, we knew that we had a week. We had no money, no sponsors, no venue and no idea if just the five of us or 50 random folks would show. But we knew that we had to stage the event and that, among other things, it would serve as a demonstration of the decentralized organizing potential of the Web 2.0 Generation."

The concept caught fire, inspiring camps in Paris; Hyderabad; Toronto; Austin; Seattle; Vancouver; San Diego; Grand Rapids, and more. WineCamp, TagCamp, MashUp Camp and other hot-topic events began popping up.

Unconferences are ad-hoc gatherings born from peoples' desire to share and learn in an open environment. They are intense events, full of discussions, demos and interaction. The wisdom of crowds supplants the wisdom of experts. They maximize value for participants, not for organizers. They are funded on shoe-string budgets. They replace slides with stories, information-sharing with collaborative learning and instruction with discovery. You should try it some time.

Why Wiki

A wiki is a group-editable Web site. Wikis are composed of Web pages you can write on, enabling fast and easy collaboration.

Why should a CLO care about wikis? Because learning is social - people learn through working with one another. Wikis encourage collaboration, and collaboration is the secret sauce of innovation and effectiveness.

Wikis are a new tool in the learning executives toolkit. Training departments of yore focused most of their energy on events and processes to push information, much of it prepackaged. Wikis pull people to learn when they feel the need. The information they find largely is created by the users themselves.

Companies are discovering wikis are a way to share knowledge, store the rules of thumb of work communities, keep documentation current, cut e-mail bottlenecks and eliminate duplicate effort. They are also lightweight technology. And they-re cheap.

Invented by programmer Ward Cunningham a dozen years ago

to help coordinate a group of programmers, wikis are largely unstructured. Until three or four years ago, wikis followed an arcane set of conventions only a programmer could love.

Nevertheless, wikis have become mainstream and are now attractive. They are still weird the first few times you're exposed to them, but it's not really the wiki that is weird; its that we are unaccustomed to collaborative work.

I lead online events that explore the application of Web technology to corporate learning. A wiki holds information about assignments, Web technology, informal learning, our blogs, our mail list and more.

Everyone is encouraged to add to the wiki, correct mistakes and document discoveries. That's fine in principle, but when it comes time to correct one of my sentences, participants shy away. People respect the sanctity of the work of others. They are not comfortable changing someone else's sentences, even if it is for the greater good.

Perhaps that is the most important reason for CLOs to understand wikis. Knowledge work is inherently collaborative. Information hoarding is counterproductive. Wikis are a great way to learn to collaborate.

Wikipedia, the poster child of wikis, is a free, online encyclopedia. It contains 5 million articles in more than 200 languages that are created and maintained by an army of volunteers. (Encyclopedia Britannica contains about 100,000 articles.)

Anyone can add an article to Wikipedia. How reliable can this be? It turns out Wikipedia is very accurate, comparing favorably to respected printed encyclopedias. You see, when a new article is submitted to Wikipedia, a team of enthusiasts checks it for accuracy, bias, redundancy and links to other topics. Wikipedia embodies the wisdom of crowds.

I was with a group of friends the night Joe Lieberman lost the primary election in Connecticut. Someone looked up Lieberman on Wikipedia. The article told us Lieberman was a senator from Connecticut and the first Jewish American to run for vice president with a major political party. The next paragraph told us, On Aug. 8, 2006, Lieberman conceded the Democratic primary election to Lamont and announced he would run in the 2006 November election as a candidate on the Connecticut for Lieberman ticket. Britannica, of course, has no entry for Lieberman, much less the results of an election 60 minutes after they are announced.

GoogleDocs is a free, online, collaborative, online word processor. It's a great way to get a feel for collaborative writing. Next time you are working on a memo, post it as a GoogleDoc. Take turns tweaking the words. Don't worry: The only people who can see it are those you invite.

You'll discover how much more effective this is than e-mailing drafts of the document back and forth. You'll pinpoint misunderstandings. And you'll discover the inherent power in close collaboration.

And by the way, a GoogleDoc is nothing more than a page-at-a-time wiki.

Content

Content used to be king, but it has been dethroned. Getting things done trumps content.

Once upon a time, the goal of training was to stuff content into people's heads. Then the information tsunami swept in. There's way too much information produced for anyone to keep it in their head.

In the pages that follow, Charles Jennings makes the case for separating information into three buckets. Bucket #1 contains that small proportion of knowledge that is core; you need to have this in mind. Bucket #2 contains fuzzy knowledge; you need to know the general lay of the land and what's important. Bucket #3 is knowledge you need to know how to find; you can search for it. There's no reason to memorize it. In fact, it may change, so searching for the latest copy is preferable to memorizing yesterday's information.

What People Need to Know

Knowledge *was* power. "Access to knowledge is power" is more fitting in today's information-swamped world.

"In 2009, more data will be generated by individuals than in the entire history of mankind through 2008. Information overload is more serious than ever."[33]

---

33 Andreas Weigend, former chief scientist at Amazon.com writing in the Harvard Business Review, May 2009

Andreas Weigend knows a thing to two about data and the social data revolution, about its impact on business and its role in information overload. In his job at Amazon he had to be smart about using information if he was to help his employer make best use of the vast volume of the stuff that was arriving in its data centres every few seconds.

Social data

Social data is information produced by anyone. Some originators may be acknowledged experts. Others may simply be passionate about a topic. Either way, the data they produce can provide significant value to others. Amazon has thrived on the back of contributions and recommendations by readers and purchasers. Early on the company found that users often trusted recommendations by other users more than they trusted promotional or 'expert' views. Weigend said "by enabling users to actively contribute such explicit data, Amazon.com succeeded in leveraging knowledge dormant in its large customer base to help customers with their purchasing decisions".

"Being able to find just the right information or source of knowledge at the just right time in the just right context is far more useful than recalling something we've learned some time ago and hoping it is still relevant and 'right'."

Other organisations have used this collaborative knowledge sharing extremely effectively. Wikipedia created a transparent knowledge creation environment by allowing open discussion and online collaboration. Many other organisations have rebuilt their customer service models to encourage user communities to share knowledge about problems, issues and workarounds as they have found the 'wisdom of the crowds' better serves customers than a small, over-burdened customer help line.

But Weigend's world was not just about managing information, one of the base metals of knowledge. It was also about managing and connecting people, the caretakers of the gold. In fact it was primarily about connecting people - connecting people and helping them make their own connections between their data so it can be exchanged, made sense of in new contexts and some of it used to develop knowledge, skill and action, often in ways the originator had never thought of.

Implication for L&D: Less is more

So what are the implications of this tsunami of information on the way we go about training and development?

Firstly, every L&D professional needs to cast aside any belief that the more information and knowledge we have in our heads the better equipped we are to do our jobs or live our lives. It simply isn't true in today's world. The old adage 'knowledge is power' no longer sits comfortably in a world where information is swamping us and new knowledge is being generated and becoming obsolescent at rates never known before.

Access is power

Today, *access to knowledge is power*. And if this also means access to the person or people with the knowledge or the raw information, even better. Being able to find just the right information or source of knowledge at the just right time in the just right context is far more useful than recalling something we've learned some time ago and hoping it is still relevant and 'right'. With the increasing speeds of change and the ongoing knowledge explosion, what we learned three months ago is more likely to be out of date or simply wrong today than was the case even two or three years ago. We're living in exponential times.

Living with dynamic knowledge

As we continue to move from industrial to ***knowledge-based economies*** the half-life of much of the information that we use on a daily basis will continue to get shorter. The currency of most of the knowledge we use will have smaller and smaller windows of usefulness.

The implication of this trend for the current content-rich model of training and development that's used so widely today is really profound. In short, not only is less more, but in many cases nothing is better than any at all! That's a difficult pill for many L&D people to swallow.

"The message this sends for L&D is that our jobs as enablers of performance clearly need to change from being knowledge dispensers to becoming learning guides."

But think about it in practice. Is it better to get people to commit information to memory, knowing that it will be short-lived (and possibly out of date when they come to use it), or help them become skilled in the approaches and techniques to find the current, correct information quickly when they need it? Think for a few seconds and it is obvious that the second strategy is the better one. Teach people to fish rather than providing them with fish. What use is there in someone trying to remember their tax coding, when it may change two or three times in a year? Surely it's better simply knowing where to find the current (correct) coding when you need it. Having the metadata and the search skills is far more useful than memorising the detailed information in this and many other situations in the day-to-day pursuit of our work and life.

The message this sends for L&D is that our jobs as enablers of performance clearly need to change from being knowledge dispensers to becoming learning guides. Helping our colleagues navigate their way through information and mis-information. Through what is currently 'correct' and what may have been correct some time ago but isn't any more.

New focus for training: Forget the ephemera and get down to core skills

L&D needs to move from providing detailed task-based information to helping people develop a core set of useful generic skills that will provide them with the tools to find, analyse and make decisions to act at the point in time they need to act.;

This is a very different world than one focused on producing modules, courses and curricula full of ephemeral information – detailed content that has a relatively short half-life and is unlikely to be remembered in any detail beyond a post-course assessment, even if to that point.

We need to remember Herman Ebbinghaus' findings from 1885 - 125 years ago - that on average we will forget about 50% of what we've 'learned' within 60 minutes if the information has no context and we don't have the opportunity to reinforce it through practice.

The core skills we need

So, what are the core skills we need to help people develop so they can operate in this ocean of information?

To be honest, I don't have a definitive list. But I think I know some of the capabilities L&D should focus on. If we help people develop these, at least they'll be on a solid footing to extract positive and practical use from the volumes of information they come across each day:

Search and 'find' skills
To find the right information when it's needed
Critical thinking skills
To extract meaning and significance
Creative thinking skills
To generate new ideas about, and ways of, using the information
Analytical skills
To visualise, articulate and solve complex problems and concepts, and make decisions that make sense based on the available information
Networking skills
To identify and build relationships with others who are potential sources of knowledge and expertise, within and outside the organisation

People skills
To build trust and productive relationships that are mutually beneficial for information sharing

Logic
To apply reason and argument to extract meaning and significance
A solid understanding of research methodology
To validate data and the underlying assumptions on which information and knowledge is based
Of course there will be other core context-focused skills that people need to learn. They will tend to be complex skills that need lots of guided practice to master.

However, that doesn't change the fact that, going forward, L&D will need to focus less on content and more on developing core capabilities and skills.

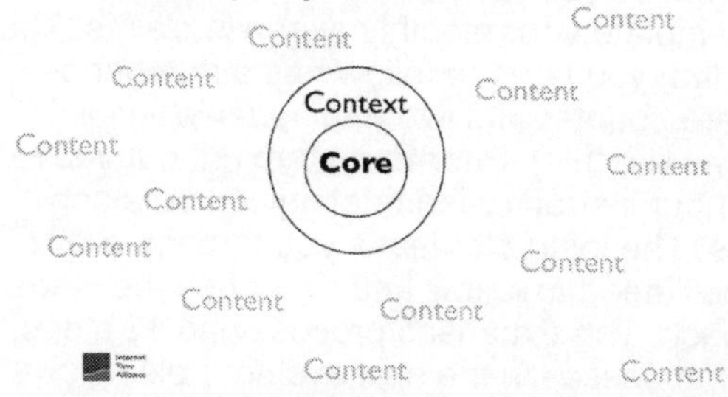

The Core of Learning Content in the Internet Age

There is an argument that we all need to learn less if we want to know more.

The 'learning' referred to here is what we know as formal structured learning activities - classes, courses, programmes, and eLearning.

The argument goes like this.

Although formal learning only constitutes about 10-20% of the actual learning that occurs in organisations, it's the visible part of the iceberg and the part where most of the budget and L&D resource is focused.

When we look at the structured learning taking place in organisations we find that the vast majority is **content-rich** and **interaction-poor**. The further up the hierarchy we go – from K12 to college through University and into training and learning in our working lives – we notice the majority of the structured learning we're offered contains lots of content for us to 'know' but very little opportunity for us build capability to 'do'. Yet action and 'doing' are at the heart of the value that people bring to themselves, to their work and to their organisations. Knowledge may provide scaffolding, but we've learned over the past 30 years or so that most of the knowledge we need to 'do' doesn't have to be stored in our heads. There's research that proves this point, but we only have to think about a common scenario to realise it ourselves.

Consider this. Your organisation has just rolled out a new online Finance system that requires you to use a new set of processes and forms when you complete your monthly expense claims. The new expense process that you need to follow has a number of steps, some of which are counter-intuitive (I'm sure we've all been faced with systems like this). Prior to system roll-out you're required to attend a 2-hour instructor-led briefing/course along with all your colleagues. The instructor leads you through all six new processes that you'll need to follow and describes the steps you'll need to take in each. The expenses process had 12 steps. Some of the other five processes in the new system (raising and signing-off purchase orders, receiving goods etc.) have more steps, some have less. The course is content-rich. You are shown screen-shots of the new system and the instructor steps through each process (without giving participants the opportunity to practice on the system itself as go-live day is still in the future and the system isn't yet stable). At the end of the course the instructor hands out a bound folder with all the screen-shots and descriptions of the processes.

When the time comes for you to complete your first expense claim (6-7 weeks after the training) do you:

a. Recall the processes you had been taught and easily step through them?

b. Find the folder and step through the processes from the screen-shots and descriptions?

c. Ask a colleague if they have used the system, if they have, get their help?

d. Call the helpline?

The chance is that you do either c. or d.

Why?

There are a couple of reasons. Firstly, very few people would be able to recall task detail weeks after being instructed. Even if you were tested and proved that you had 'learned' the processes at the end of the training. Post-training tests demonstrate short-term memory recall, not behaviour-changing learning. Hermann Ebbinghaus illustrated this and the exponential nature of forgetting in his famous 1885 experiment. In short, we forget around 40% of non-contextual information within the first 20 minutes of learning it if we don't practice and reinforce the learning almost immediately. If you didn't have the opportunity to practice the new Finance system processes, they were mostly gone from memory the next day. If you did, then didn't have the opportunity to use the system again for a number of weeks, you've lost it from short-term memory again.

The second reason people ask others or call the helpline is because the vast majority of people simply don't turn to detailed manuals when facing a problem and can't remember the solution. They are more likely to turn to other people for help. Even if you pulled the folder off the shelf it's likely that the amount of detail and the number of processes would have made it difficult to follow, and you will have lost the context with which they were described in the course anyway.

Part of the problem is that with learning we tend to concentrate too much on content and 'knowing' and too little on action and 'doing'.

Traditional Model – Content-centric learning

The standard approach has been to expect people to learn all the content in a structured learning event – whether it's an ILT or eLearning module, course or programme. Then ratify this learning through some type of assessment. The assumption is that if you pass the assessment, you've 'learned the topic'. This is a naïve view of the learning process. Learning is about behaviour change, not short-term knowledge acquisition.

Most people who sit down to design learning experiences (even trained 'instructional designers') think first about the content. 'How much content can I transmit to the recipients in the time I've allowed?' or 'Which content do I need to produce to meet the learning objectives?' The knee-jerk reaction is to start with the content because somehow we seem to think that learning revolves around content. Content is information which we believe somehow transmogrifies into knowledge that will be useful to 'do' at some time in the future.

What's Worth Knowing?

If we break what we need to know about using a process or procedure, for example, into its component parts we can start to get an understanding of what we need to learn and commit to long-term memory and what we don't.

Firstly, there are some things that we simply have to commit to memory. These are the **core concepts**. In the diagram above the examples of core concepts are things such as 'what does my job involve?' and 'what relationship does my role have with other departments?' This is what I'd call the DNA of the role. Other core concepts that need to be committed to memory may involve some basic formulae, tools, marketplace practices and 'the way we do things around here'. This is the content that any good new hire or induction training programme should include. These core concepts only change rarely. Structured learning/training works well to help with this memorisation.

Then there are things that we need to be familiar with, but don't need to commit to memory in any detail. These are **contextual elements** that may vary depending on the context in which we need to use them. The Finance system processes are good examples of this. They are probably too complex to be learned correctly, and they are likely to change over time or depending on the role of the person using them. There's no point committing the detail to memory, but it's helpful to be familiar with the general structure and steps.

Finally there is the **detailed task-specific content**. The 12 steps in the process map and the field-level forms in the case of the Finance process. This is 'stuff' that you simply shouldn't waste time learning, or trying to learn in a formal way. In many situations, task-specific content changes constantly. What was correct and up-to-date last week may not be correct and up-to-date today. It is simply a waste of time to include this content in structured learning/training courses and programmes. You may learn it by repeatedly doing it, and then you have the problem of 'unlearning' it when the process changes.

So, what's the answer?

Find/Access Model – Content-right learning & Content-light learning

The answer is that in today's rapidly changing world we need to learn just enough to be prepared to meet that rapid change. This means, in the words of John Seely Brown, we need to rethink what we need to learn, and how we learn. If most of what we learn is going to be rapidly made obsolete by change, then we need to change our learning models.

This brings us back to the initial premise – if we want to know more, then maybe we should learn less.

The Find/Access model addresses this challenge. This model takes a lot of the content out of 'learning' and moves it into the 'familiarise' and 'find' categories.

The Find/Access model focuses learning only on core concepts. Basic conceptual tools such as **critical thinking skills**, **analytics skills**, **logic**, **search skills**, **data validation skills**, **research methodologies skills** and so on fall into the **core concepts bucket**. This is the 'stuff' we need to learn.

Armed with the skills developed in the core concepts bucket, dynamic and detailed content can be obtained when it's needed from 'the cloud' or from other sources –from colleagues, helpdesks, experts and so on.

There's no need to incorporate the vast majority of the dynamic content we need in structured learning courses and events. In fact, doing so simply distracts and consumes time – which may be a benefit to the providers of learning courses and events, but is of little use in the process of improving performance.

However, we should be careful not to throw the baby out with the bathwater. To take this step we first need to ensure we have both the core find skills – the 'MindFind' skills (as my co-authors David James Clarke IV, Cameron Crowe and I describe in our forthcoming book *MindFind*) – and the tools to connect us to the information sources we need at the time we need them. Fortunately, Web application developments over the past 3-4 years are making this second task much easier for us.

Third Order Find Skills

As professionals involved in learning and performance improvement, we need to focus on helping others develop capabilities and skills in the **core concepts bucket** – the critical thinking skills, the analytical skills, logic, the search skills, and to develop some understanding of research methodologies.

(I'm sure there are other skills and capabilities that should be in this bucket and welcome any comments and suggestions you might have)

Fortunately, the development of third order approaches to the organisation, categorisation and labelling of information allows us to find what we need much more easily now than in the past. This is critical, and the designers of every structured course should reinforce the development of third order find skills and the use of third order find approaches. David Weinberger explains these third order approaches very clearly in his excellent book '*Everything is Miscellaneous: the power of the new digital disorder*'. Weinberger describes how tagging and metadata (third order classification) allow us to find information from our own contextual standpoint, rather than having to fit into some classifier's context. Those of us who spent weeks and months shuffling academic library index cards in the past will understand how liberating the use of metadata has been.

As we develop these third order find skills the misplaced need for vast amounts of content in structured learning will fall away. We'll need less structured learning overall. We'll place more focus on learning by doing (through experience and practice), through interacting with others (network-building and conversations) and through reflecting on our actions. As a result, although we'll be learning more overall, our structured learning will decrease. We'll know more and the knowledge we need will be more relevant for action.

When it's just so obvious NOT to train it's painful to watch it happen

The amount of time, effort and money wasted on formal ILT training prior to rollout or upgrade of enterprise platforms (particularly ERM and CRM) and other new software systems is really quite amazing.

Some managers and L&D people just don't seem to get it.

It reminds me of the remarkable insight of the author Aldous Huxley when he said *"I see the best, but it's the worse that I pursue"*

The evidence has been around for a long time that formal

training on detailed task and process-based activities in advance of the need to carry out the task or use the process is essentially useless.

The logic and evidence both point to the fact that the "*we're rolling out a new system, so we've got to train them all*" approach employed by many (read 'most') organisations, and offered as a service by training suppliers across the globe, is both inefficient and fundamentally ineffective.

You might as well throw the money spent on these activities out the window. Actually, a better option would be to spend the diminishing L&D budget on approaches that do work. Not only would new rollouts and upgrades come into use more smoothly, but am prepared to bet that it would leave budget over to use for other things, or to take as savings (perish the thought!)

Even if you've never been involved in training for rollout and upgrade and then finding that users demand re-training or simply call the help desk as soon as go-live happens, it helps to be aware of some fundamental truths about this flawed model.

Truth 1: Too much information for any human to remember

Most pre go-live training is delivered through ILT or eLearning and is content-heavy. The instructional designers and SMEs feel the need to cover every possibly eventuality and load courses with scenarios, examples and other 'just-in-case' content.

I have seen multiple PowerPoint decks of 200-300 slides delivered over 2-3 days for CRM upgrades. Few humans can recall this amount of information for later use, or even a fraction of it. Maybe if they have photographic memories they can, but designing for photographic memories is not really a sensible strategy. The rest of us just park most of what we do remember at the end of the session in the 'clear out overnight' part of our brains.

And all those expensively-produced User Guides are simply a waste of the Earth's limited natural resources. They tend to be too detailed, linear, full of grabs of screens that the user will never refer to, impossible to navigate, and the last thing people reach for when they need help in using a new system. They are far more likely to reach for the phone and call the Help Desk. Training User Guides are quintessentially shelfware. Usually the only time someone picks user guides off the shelf is to throw them in a bin (hopefully one marked 'recycling') during a clear-out or an office move.

Truth 2: Too much time between the training and use

Embedding knowledge in short-term memory and long-term memory are two very different processes. Even the information that can been recalled immediately after training - and that's likely to be minimal – will be lost if it isn't reinforced through practice within a few hours.

Practice and reinforcement are required for the neurological processes of conversion to long-term memory to occur - chemicals in the brain such as seratonin, cyclic AMP, and specific binding proteins do that job.

Do you think Tiger Woods' brain retained the details of how to arrange his body to hit a ball 400 yards without practice and reinforcement?

Truth 3: Post-Training Drop-Off

Harold Stolovitch & Erica Keeps carried out some very interesting research on desired vs. actual knowledge acquisition and performance improvement. The work uncovered some important observations.

The graph above shows the results. During the training event, following an initial dip - the 'typing/golf pro dip' – where performance drops as new ways of carrying out tasks are tried out, knowledge and performance then improve to the end of the training session. The individual walks out the door knowing more and being able to perform better than when they started the training.

Then the problems start.

The drop-off following the training event (called 'post-training re-adjustment by Stolovitch and Keeps) can kick-in very quickly, possibly in a matter of hours. You finish a day's training course, go home, sleep, and by the next morning a lot of what you had 'learned' has been cleaned out of your short-term memory. Bingo!

Then next day you get back to work and try to implement what you learned in the class. The trouble is, you can't remember exactly what to do, you don't have any support (that trainer who you called over to prompt you when you went through the exercises in class yesterday isn't there), so you try a few things, find they don't work (unless you're lucky) and then you simply go back to doing what you did previously....

The result?

Performance improvement = zero

Value added by the training = zero

Return on investment = zero

Upwards - Following the Dotted Line

The only way knowledge retention and performance can follow the dotted line upwards is if plenty of reinforcement and practice immediately follows the training. Even better if this is accompanied by some form of support – from line managers setting goals and monitoring performance, from SMEs providing on-demand advice and support, or even from learning professionals providing workplace coaching.

An even better (and certainly cheaper) option is simply to cut out the training and replace it with a support environment from the start.

Where Performance Support Trumps Training

There are some very good **ePSS** (electronic Performance Support Systems) or **BPG** (Business Process Guidance) tools available now. They are economic and generally straightforward to implement and trump training every time for following defined processes found in ERP and CRM systems and other software products

ePSS/BPG tools provide context-sensitive help at the point-of-need and "act like a GPS system rather than a roadmap" as Davis Frenkel, CEO of Panviva Inc., the company that produces the very impressive SupportPoint BPG tool, explains. "When you're learning to follow a process, you just want to know the next 2-3 steps you need to take. You don't want to have to remember the entire 20-30 process steps and all the options", Frenkel says. I think he's absolutely right and it's a good analogy.

A GPS tells you that you need to 'turn left at the next intersection' or 'take a right turn then keep straight ahead'. It instructs incrementally, and doesn't tell you every turn on the journey when you set out.

When there's no access to GPS and the driver has to revert to a map (and doesn't have a flesh-and-blood GPS sitting beside them reading the map and instructing in increments) they will tend to read and memorise just the next 2-4 turns on the journey and then re-read the map to get the next set of instructions. Job done, destination reached.

So why don't many organisations and L&D folk wake up to the failings of using the wrong approaches to achieve their required outcomes?

Why are millions of $/£/€/¥ spent every year training employees on using enterprise systems in this way when there's evidence to prove that it simply doesn't work?

Forever Beta

Astute CLOs keep all their programs in beta. A dozen years ago, software developers said a program was "in beta" if it was nearly finished but not ready for release. ("Alpha" meant the application was a collection of scraps that only a developer could run.)

Netscape changed the meaning of beta forever. Instead of limiting beta tests to a small, handpicked group of users outside the company, Netscape posted beta releases on the internet. Anyone could download the latest beta version. Many of us did. Improvements in the Web's early days came fast and furious, so we downloaded betas time after time after time. Netscape received feedback and suggestions from thousands of users. This accelerated product development, and that led to even more frequent beta releases. Running the most recent beta version was a sign of reckless courage.

Traditional software companies continued to release new versions every year or two rather than incrementally. Customers might not see new features until a year or two after they appeared in beta. This exacerbated customer frustration over missed deadlines. Journalists published lists of vaporware. At one point, Microsoft was more than a year late delivering a promised release of Windows.

Years later, Google became the poster child for the perpetual beta. Google Search was beta for more than a year. Unlike Netscape, which offered an official release alongside the betas, Google offered only beta. Google Labs highlights programs that are pre-beta experiments.

Google is not simply releasing products before they are finished, because from the word "go", Google's betas have been more reliable and polished than most firms' final releases. Rather, Google is setting high expectations. The implication is that what's good enough for other software companies is only a beta release for Google.

Beta users have a different relationship with vendors. Their mindset is different. Their input is valued. What used to be a complaint becomes a suggestion for improvement. The developer and the user are partners, working together to improve the product. This is why Tim O'Reilly says that the perpetual beta phenomenon is a core aspect of Web 2.0.

A developer who calls a release beta recognizes that nothing is ever finished. There's always room for improvement. This lack of arrogance is endearing, but something more profound is going on.

Everything is connected to everything else. That's the heart of the network age. And it's why every product is beta. The world is forever changing: Everything flows. Thus, when a company says a product is beta, it demonstrates its recognition that nothing lasts forever and there's always room for improvement.

Peter Drucker said the purpose of business is to create and maintain a customer. A developer who says, "Here's what we've got now, but something better is on the way," forms a relationship of mutual self-interest with the customer. The developer who says, "This product is final. We won't be doing anything more with it. This is as good as it gets," gives the buyer no incentive to participate in a continuing relationship. Beta empowers the customer to decide what's good enough. Nothing's set in stone. Nothing is absolute.

It's even more important to label learning beta than software. All learning is co-creation, a product of a learner and an outside agent.

A professor gave her class a paper on urban sociology to read, explaining that they would be tested at the end of the hour. The professor gave another class the same paper and instructions plus a warning that the material was controversial; it might not be correct. In other words, the paper was beta.

The group that read the beta paper scored higher. Why? Because uncertainty engages the mind.

This is why it makes sense to label all learning activities beta. Engage the learners' minds. For that matter, mark plans beta: It will invite participation. And make your department beta — after all, everything is an experiment

Environmental Design

The front page of a recent issue of The New York Times displayed a heart-rending photograph of two polar bears stranded on tiny chunks of glacial ice floating in the Bering Sea. The accompanying headline reported, "Science Panel Calls Global Warming 'Unequivocal.'"

Yet, many of our leaders and scientists continue to demure. They need more proof and say, "Why not put things off until next year?"

Informal learning can be as controversial as global warming. Recently, I shared my thoughts on informal, networked learning with 100 learning professionals.

One attendee wrote, "Too bad this bad experience is how I ended this great conference. Your session was too scattered for me." Another, however, said, "Bravo. Every speaker here has talked about how we need to change the way we teach, but no one had a plan. Now I have the blueprint. Thank you."

The naysayers tell us, "If it ain't broke, don't fix it." They complain their bosses would never buy informal learning. They think change is incremental, and we can wait for the day when there's overwhelming proof informal learning works. "Business as usual" rules the day.

How can learning professionals' opinions on informal learning be divided and cocksure? I attribute it to taking an all-or-nothing attitude about an area rife with shades of gray.

Informal learning and formal learning are aspects of an overall spectrum of learning as a whole. Imagine an audio mixer in a recording studio, one of those units with dozens of sliders that enable you to boost the vocals, downplay the guitar, etc.

> Leadership cannot really be taught, it can only be learned.
>
> *Harold Geneen*

The Learning Mixer

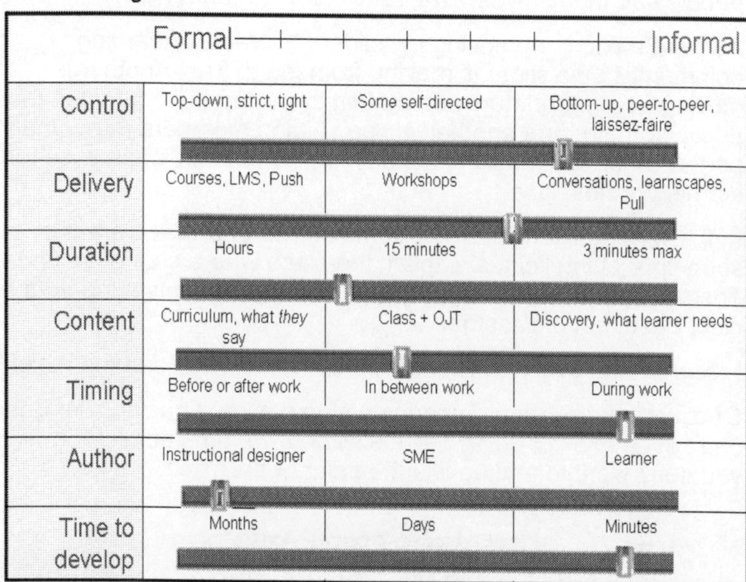

Our "learning mixer" has sliders for characteristics such as content, delivery, duration, authorship and development time. You don't achieve the best mix by moving all of the sliders to the top or to the bottom.

The "delivery slider" moves from courses and push (formal) to conversations and pull (informal). Duration goes from hours (formal) to minutes (informal). Subject matter ranges from curriculum (what the organization says — formal) to discovery (what the individual needs — informal) Timing goes from outside of work to during work. Development time ranges from months (events — formal) to minutes (connections — informal).

Learning professionals who favor using formal learning exclusively (or informal learning exclusively) are denying themselves the opportunity to mix the ideal combination for the situation.

After the conference presentation mentioned earlier, I decided to eat my own dog food (although I prefer to think of it as "drinking my own champagne").

I realized I hadn't set the sliders quite right for the "unworkshops" we've been conducting on learning Web 2.0. The objective was for participants to adopt a new self-image as Web learning professionals. Workshops are not the road to redefining how people see themselves. That requires community.

As I write this, I am moving my sliders to create a learning community. One slider is moving from fee to free. Another is moving from proprietary information to putting our content in the public domain. And another will be serving members rather than participants. The resulting melody is a community of practice for learning professions.

In the words of Tom Stewart, communities of practice are the shop floor of intellectual capital, the place where stuff gets made. The major raw materials are conversations, so I'm setting up a clubhouse, not a classroom.

I recommend every CLO push the sliders on the "learning mixer."

Of course, I also recommend you stop driving a gas guzzler and don't even think of going outside without wearing sunscreen — you don't want to end up like the polar bears.

Community

Professional Development

Long-term professional development often involves working and growing with peers.

The book *Kitchen Confidential*[34] by Anthony Bourdain describes how he became a professional chef and how he continues to support the community of professional chefs. No one issues membership cards to professional chefs but they are not difficult to recognize. They wear funny looking hats and white tunics. They carry a set of knives that no one else is allowed to touch. Their fingers bear scars from calling it too close with those knives.

When chefs travel, they meet with other chefs. They eat together. They share techniques. Were it not for this sharing, we would not enjoy the broad, international array of foods on our

34 Bourdain, A. 2001. *Kitchen Confidential.* Harper Perennial

tables (because chefs shared their sources and uses of exotic ingredients). When a top chef wants to move to a new job in a particular location, he tells a few chefs, the grapevine spreads the word, and within a week he has several job offers.

In the book, Bourdain describes starting out as a dishwasher in a restaurant on Cape Cod. Then he lands a job as a fry cook. From that point on, the chef running the kitchen he's working in is looking out for his career. When will the kitchen worker be prepared to advance from washing lettuce to making salads? What does she need to know to advance to pastry chef? How can the chef help the dessert chef advance to sous chef? Good chefs take developing their staff very seriously. They see that their apprentices learn to create satisfying yet economical food.

Chef

Anthony Bourdain

Anthony Bourdain decided he needed to accelerate his development so he attended the Culinary Institute of America for formal training. This enabled him to understand the interrelationships of ingredients and cooking and customers. The curriculum at CIA taught him frameworks for various cuisines; he learned practices that would have taken years to learn on the job. And indeed, when Bourdain went back to cooking, he rapidly advanced up the ladder to become a chef.

Chefs are a community of like-minded individuals who identify with one another, advance the practice of their profession, and help new entrants join the profession.

Ten years ago, the common wisdom was that you could not establish a community of practice. If you found one that was working, the best you could do was to nurture it. It was like truffles. They grow wild. You want truffles, you put a pig or well-trained dog on a leash and encourage it to dig around the roots of oak trees in southern France or northern Italy.

The authorities were wrong on both counts. Half the world's truffles are cultivated on truffle plantations in Spain. Thousands of corporations have established thriving communities of practice that advance both the careers of their members and their shared body of knowledge.

Knowing the tricks of a trade does not make you a professional.

Beyond acquiring know-how, a professional hangs out with other professionals, builds relationships with others in the profession, and contributes to the collective wisdom of the profession. Most importantly, the professional knows deep inside that she has joined the profession.

Become who you are! *Nietsche*

The cook becomes a chef when she *feels* she's a chef. Professional firefighters, insurance salespeople, plumbers, accountants, and architects don't just master subject matter; they become members of their profession.

How does one become a professional?

Professionals learn from one another. They learn from watching other professionals, from experimentation, and through following the advice of mentors. In time, they pay back the community by shifting from “what's known”
to “what's next.”

Experience is the best teacher. You can't become a chef without working and learning in a kitchen.

Many professionals accelerate the rate at which they gain experience by enrolling in formal courses. Formal learning, where an outside authority chooses the subject matter, is a great way to see the big picture of a new field, master its concepts, get to know the ropes, and learn to talk the talk. Mind you, formal learning doesn't teach everything. No chef has every recipe in her head; that's why she has cookbooks.

How do workers learn to do their jobs?

Most people figure out how to do their jobs from the people they work with. They ask questions, they try things out, they ask for help, they tap into the grapevine, they snoop, they copy the behavior of people who seem to being doing things right. Anthropologists who have studied workplace behavior tell us this "learning at the school of hard knocks" is four times more important in developing talent than training in workshops and classrooms.

Learning is social; people always learn from one another. They have many, many times more contact with co-workers than with instructors, so it shouldn't come as a surprise that the workplace is where workers figure out what works.

While at first it seems haphazard, this informal learning is generally more effective than what goes on in organized workshops and classes. Why?

Rather than getting ready to deal with a situation that may or may not occur, impromptu learners are figuring out what they need in order to solve an immediate problem. Workers remember things they choose better than things instructors tell them to learn. They trust their peers more than instructors. Perhaps most important, self-motivated workers apply what they've learned immediately. When humans learn something and don't apply it, they forget their lessons before they have an opportunity to use them. Not only that, but people learn better in five-minute chunks than from one-hour sessions.

Strangely, this self-directed problem-solving flies under the radar in most organizations. Corporations invest in training and workshops and put nothing into improving the impromptu side. They also concentrate on novices, leaving experienced workers - the high performers - to fend for themselves. Why do corporations invest in the areas where it does them the least good? I blame schooling.

You *can* teach old dogs new tricks. They just don't learn them in school. With the workforce we'll have for the next decade, we better get good at working with the older dogs.

Stories of Working Smarter

Dirty Words

Top executives have little time so it's important to have a one-minute elevator pitch ready for chance encounters with them. Execs respond better to concrete examples than abstractions.

Learning professionals know they shouldn't use training jargon (e.g. Kirkpatrick levels, Gagne, kinesthetic) when talking to executives. Many chief learning officers fail to realize they should also purge some common words from their vocabularies because they trigger negative thoughts among decision-makers.

Comedian George Carlin had a skit about words you were not allowed to say on television. Most of them were four letters long. His words were dirty; ours are bad for business. Here we go:

> **Learning** is a dirty word because executive managers have a hard time hearing it. You think of improving skills and increasing knowledge. They think of classes, teachers, and school. They remember how ineffective school was at getting things done. You forget most of the lessons before you have a chance to use them. *Learning* taints the conversation. Better to speak of collaboration or boosting brain power. I changed the name of my new book from *Informal Learning in the Cloud* to *Work Smarter*.
>
> **Learner** is banned because no one but the training community uses the term. They are workers first, and learners second. Talking about *learners* conjures up the bad old days of taking people off the job to learn. Increasingly, learning takes place on the job. In fact, I foresee work and learning converging at an astonishing rate.
>
> **Social** learning is the hottest thing since electricity among web enthusiasts. However, MIT's Andy Macafee warns that executives who hear *social* flash on scenes of Woodstock and other non-business activities.
>
> Likewise, executives hear the word **informal** and take it to mean haphazard. Most job-related learning is informal, and there are enormous opportunities to make it better. Collaborative networks, expertise locators,

reducing fear of failure, graphic design, workspace architecture, and many other techniques increase the productivity of informal learning. Better call it collaboration if you want to sell it.

You have probably stopped using the word **training**, but just in case, let's review why it's inappropriate. *Training* is something you do to someone. *Learning* is something people do for themselves. You hope that people learn from training, for that's the objective. Talking about training can blind you to alternative means of learning.

Despite growing evidence that **eLearning** can produce superior results than the classroom, early failures sullied its reputation. eLearning circa 1999 was for the most part deadly dull and uninspiring. People stayed away in droves. Completing an eLearning course was the exception rather than the rule. Avoiding eLearning because of a bad early experience is like going to a movie and saying you'll never go to another one of those because movies are bad.

Stories

This compilation of examples of Working Smarter is a work in progress. Use them instead of dirty words. Please share stories with us for the next edition.

Thanks to Dave Wilkins, Jane Hart, McKinsey, Jay Cross, Bill Ives, Jon Husband,Twitter.com, and others for the examples collected here.

Stop the Presses

The New Social Learning
A Guide to Transforming Organizations Through Social Media
By Tony Bingham and Marcia Conner
Berrett-Koehler Publishers, San Francisco
2010

An acquaintance who was appointed chief learning officer of one of the UK's major banks three weeks ago asked Jay where to find some great examples of social & informal learning. He knew from experience that the way to sell the new learning is through examples rather than logic. It's easy to pooh-pooh "social learning" but impossible to argue with success.

The first thing that sprang to mind was *The Working Smarter Fieldbook*. This edition of the unbook was coming out the next week. Believing in the power of examples (and the facile misinterpretation of labels), we had beefed up the Fieldbook with dozens of new stories about successful implementations. Then I bit my tongue. On the flight to Europe, I'd read Marcia's new book.

The New Social Learning has the best examples of humanizing learning and leveraging network effects we've read anywhere. Better than ours. Examples of what? Communities. Story sharing. Twitter. Collective intelligence. Immersive environments. Organizational transformations. The usual suspects.

Wait – there's more. After succinct descriptions of what's going on and why it matters, the book addresses the organizational roadblocks that inevitably arise and provides logical workarounds.

If you follow the posts from The Internet Time Alliance, you know we are generally in the front lines of the struggle to wrest control from industrial-age fuddy-duddy managers who perpetuate obsolete people practices. We take a lot of crap for trying to force staid companies to wake up and smell the coffee. Marcia's book gives us the ammunition to respond to these slams:

- Is this learning?
- People will say inappropriate things.
- People will post incorrect information.
- Our people need training, not socializing.
- These systems compromise classified information.
- This can't be governed.
- Our management team will never sign off on this.
- People will waste precious time.
- Employees will give away company secrets.
- Some people will just lurk.
- People will post inappropriate videos.
- The value of media sharing can't be measured.
- In person is always best.
- Video isn't for serious businesses.
- Videos are for fun, not real knowledge transfer.
- (Re: Twitter) I have too much to say.
- I don't have time.
- It's only for young people with ti eon their hands.
- It's overwhelming.
- Answers are hit or miss.
- I don't know how to use it.
- Finished content is more valuable to works in progress.
- It's risky to let anyone post anything.
- Our information is unique. There's no way to share that.
- We have a wiki but few people contribute.
- (Re: Second Life) It all seems too sic-fi, too unreal for my organization.
- This is all too expensive.
- This doesn't create lasting change.
- It's not natural.

- No one will be interested.
- People aren't paying attention.

Tony and Marcia give well-reasoned rebuttals to these slams. They have more patience (and tact) than we do, for Jay's response to most of these would be "**Bullshit!**" Or "You don't know what you are talking about." The loudest criticism emanates from people who have no experience with what they are criticizing.

They close out each chapter with sound, practical recommendations.

We'll continue on with our examples, but if you want the full dose, read The New Social Learning, too.

IBM's Social Media Program
Seeking Innovation anywhere and everywhere

"Be yourself." It's one of the rules of social media. If you're blogging, tweeting or Facebooking for business, be real—or you won't be followed. Yet, how do you pull off *authentic* while maintaining the company brand message?

It's tough enough for a small business. What if you're #2 on *Business Week*'s best global brands list, with nearly 400,000 employees across 170 countries?

At IBM, it's about losing control.

"We don't have a corporate blog or a corporate Twitter ID because we want the 'IBMers' in aggregate to be the corporate blog and the corporate Twitter ID," says Adam Christensen, social media communications at IBM Corporation. "We represent our brand online the way it always has been, which is employees first. Our brand is largely shaped by the interactions that they have with customers."

Thousands of IBMers are the voice of the company. Such an

approach might be surprising for #14 on the *Fortune 500*. IBM lets employees talk—to each other and the public—without intervention. With a culture as diverse and distributed as IBM's, getting employees to collaborate and share makes good business sense.

"We're very much a knowledge-based company. It's really the expertise of the employee that we're hitting on," Christensen says.

No Policing

IBM does have social media guidelines. The employee-created guidelines basically state that IBMers are individually responsible for what they create and prohibit releasing proprietary information. But the document **lacks any mention of brand messages or values.** Nor does IBM corporate regulate employee social media activity. Only three people hold social media roles at the corporate level, and oversight isn't part of their jobs.

"***We don't police***. *The community's largely self-regulating, and so there hasn't really been a need to have someone go about and circuit these boards and blogs,*" Christensen said. "*Employees sort of do that themselves… And that's worked wonderfully well.*" .

The Payoff

IBM invests in creating its own social media tools. But it's earning that back by monetizing some of those as part of the IBM product portfolio. The other part of the investment equation —employees' time—doesn't seem to be a concern, according to Christensen. That's because collaboration and knowledge make IBM what it is. And that's a company with $12.3 billion in earnings on more than $100 billion in revenue with a 44.1% gross profit margin in 2008.

Christensen says to date there's not an effort to tag a return on investment to its social media efforts.

"*I think if you'd ask any senior executive at IBM, '**How important is it for our employees to be smarter?**', inherently they* *understand that these tools can play in helping with that,"* Christensen said.

"I don't see myself rarely or ever having that hard conversation on the value of engaging employees in these spaces."

Booz Allen

In 2007 a perfect storm of events converged to prompt the creation of Hello.bah.com (Hello) as Booz Allen's enterprise 2.0 knowledge sharing program, a suite of web-based enterprise tools designed to strengthen collaboration, connectivity, and communication across geographical and cultural barrier

Booz Allen's strength lies in its people and intellectual capital. The firm had grown in recent years to around 23,000 staff, yet a 2007 staff survey found that while people still felt affinity to the firm, the strength of this affinity was slipping for the first time.

Since August 2008, more than 80% of the firm has logged into Hello and more than 53% of the firm has contributed original content. There are more than 4,000 individual searches a day.

Communities provide one of the most valuable components of Hello yielding new knowledge and intellectual capital for the firm. Any one can go to a community to find all related content aggregated in one place, regardless of what format it entered Hello (blog, wiki, etc.). There are over 480 communities now and they act as the glue for the system.

Hello has helped bridge the geographic divide of staff located in more than 100 US offices and client sites, building relationships and fostering collaboration across teams. Stronger staff relationships yield stronger clients solutions and lead to growth in business.

Hello allows individuals to keep their profiles and availability current. It also makes it easier for those in need of staff to find these profiles. This increased self-service with better real time data allows the staffing people to address more strategic issues than the tactical tracking of current availability.

Booz Allen has won several multi-million dollar contracts based on the firm's experience with Hello and technology infrastructure as many government agencies are faced with the same challenges

The learning group at Booz Allen has since requested that the proper use of Hello be included in new employee orientation. This should significantly reduce the on-boarding time and decrease the connection curve for new employees.

Océ

Océ is a global printing company with over 21,000 employees.

The recession helped propel E2.0 initiatives at Océ. As a result of the economy, Océ had a very small budget to improve communications within the company. They had to take big steps back to look at ways to improve innovation, collaboration, and knowledge sharing across the entire organization;

Everything was very isolated and information was very silo-ed. People were not taking to each other and everyone kept to themselves. Sharing and collaborating over organizational entities was not easy. Océ had a lot of work to do but no budget.

A new manager of Internal Communications was pretty much starting from scratch. As a result, an internal communications plan was written with a focus on all things digital. The goal was to get employees to communicate, share best practices, and improve innovation. Océ really wanted to create two-way conversations, while being able to connect people across the organization.

A few people at Océ recognized the fundamental change underlying Enterprise 2.0 movement and how it would change the way Océ does business. This small group of people wrote a plan called "Markets are Conversations" based on books such as *The Cluetrain Manifesto, Wikinomics, Grown Up Digital,* and *The Wisdom of Crowds.*

They overcame this culture of closed communication by leading by example. This meant a few things; the first was to show peers that other organizations have successfully adopted an open culture of sharing ideas and expressing doubts and uncertainties. The second is that the leaders had to "walk the talk" and lead by example. They had to ask questions and openly express their doubts, uncertainties, and need for help.

At one point, a small department called "The New Media Lab" was formed to enable the use of social media while helping to implement new social media tools and ideas. The "Lab" was comprised of a group of employees that were interested in new tools, technologies, and strategies. They tested everything on themselves first before deciding to roll anything out. Unfortunately, over time everyone dropped out of the Lab due to lack of interest, time, or understanding.

Océ admits that currently their organization structure has not changed much at all, which is making things a bit difficult. This is becoming an issue not just with Enterprise 2.0 but with their external facing social media efforts as well. There are different Twitter accounts, various blogs, many wikipedia entries, and bits and pieces of scattered information. This is a problem because new things are happening but the organizational structure is not adapting. There still needs to be alignment between new technology use and strategies and how the organization is structured to support these things.

Undoubtedly the experience to date reflects many of the concerns and issues that are addressed by the plethora of advice (including ours) about new forms of workflow, business process changes and adoption.

We thought it was useful to include this reported case exactly because the points discussed are so often concerns when considering or planning a pilot project or an implementation. We'll follow and report developments with Océ as we learn of them.

Pitney Bowes & Yammer

Celebrating its 90th year of innovation, Pitney Bowes is a $5.6 billion company that employs 33,000 worldwide and provides software, hardware and services that integrate physical and digital communications channels. With its focus on productivity, Pitney Bowes is increasingly helping other companies grow their business.

With the motto “Every connection is a new opportunity™” the company understands the importance of maintaining an interconnected workforce for it's 33,000 employees, and the Management Center for Learning & Performance has taken note of Yammer's impact on the company.

Mike Petersell, the director of Pitney Bowes' Management Center for Learning and Development, identifies Yammer as a pivotal element of employee learning. The employee learning process is often most efficient and effective when it occurs in a non-formal and natural way, which Yammer facilitates perfectly.

Employees at Pitney Bowes have taken to using tags and groups to categorize information, a process that contributes to the company's view of its Yammer network as a crucial tool for employee access to information. Petersell sees Yammer's value in the connections it makes possible: "I recognize that what makes people most successful is not what they learn from the content of the programs we provide, but what they learn from one another."

Results and Benefits

- Better Employee Learning: Yammer facilitates and augments the highly valuable "casual learning" that happens every day within Pitney Bowes.
- Easily Searchable Knowledge Base: Each discusslon is archived and accessible to all within the organization for future access.

Telus

TELUS considers its team members vital to providing superior customer service. Therefore, it places a high value on learning (leadership and professional development, business and sales, technology, and health and safety learning). Until recently, TELUS handled learning primarily by outsourcing instructor-led experiences for team members. Much of what the company's individuals learned depended on the knowledge presented by the instructors, and the company was concerned that this was limiting the development of its team members.

TELUS decided to shift its corporate philosophy from one focused on formal, classroom-based learning to one that also included informal and social learning. As defined within the company's "Learning 2.0" initiative, informal learning would include webcasts, books, mentoring, coaching, and job rotations, while social learning would comprise videos, blogs, microblogs, and wikis.

In 2009, the company's learning budget was roughly $28.5 million, 90 percent of which it dedicated to formal learning. TELUS set a 2010 budget of about $21 million, but Pontefract aims to adjust the ratio to 60 percent formal and 40 informal and social learning for the year.

Introducing informal and social avenues of knowledge sharing has become more important to TELUS because its current work force is made up of increasingly younger team members who consider social networking to be a basic communication tool. About 40 percent of team members are in their 50s and 60s; 35 percent in their 30s and 40s; and 25 percent in their 20s. "*Within the next 10 years, we could see 40 percent of our work force retire,*" says Pontefract. "*We're establishing what we call a 'culture of collaboration' to give team members multiple ways of comfortably sharing their knowledge, no matter what their age or title. We recognize the importance of their intellectual property and of communicating it throughout the organization.*"

Internal surveys returned positive results, with 99 percent of the 7,000 team members surveyed reporting that they understood the three categories of learning—formal, informal, and social—and 97 percent agreeing that learning can successfully take place in all three ways.

TELUS is creating a culture of collaboration in which team members have easy, ongoing opportunities to share what they know. "*With its many social, learning, video, and other collaboration facets, employees will gather around our 'virtual water cooler' to swap acumen and experience, ideally checking with each other before turning to outside classroom instruction,*" says Pontefract.

Although the company's learning budget for 2010 is $21 million, TELUS anticipates saving 20 percent of that—nearly $5 million in 2011 as a result of its shift toward informal and social learning.

TELUS expects to further streamline its learning budget as team members become better versed in all the options for informal and social learning. In fact, the company's three-year plan is to move to a situation in which formal learning accounts for just 50 percent of its total learning budget.

TELUS team members will have faster access to the specific skills and knowledge areas with which they need help.

The company also is focused on enhancing its processes through collaboration, which means that team members' shared insights will result in positive business changes, such as bringing products to market faster and better understanding customer feedback.

The company expects that its shift to a culture of collaboration will not only empower team members and contribute to an increase in team member attraction and retention, but also counter the stereotype of telecommunication companies as being entrenched in old ways of doing things.

Central Intelligence Agency (CIA) - Intellipedia

The CIA reorganized of the intelligence bureau after 9/11 and the path of change for a secretive organization becoming more open to sharing information internally.

The CIA case was covered by David W. Gardner, C.G.Lynch and Tom Davenport of Harvard University. These reports focused on the CIA's implementation advice for introducing and adopting a Wiki into a large organization.

The CIA's Intellipedia, built on wiki technology, was founded in April 2006 and is a central repository where 16 agencies collaborate on key topics and challenges facing the intelligence community.

The two CIA officials who lead the Intellipedia stressed the importance of administering access, starting small and moving information out of narrow channels like e-mail and into broader platforms like wikis .

1. Set access policies.
Because most people associate wikis with Wikipedia, you need to establish that there will be access controls about who views (and just as important) who edits information on a wiki. With Intellipedia, for instance, there are three different versions. One is generally viewable by most agency employees, another is secret, and a third is top secret. Within each of those versions, some people have editing access and others only are allowed to view. Some aren't allowed writing or viewing access depending on their security clearance.

The beauty of the wiki model, Dennehy says, is that all edits can be easily tracked and made available in version history. "*We're often asked in the intelligence community, what did you know and when did you know it?*" Dennehy says.

2. Start small.
Implementing social software is more of a cultural challenge than a technical one. Many of the disparate intelligence agencies had held onto their own data and didn't share it with one another for years, so changing that paradigm can be difficult. Given this reality, it's important to start small.

At the CIA, the first wiki page they created was a list of acronyms. Since the intelligence community is riddled with them, it became a page people were willing to update (**and saw immediate value from**). "*It's very simple, and gets to people who are uncomfortable with the tools to quickly make and edit and publish it,*" Dennehy says. "*If you make those barriers small, they're more likely to adopt.*"

3. Move information out of traditional enterprise tools such as e-mail.
In order to change what tools people use to consume and disseminate enterprise content, it's important to show first that you aren't making more work for them.

.. and make the information social (see access policies, above) ...

"*Move processes out of channels and onto platforms,*" Burke says."*If we can take those and replace it with platform based tools, we can capture them on the network.*"

Pfizer

Workers at Pfizer routinely post articles to a wiki called Pfizerpedia that's grown to feature more than 10,000 articles and numerous how-to videos.

Pfizer enterprise 2.0 technology manager Simon Revell on the adoption of wikis, blogs, and other social computing tools at the conservative pharmaceutical maker. "*We had to challenge the culture,*" Revell said at the Enterprise 2.0 conference. "*We had to get them through the fear barrier.*"

Workers at the company now routinely post articles to a wiki called Pfizerpedia that's grown to feature more than 10,000 articles and numerous how-to videos. They also access bogs to communicate with managers working in different time zones and regularly rely on RSS feeds for external and internal news related to their jobs.

"*You're handicapped if you're not thinking about RSS*," said Revell.

Even Pfizer's ultra-cautious regulatory affairs group is using the wiki to generate ideas. "*They've embraced it*," said Revell.

Starting with small projects targeting limited groups of users was key to overcoming resistance at the company to social computing. And "*We didn't refer to the blogs as blogs*," said Revell, conceding that, for some in the company's upper management, the term still connotes "*something that's frivolous*."

There's also the fact that blogging does not come naturally to some workers. "*Blogs are one of the most difficult aspects of Enterprise 2.0 to get off the ground.*".

To overcome resistance, a colleague of Revell's worked up a graphical slide deck that depicted how "Charlie", a fictional Pfizer employee, could use social computing tools to accomplish daily tasks and become more productive.

The slides found their way on the Internet and "Meet Charlie" became a viral hit, garnering more than 120,000 views.

It all started, said Revell, with a few "corporate punks" and a campaign that "was designed to be edgy."

EDR's Commonground

EDR is a large provider of environmental information and reports for commercial real estate professionals in New England.

In mid-2008 EDR created *commonground*, a social network (B2B) for environmental and property due-diligence professionals. EDR's goals in creating this online social space were to 1) enhance its brand, 2) develop more solid relationships with customers, 3) improve its marketing effectiveness, especially on the Web, and 4) generate new sources of recurring revenue.

EDR's key tips:

1. Agree on the Strategic Business Drivers
2. Report on the basic metrics regularly (at least bi-weekly)
3. Report Key Findings ad-hoc, as they occur
4. Make time to communicate - up, down and across the organization
5. Ongoing research about how to improve data quality

Based on one year's activities, here's the “return” EDR feels it has obtained from it's (now) asset.

- Featured as a top 10 initiative in the DMGT '09 annual report
- Referred to - now - as an "asset" rather than "initiative"
- Customers saying they are receiving real-value answers, jobs and business
- Significant search engine optimization improvements
- Environmental Business Journal award in February 2010
- Member referrals are increasing considerably (viral effect kicking in)
- EDR's first monetization effort exceeded initial expectation

Social Snippets

Here's a collection of very brief stories .. pointers, really ... to stories McKinsey (the consultancy) has gathered together in a study titled “Clouds, big data, and smart assets: Ten tech-enabled business trends to watch.” It's a great example of a blog post packing lots of potential information into a short space online – “pointage” or “linkage”, as some of us call it - tempting those interested to follow links and explore the stories.

The McKinsey study' s headline ...

“Advancing technologies and their swift adoption are upending traditional business models. Senior executives need to think strategically about how to prepare their organizations for the challenging new environment”

“Across the board, the stakes are high.”

Another key recommendation is that brand owners aiming to meet the challenges of the digital era should focus on co-creation, open innovation and consumer insights, according to a study.

McKinsey reports that as of mid-2010 there are currently 4bn cellphones, 450m mobile web users and 68m people posting blogs and product reviews online.

One key response to such trends is "*distributed co-creation*" - or generating ideas for possible new goods, services and advertising campaigns in partnership with the internet audience.

McKinsey revealed that 70% of senior executives believed online communities provided a chance to create significant value.

Procter & Gamble, the FMCG giant, has leveraged this opportunity via its Vocalpoint.com site dedicated to mothers, who can share their views about its brands with friends and other netizens.

"*In markets where Vocalpoint influencers are active, product revenues have reached twice those without a Vocalpoint network,*" McKinsey said.

Building an internal, corporate social network can also pay dividends, and Dow Chemicals has even extended this strategy to include retired employees.

Amazon's Mechanical Turk platform offers "*businesses and developers access to an on-demand scaleable workforce*" of experts and enthusiasts.

Such an approach to can be applied more broadly, with Bechtel, the engineering firm, having established an in-house "*open-collaboration*" database of information.

As a consequence, Bechtel found 25% of the material required for new projects actually already existed in most cases, lowering launch costs and reducing lead times.

The notion businesses could become a "*full-time laboratory*" is another growing trend, given the wealth of insights contained by sources from social media to mobile GPS.

This transition towards "*big data*" is evidenced by the fact that the amount of available information is doubling every 18 months, allowing companies with suitable analytics software and the flexibility to react.

Amazon, eBay and Google are some of the pioneers in the field, assessing details like where to locate buttons on websites and the order in which content should be displayed to confirm what drives engagement and sales.

Elsewhere, Capital One, the financial services specialist, appointed a team of analysts, IT staff and marketers to segment its customers and develop products, participating in around 65,000 tests a year.

Ford, PepsiCo, and Southwest Airlines all operate systems to monitor the buzz on properties like Facebook and Twitter, helping them gain a real-time appreciation of shopper perceptions and habits.

The evolving climate also means corporations can profit from "*imagining anything as a service*", McKinsey continued.

This is shown by Alibaba, a B2B exchange in China that has signed up 30m enterprises keen to promote their own capabilities or locate partners.

"*Its network, in effect, offers Chinese manufacturing capacity as a service, enabling small businesses anywhere in the world to identify suppliers quickly and scale up rapidly to meet demand,*" McKinsey argued.

Mixed advertiser-funded, subscriber and "*freemium*" models have built on similar trends, and photo-sharing site Flickr, music portal Pandora and communications firm Skype show how this delivers results in practice.

Further benefits can come from "*innovating at the bottom of the pyramid*", a tactic championed by General Electric, which has constructed R&D centres in emerging markets to achieve this goal.

Safaricom, the telecoms provider, has moved into the banking space, giving eight million African customers "*virtual cash*" on their handsets, as most of this demographic lack the funds or documents to open bank accounts.

Each one teach one

In the wind turbine business, when a windmill stops generating power, cash flow drops to zero.

Fixing broken wind turbines is a tricky business. There aren't many turbine repair schools around. Working on turbines takes mountain-climbing skills and engineering know-how.

Often a repair person comes upon a new and confusing condition -- while 60' off the ground.

The president of a large turbine company installed Yammer, a low-cost messaging service like Twitter except that it runs on private networks. All repair people were supplied with smart phones. Anyone who needs help fixing a turbine can send a message to his colleagues for help. He can transmit photos or even videos of broken parts. The old hands help more recent hires learn their trade. The company figures the increased uptime of turbines generates $3 to $5 million a year.

Intelpedia

A product manager at Intel asked why they couldn't set up an in-house version of Wikipedia just for Intel use. A web enthusiast in the IT group set it up with free, open-source software.

Originally intended to capture Intel's history and artifacts, news of "Intelpedia" spread like wildfire. It was the only place in the company where you could give and take information company-wide. For example, it became the authoritative reference on the acronyms used by different Intel divisions. Intelpedia was where teams came to coordinate projects. Users policed the content, fixing errors and explanations when they came upon them.

Intelpedia provides more value than any knowledge management system. The content is relevant because it's provided by the very people who do the work. 20,000 employees participate, visiting the site more than a million times a year. Intelpedia saves Intel a minimum of $20 million a year by simply making it easy to find information.

The value of not reinventing the wheel

IBMers George and Martha each need information buried in a

proposal IBM had made to Mt. Vernon Industries three years ago.

George searched through his office file cabinets. He asked a colleague in the next cubicle if he knew where the old proposal might be. Then he asked people in the coffee room. This is typical. Knowledge workers ask the people nearest them for help rather than the people most likely to know what they're looking for. They spend a quarter of their time searching for information. They spend an equivalent amount of time evaluating what they find. George never found the proposal he was looking for, so he had to re-create the information he sought. This is typical, too; knowledge workers spend 13% of their time creating documents, 90% of which already exist. This barely leaves enough time,14%, for them to do their email.

Martha tapped into IBM's online Blue Notes directory. She quickly identified the person in charge of the Mt. Vernon deal and noted he was in his office. Ten minutes later she had an electronic copy of the proposal.

More for less

Jack and Jill are sales reps for Widget Corporation. Jack found out about Widget's latest product from a 50-minute presentation at Widget's annual sales meeting. Jill missed the meeting and heard about the product on a 10-minute video narrated by a project manager.

Jack is only human. His mind started to drift 10 minutes into the presentation. He was hung over and sleep-deprived, awful conditions for remembering anything. Jack forgot two-thirds of what he learned about the new product because he didn't revisit the information until a week later.

Jill watched the video presentation of the product at her leisure before visiting a prospect. She wanted to get as much insight as possible before the call, so she gave the video her full attention. She downloaded it to her laptop and reviewed it the next day. She repeated a few key phrases she wanted to have in her head during the call.

Who's more likely to close a deal, Jack or Jill? The odds are that Jill remembers two or three times more than Jack.

Time is money

Sam joined Sun's sales force in 1998; Janet signed on in 2000.

A week after being hired, Sam attended a week-long training program at Sun's main campus. He and the other 120 people joining Sun that month endured rigorous dawn-to-dusk training on product features and benefits. Boot camp. After a while, Sam felt information was flowing in one ear and out the other. Fifteen months later, Sam and half of his class were selling at quota -- $5 million/year.

Jerry, a staffer in sales support, re-configured Sun's sales training before Janet arrived.

Janet studied product features online and wasn't permitted to come to headquarters until she passed proficiency tests. A challenging case study that required hands-on coordination was the centerpiece of her week of at the home office. Additionally, there was time for pep talks -- and for learning the new product information system. Janet became the mentor on the system for her branch, and later this gave her face time with the seasoned sales staff. Janet and half her class were selling at the $5 million/year rate in six months, nine months earlier than Sam's group!

Time-to-performance is a handy metric, for it quantifies the effectiveness of preparation. In Sun's case, their 1,440 new hires/year shorted time-to-quota by 3/4 year; 1440 x 3/4 x $5,000,000 = $3.5 billion in incremental sales. You might want to look for places in your organization to speed up time-to-readiness.

Different strokes

Huck just joined the Mississippi Bank as a credit analyst; Jim is the bank's senior loan officer.

Huck is signed up for a batch of online courses and face-to-face seminars. He needs to learn frameworks, risk profiles, new terminology, the bank's loan policies, how to make loan decisions, and what documentation is required. He and the bank want Huck to be producing quicker than the ten year apprenticeship these training programs replaced.

Jim already knows the lay of the land. He mastered everything Huck will learn years ago. Jim learns from chatting with friends and swapping stories. He hasn't attended a course or workshop in a decade; that's not the way experienced people learn.

Two years ago the bank realized that it was foolish not to assist their seasoned players with their learning; they knew that offering classes was not the right approach. A 2% improvement in the performance of someone like Jim makes a large contribution to the bottom line. The bank installed a web cam and showed Jim how to converse with colleagues in other locations. Jim now leads monthly online sessions where lenders share lessons learned.

Weak ties are strong

A sociologist discovered that job-seekers in Silicon Valley invariably find their jobs through friends of friends, so-called "weak ties." Since every friend has dozens of friends you don't know, there are a lot of them. Also, they come from different professional groups, have different contacts, and see things unknown to your inner circle. Since things happen through these "weak ties," how do you get to them?

Blogs enable people to share their views on professional matters and their personal lives. Bloggers share tips with one another on who's worth reading. I reach fifteen times as many people I've never met as people I know.

The weak ties phenomenon has some mysterious corollaries. If people you don't know but your friend knows lose weight or quit smoking, you're more likely to as well, even through you're complete strangers. Likewise, if your unknown weak ties are happy, the odds are better that you're happy, too. People concerned about connections blog to keep their hand in the game.

The 80/20 rule at work

Every year, a company hires 1,500 seasonal workers to assist clients with their taxes. The newbies start with a crash course in preparing tax returns. Nonetheless, the first month with a new crop of workers is always rocky, as they stumble to answer questions.

The company applied the 80/20 rule to identify the most common questions. From this they assembled an FAQ (list of Frequently Asked Questions). You don't need to memorize something if you know where to find it.

New hires using the FAQ as support shaved 10% off the time of the average customer call, an aggregate labor cost saving of $3 million. Plus, the customers received speedier service from company reps who spoke confidently.

Spread the word (cheap), save lives

Two West Point classmates in Iraq realized that their peers would become more effective were they able to share their evening conversations about what they learned in the course of combat each day with their fellow officers.

Without Army permission, they set up a public blog. They described new ways booby traps were being disguised. They reported successes working with civilians. They even gave tips on what candy to eat (stopping to unstick candy stuck to its wrapper makes a soldier an ideal target for a sniper.)

The blog became a must-read for most company commanders in the war zone. The reports on the blog were up to the minute. They were expressed in an authentic, conversational voice, something the Pentagon would never have mastered. The blogs were relevant and authentic. The practice has now spread to platoon leaders.

Comply

Bank tellers John and Mary both took compliance training and tests to certify their knowledge of money laundering statues.

The week before, Mary attended a brown bag session at lunch where her branch manager showed video clips of drug dealers and gangsters trying to make illegal deposits. Three times a week for six weeks after the test, Mary received a question in email to reinforce her knowledge. At a staff meeting, her branch manager told her about a failed attempt to deposit $80,000 in small bills at a nearby branch.

John went to compliance training cold. He passed the test and had no follow-up.

The odds are that Mary will remember two to four times as much about money-laundering regulations as John.

Tap into collective intelligence

Six thousand software engineers in a private, worldwide

telecommunications firm kept up to speed with their ever-changing field by reading journals, blogs, specialty bulletin boards, conference presentations, RSS feeds, and internal reports. They each spent two to three hours a week scanning these sources but could never be certain they weren't missing some important new development.

Senior management appointed a director of technical excellence to review the situation. He identified nine communities of interest, that is, broad subjects the engineers identified with. He recruited a respected thought leader in each area to monitor news and trends for everyone in their domain.

The thought leaders were given time to review the news. Members of their communities sent them tips to follow up. The leaders were supported by bloggers who refined the copy and made the presentation of information sing. Three times a week, sometimes less but never more, updates arrived in the Outlook accounts of people who subscribed to them.

Two-thirds of the engineers, about 4,000, took part in the program. Two hours a week saved over the course of a year mounts up to a couple of weeks. The new way of distributing news was freeing up 8,000 weeks of billable hours, something north of $25,000,000.

I think, therefore, where are my keys?

Human memory degrades over time. (What was trigonometry all about?) A strong memory may stick with you, but regular memories fall away exponentially unless they are reinforced. A week after a workshop, 90% of the topics you have not revisited will have disappeared. The speed of forgetting is exponential: the sharpest decline is in the first twenty minutes, then in the first hour, and then the curve evens off after about one day.

In a workshop during his first month on the job, Romeo learns his company's sales process, knowledge about its products, features and benefits, effective sales pitches, promotional campaign, seasonal contests, how to process orders, competitive advantage, pricing, prospecting techniques, the order entry system, delivery forecasting, the company's quota system, and a few "war stories." It's intense (and stress destroys memory, too.) He wonders how much of this is going to be useful on the job. By the time he needs to use the order entry system or describe the benefits of one of the more obscure products, his mind is a total blank. This is the rule, not the exception. Studies find that only 10% to 15% of what sales people learn in a workshop ever appears on the job.

Juliet joined the company the day after Romeo's workshop ended. She'd have to learn the ropes by jumping in. Luckily, Juliet's boss was a generous, gifted mentor. When Juliet needs to do something, for instance, quote a price, she would find out what she could from the company intranet. She would ask the veteran sales people. And if that failed, she'd ask her mentor for help. She's after only as much as it takes to do the job, not the lore and history that surrounds it. As soon as she learns what she needs to know, she applies it. This application of what she'd learned reinforced what she'd learned and strengthened her memory. She trumped the forgetting curve.

Juliet will spend more time and effort learning her job than Romeo, but her knowledge is much more likely to be there when she needs it.

People like us

A little known secret is that people learn from people like themselves. Children learn more from children they play with than they do from their parents. That figures. You identify with your friends; authority figures are another category. Consider: Which has more credibility with you -- a prepared statement by your CEO or a rumor from the grapevine? We naturally expect the really skinny from our friends and cockamamie bullshit from the other classes.

Orville listened to four presentations about the company's exciting new technology. The head of engineering explained its technical chops. The product manager told him why the new offering outshone the competition. The sales manager described the incentive rewards for early orders. The division executive showed how the new products were the lynchpin for making the year's numbers. Then he continued whittling away at the day's email.

Wilbur went online to the company's learning exchange. The exchange enables anyone in the sales force to upload off-the-cuff presentations with ease. He watched his division's top sales person deliver a compelling five-minute pitch she'd used to close a massive engagement. He watched his friend Amelia explain why this was a natural follow-on sales for customers who bought into the firm's cloud vision.

Who do you expect to do a better job the next day? Orville blew a day of selling (opportunity cost = $20K?); Wilbur learned what he needed in the evening. What's the ROI on formal presentations these days?

Empower your ecosystem

One of the world's largest enterprise software companies knew it lacked the capacity to support the next release of its platform. The company set up an online network where customers could ask questions and software consultants, whether on the payroll or independents, could respond.

Customers rated the quality of the answers they received. Consultants competed for points based upon the quality of their answers. Customers received good advice; consultants received recognition and a way to market their value.

Both response time and the quality of response improved from when the old days when the company answered all customer queries by itself. More than 1,000,000 queries from the firm's 95,000 customers have been answered in the system. Most inquiries are fielded by independent consultants, not employees. The network recently reached 2,000,000 members.

SAP offers three distinct communities that provide information, trusted resources, and true co-innovation. With more than 1.3 million members in over 200 countries, members have access to the 6,000 posts per day by world-class members. With over 500,000 unique visitors monthly — and one million topic threads — the SAP communities create fast, high-quality responses to customer queries.

SAP Developer Network (SDN)

SDN is an active online network that offers deep technical content and expertise for SAP developers, analysts, consultants, and administrators on SAP NetWeaver.

Members of SDN have access to technical articles, white papers, and how-to guides, as well as some 200 moderated forums, expert blogs, software downloads, extensive eLearning materials, and a Wiki that supports open communication. As a member, the more you participate and contribute, the more you get in return through the Contributor Recognition Program.

The rewards for the software company are beyond counting. $100 million? How can you place a value on keeping a €10 billion company prospering? What's it worth to outsource customer service for peanuts?

Wikipedia

Fifteen years ago, two groups started to write encyclopedias. One had deep pockets, paid an army of experts to write articles, and backed their with extensive global advertising. The other was put together by thousands of unpaid, amateur freelancers, and no advertising.

Last year Microsoft's Encarta went out of business. In March 2009, Microsoft announced it was discontinuing the Encarta disc and online versions. The MSN Encarta site in all countries except Japan was closed on October 31, 2009. Japan's Encarta site was closed on December 31, 2009.

Since its creation in 2001, Wikipedia has grown rapidly into one of the largest reference web sites, attracting nearly 68 million visitors monthly as of January 2010. There are more than 91,000 active contributors working on more than 15,000,000 articles in more than 270 languages. As of today, there are 3,213,092 articles in English. Every day, hundreds of thousands of visitors from around the world collectively make tens of thousands of edits and create thousands of new articles to augment the knowledge held by the Wikipedia encyclopedia.

Xerox Sales

In 1974, Xerox opened the doors of Xerox Document University outside Leesburg, Virginia, at a cost of $55 million dollars. The primary objective was training repair personnel on notoriously complex copiers that combined optical, digital, and mechanical technology in one fragile machine. Despite its investment, Xerox was not happy with the original results. Repair people were applying few of the lessons learned at Xerox Document U.

Xerox PARC hired an anthropologist, Julian Orr, to investigate. Orr found that Xerox training and documentation described a logical, consistent world. A troubleshooting roadmap showed the sequence of steps to fix a machine, but not what to do when you reached the end of the road. Orr discovered life was not so simple. Xerox machines are quirky. It's as if they have personality traits. Reps come to know their machines as shepherds know their sheep. They may all look alike to you and me, but a shepherd knows their names and behavior.

The repair people constructed narratives to explain the complicated procedures used to fix particular machines. They shared the stories at the coffee shop or bar. The repair people were training each other.

Xerox bought the repair people two-way radios. This sparked a 300% improvement in the reps' learning curve. Xerox sold the Document University building in 1994.

Ace Hardware

Ace Hardware set up a bulletin board, initially for 300 business dealers, expanded to 4,400 independently owned stores. Questions, Suppliers. Emergency help.

In most hardware stores, there's a gray-haired clerk who knows everything. For example, you fumblingly describe how you want to put a bird feeder on a pole, and the old guy says, "You need a flange fastener." Or, you want to hang shutters. "You need pintles," he advises. His acquaintance with doohickeys is endless: T-joints, pan head screws, toggle bolts, rheostats, turnbuckles, ball valves.

Although Ace doesn't share its financial results, it does say its investment in its online community has increased sales so much that it achieved a 500% return on its investment in the first six months. The company estimates that fully one-third of its dealers use the site at least weekly. Some check in every day.

FindLaw

FindLaw is a site where users find lawyers and legal advice. A big part of this site is an exchange where users can post legal questions and lawyers can provide answers. Similar in concept to LinkedIn Answers, this site is an interesting mix of emergent and formal knowledge. Obviously, the legal profession is based on established precedent, but the application of precedent to the unique vagaries of each case is emergent.

Ford Motors SyncMyRide

To reduce support costs for the Sync product, Ford Motor Company turned to their customers on the SyncMyRide site. The product has many devices that are approved by the manufacturer for use with Ford; however, customers are finding that there are other devices that can also work with it as well, and are also sharing tips and tricks on using Sync.

The site boasts over 10,000 active users (all of whom have to input a VIN to be compliant with government regulations) and over 1 million message views.

Cook Medical

Cook Medical uses discussions as a mechanism for sufferers of a particular disease to support each other and provide advice and ideas in coping with their affliction. A separate chat is used by doctors and specialist to share and identify existing and emerging best practices. As in many of these emergent stories, the community is not restricted to "employees" but extends the concept of workplace to include outside consultants and the like.

Google

Google has been using prediction markets for many years now, but even as far back as 2005 (eons ago in web time), they were having great results. Recently, there was an analysis done on the way prediction markets within Google map to social networks. Best Buy is using Prediction Markets to monitor progress toward specific goals. Workers buy and sell stock in certain initiatives based on the likelihood of outcomes. This is part of the overall strategy which also includes wikis, blogs, idea sharing, and discussions. Eli Lily has successfully used prediction markets to identify drug candidates that would make it through clinical trials. American Express conducted a Members Project to solicit ideas to make the world better. Members then voted on results with the winning idea getting funded with $1-5 million.

Proctor & Gamble

P&G has basically turned R&D on its head by soliciting ideas from the public and it's customers. Over 50% of P&G's new product ideas now come from outside the company and, at the same time, they have significantly reduced R&D efforts.

Innocentive

Innocentive was started by two Eli Lily alumni as a third party site for organizations to tap external experience in solving difficult or intractable scientific problems. It's essentially a market-place that connects seekers and solvers. Seekers post challenges and problems and associated "reward" money for solving the problem, and solvers post solutions. If the solution works, they get paid.

To date, over 800 challenges have been posted and just under 50% of these have been solved with $3 million in awards going to solvers. (Wikipedia has a good summary of references to follow).

Cisco's Idea Zone

Internal idea sharing through Idea Zone resulted in $3 billion in new market opportunities for Cisco. 400 ideas were submitted to the internal wiki and then 10,000 employees extended those ideas, enhanced them, shot them down etc… to help winnow them down to a manageable number. These were then further vetted and winnowed by members of the leadership team, resulting in 3 ideas collectively worth $3 billion in new markets.

Following the success of the i-Zone, Cisco decided to open a competition with the public to solicit ideas for new products or services that Cisco might pursue. Through this i-Prize initiative, Cisco identified a possible market for energy efficient network switching for the electric grid, in which Cisco will likely invest over $10 billion in the coming years. The winning team was led by a graduate student from Germany.

Scottrade

Scottrade has been in growth mode for awhile and couldn't keep up with either the distribution of new information to new branches or the related influx of competitor information. Formal models of information capture and delivery were taking too long and requiring too many resources so they moved to a wiki model where everyone could share best practices and new information. This solution, like many others in this list, is also a great example of how to facilitate collaboration and sharing as well.

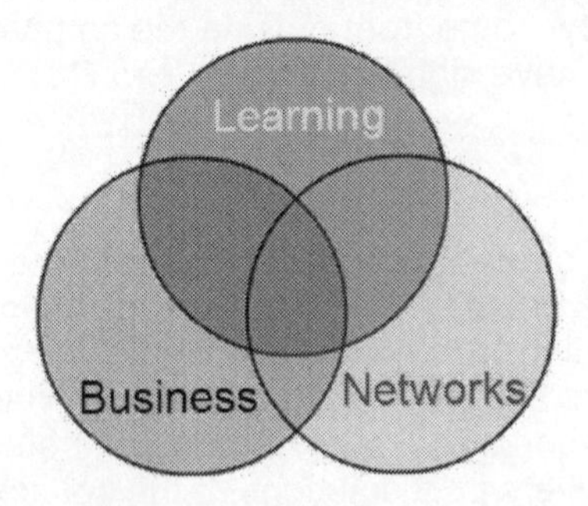

Cienna

Cienna has developed a technical partner community to connect partners to internal product resources within Cienna to drive innovation. They are doing this through idea share, virtual events and conferences, and discussions. "Conversations are strategic to so many people for so many different reasons…" The emergent part of this is the capturing of new ideas to drive product innovation.

John Deere

John Deere set up a private and exclusive community that would enable its premium tractor owners to engage in peer discussions, connect with product managers in real time, share ideas on how best to operate the John Deere machinery, and offer suggestions for new product enhancements. The community enables Deere to collect and capture insight from its most exclusive and premium market segment, which it then leverages to help improve products and develop new product features.

As with a lot of these stories, the community is about peer-to-peer collaboration and sharing among owners and about capturing emergent knowledge, ideas, and best practices. It's also, like Cienna and iRise, about breaking down the walls between "outside the company" and "inside the company."

Caterpillar

Caterpillar's Knowledge Network has 3000 active communities of practice, boasting 200% ROI for internal communities and 700% externally. Hard dollar savings? $75 million as of five years ago.

And you thought this stuff was new? By the way, five years ago, 85% of Caterpillar's valuation was based on it's intellectual capital, and only 15% came from it's hard assets. Just thought you might want to chew on this in case you have any lingering doubts that we have fully transitioned to a knowledge and network economy as opposed to an industrial one.

British Airways

British Airways uses discussions as a way for its flight crews to stay connected. Flight crews are essentially an ad hoc team thrown together for a brief period, so it's important that they share information with each other in a collective way. Sometimes the result is collaboration as when the flight crew identified issues with cups. Other times the discussions capture emergent knowledge.

Twitter 101 at Dell Computer

When company employee Ricardo Guerrero discovered Twitter at the South by Southwest conference in 2007, he thought he'd hit on a good channel for pushing out information. The rest of the team agreed.

"We thought, 'Great—this has a really short lead time, and it will let us communicate our message effectively,'" says Stefanie Nelson, manager of demand generation at Dell Outlet. "We started using it for one-way communication."

The company was surprised when people responded. "They wanted to ask questions. They wanted to share their experiences, good and bad," says Nelson, who's based in Austin, TX. "We realized that people were really interested in talking with us."

So instead of using Twitter just to let people know about deals, the company has come to think of it as a good place to interact with customers—and to raise awareness about the brand. "When we respond to people on Twitter, they get really excited, and we gain advocates."

That doesn't mean Dell Outlet has abandoned the deals. In fact, the company often posts offers that are exclusive to Twitter. They twitter only a few times a week so as not to spam their followers, and they use tracking URLs to gauge what followers find most appealing.

Increasing sales

Do the coupons work? Big time. Not only do they get retweeted and picked up by coupon sites—both of which spread the brand name—they also drive sales. Dell Outlet has booked more than $3 million in revenue attributable to its Twitter posts. In addition, the division has done research showing that awareness of the outlet has grown, too. "The uplift has been more than we dreamed," says Nelson.

Connecting with customers

Dell now has more than 80 Dell-branded Twitter accounts (including @dellhomeoffers for new system deals) offering everything from videos of new technologies to promotions for Asia-Pacific customers. It also encourages employees to twitter, and has well over 100 employee accounts. Dell uses many of those accounts (with names like @StefanieAtDell), primarily for customer service exchanges that require direct messages (Twitter's private channel) and to reach out to people who are twittering about Dell (which they find via Twitter search).

BesyBuy's Twelpforce

Best Buy wanted to be a resource for customers beyond their experience in the stores. They knew technology people enjoy today is sometimes challenging to use and learning the details of product features, benefits and sharing can make heads spin. The company developed a unique way to connect with customers through their @twelpforce account to provide real-time interaction.

Best Buy empowered the "blue shirt" members of its Geek Squad tech support service and corporate employees to staff their @twelpforce account on Twitter. People use their own Twitter account to ask questions directly to @twelpforce, and any Best Buy employee, working on company time, can provide answers using an @reply to the customer. By tagging their tweets with #twelpforce, the answer is sent through the @twelpforce account, allowing anyone to search the feed for topics they are researching.

As of 1/11/09, @twelpforce has provided over 19,500 answers to customer inquiries. They've had a tremendous response from employees as well, with over 2,300 signed up to answer questions.

Best Buy's thought at the beginning was simple...Be Relevant.

Give customers something of value so they find themselves invited into conversations, and welcomed into the purchase/ support cycle. They wanted to leverage Twitter and the real people behind @twelpforce to set them apart from competitors by sharing knowledge on-demand.

It also provided an opportunity to expose employees and the Best Buy Brand to social media. Through conversational employee/customer interactions via Twitter, they hoped to humanize their entire organization. Twitter let the employees be authentic, transparent, and bring more of "themselves" to the table. They felt the @twelpforce initiative in particular was a game changer since it was the first time a company used Twitter to create real-time customer service.

Next up is an effort to localize this exchange of information. Best Buy wants the majority of communication to shift to specific employees sharing locally relevant seminars and product sale information with their followers while the @twelpforce account will continue to serve as a main knowledge center.

British Telecom Dare to Share

"It does not replace the company's existing learning programs so much as augment them with informal learning opportunities and with social collaborative opportunities.

From a technology platform perspective, the approach is equivalent to an enterprise wide YouTube system with a strong social dimension. Dare2Share leverages Microsoft Sharepoint to enable employees to create, find and view learning segments (podcasts, documents and links), and also discuss and debate the content being created. Perhaps more important than the platform, however, is the attitude and learning culture that this approach creates across the organization. The free-form environment encourages people to experiment, innovate, collaborate, communicate and share their experiences and knowledge in engaging ways. This knowledge sharing has a positive impact on how other employees serve customers, find information or solve problems."

The Business Case for Social Learning, Accenture, Point of View, April 2009

Pearson People Development

"Problem: Pearson's learning strategy of face-to-face training for its global company of over 35,000 needed to change due to restrictions on travel on and after September 11, 2001

Solution: Implemented an online, virtual meeting environment to increase telecourse interactivity. Began a virtual book club utilizing collaborative software for brainstorming and decision making

Results: A shift from face-to-face culture to a virtual business culture. The role of Pearson People Development changed to being a learning enabler. Substantial cost savings from reduced face-to-face meeting time. Increased employee engagement because of the benefits of the new virtual processes, such as reduced stress and time"

PearsonPeopleDevelopment Case Study (PDF), Corporate University Exchange, November 2009

SFR

"French mobile phone company SFR implemented ActiveNetworker from Jobpartners to support its new social network. My SFR comprises a company blog, a central space for discussion, and the ability to build profiles that allow employees to share information on career progress, learning and development and aspirations. They can also join groups of interest ... ActiveNetworker has been well received and SFR is averaging 80,000 visits per week from the 10,000 employees that are using it.

Social networking: E-learning on the social, Sue Weekes, Personnel Today, 18 November 2009

Agilent Technologies

As early as two years ago, the global measurement solution provider introduced Wiki as a collaborative learning software to its workforce across the world. Its intention? Enhance group learning within its corporate environment. ... Christopher Goh, Agilent's director of global learning and leadership development, believes leveraging on such social networks allows his company to "facilitate collaborative learning and knowledge sharing" amongst its employees, especially the younger generation. "This medium augurs well with Gen Y learners who are tech-savvy and used to collaborating with each other in a networked environment.

Wiki is used as a support group learning platform in one of Agilent's core leadership programmes after participants completed the initial traditional classroom training. A Wiki site would be set up to allow participants work in teams to resolve their common leadership challenges, which had been discussed in the classroom. According to Goh, the participants will then work together over the web for 10 weeks after the training.

The Corporate Classroom, MarketingInteractive.com, 1 October 2009

Worldwide Fund for Nature: learn2perform

"learn2perform was set up for the People Development Team at WWF international in Geneva to provide a social learning and collaboration platform for WWF staff around the world. Staff members can set up an account in order to use a range of social media tools to manage their own personal learning, as well as set up group spaces to support team or project work. This site runs alongside WWF's e-campus where staff can access self-paced online course

"learn2perform has been set up to offer a range of social media tools useful for working and learning individually and collaboratively: creating blogs, bookmarking internal and external resources, an rss feed reader, uploading and sharing files, creating and editing web/wiki pages, providing member's news on the Twitter-like wire as well as messaging and online chat"

All things Elgg, 29 August 2009

Nationwide Insurance

"An internal micro-blogging tool fashioned much like Twitter, Yammer is accessible only by your staff. Employees at Nationwide Insurance find it so useful that 7,000 of its 36,000 employees have jumped on it in the last year without prompting from internal communicators.

How? The director of social media at Nationwide, Shawn Morton, tried Yammer and initially thought it wouldn't be useful because it was too similar to Twitter and Facebook. Then, several senior leaders, including the president and chief technology officer tried it, which set off a chain reaction within the company. "We went quickly from a dozen users to thousands of users over the course of the next few months," Morton says. "It's growing all by word of mouth."

At Nationwide, Yammer links rank-and-file with the C-suite, Ragan.com, 23 November 2009

Connectbeam

"This company saved $50,000 because of its Connectbeam implementation. Here's a bulleted summary of the story:

2) An employee created a wiki page explaining how to get a discount on software
3) Wiki page was shared on Connectbeam
4) Employees in other departments Googled the name of the software app
5) The wiki page was returned alongside the Google search results
6) Other employees clicked on the link to the wiki page, learning how to get the discount
7) Result = $50,000 savings to the company "

How Connectbeam saved $50,000 for a company, Connectbeam blog, 24 November 2008

****

Jane Hart's 100+ Examples of the Use of Social Media in Learning (by tools). http://c4lpt.co.uk/handbook/examples.html

Why These Things Work

Every one of these stories describes social or informal learning. Lessons are learned; people perform better.

The techniques are non-traditional, to be sure. We've looked at blogs, wikis, FAQs, instant messaging, crowdsourcing, sharing ideas, discussion among colleagues, discussion with experts, discussion with customers, learning on demand, chat, prediction markets, outsourcing innovation, communities of practice, subject matter networks, collaboration, expertise location, video learning, podcasts, coaching, use-generated content, experiential learning, mentoring, and peer-to-peer learning.

All this results in Working Smarter. These examples work because learners choose what they need to know; it's relevant; they're motivated to continue until reaching a solution; learning is immediately reinforced in practice; and the content is practical, ground-level knowledge.

Kevin Wheeler, George Siemens, Jay Cross, Charles Jennings at Online Educa Berlin

Rethinking learning in organizations

Connections

Everything is connected. You're linked to telephone networks, satellite networks, cable feeds, power grids, ATM networks, the banking system, the Web, intranets, extranets and networks that are local, wide, wireless, secure, virtual and peer-to-peer.

Social networks interconnect us in families, circles of friends, neighborhood groups, professional associations, task teams, business webs, value nets, user groups, flash mobs, gangs, political groups, scout troops, bridge clubs, 12-step groups and alumni associations.

Human beings themselves are networks. Scientists are still conceptualizing the human protocol stack, but they affirm that our personal neural intranets share a common topology with those of chimps and other animals. Once again, everything is connected. Learning is a whole-body experience.

Intel CEO Craig Barrett once said, "We're racing down the highway at 150 mph, and we know there's a brick wall up ahead, but we don't know where." We still don't know where that wall is, but today the car would be hurtling along at 1,800 mph.

In a world where we don't know what's coming next, what constitutes good learning? We're in whitewater now, and smooth-water sailing rules no longer apply. In whitewater, successful learning means moving the boat downstream without being dumped, preferably with style. In life, successful learning means prospering with people and in networks that matter, preferably enjoying the relationships and knowledge.

Learning is that which enables you to participate successfully in life, at work and in the groups that matter to you. Learners go with the flow. Taking advantage of the double meaning of "network," to learn is to optimize one's networks.

The concept that learning is making good connections frees us to think about learning without the chimera of boring classrooms, irrelevant content and ineffective schooling. Instead, the network model lets us take a dispassionate look at our systems while examining nodes and connections, seeking interoperability, boosting the signal-to-noise ratio, building robust topologies, balancing the load and focusing on process improvement.

Time is all we have.

Barnaby Conrad

Does looking at learning as networking take humans out of the picture? Quite the opposite.

Most learning is informal; a network approach makes it easier, more productive and more memorable to meet, share and collaborate. Emotional intelligence promotes interoperability with others. Expert locators connect you to the person with the right answer. Imagine focusing the hive mind that emerges in massive multiplayer games on business. Smart systems will prescribe the apt way to demonstrate a procedure, help make a decision or provide a service, or transform an individual's self-image. Networks will serve us instead of the other way around.

For tech networks, foundation meta-processing skills will foster the growth of self-determined learning. Personal knowledge management systems will store memories and facilitate rapid knowledge sharing across one's network. Alter-ego agents will seek out and present us with a balance of normal alerts and fringy out-of-the-box wake-up calls.

Learning is not enough

Learning is a necessary but insufficient condition for working smarter.

Dictionaries define learning as acquiring knowledge and skills. But we all know skilled, knowledgeable people who don't get things done.

The academic literature abounds with models that usually march through four sequential steps. They leave out application of what's been learned. You could spin around a circle like this without ever accomplishing anything.

Of course, learning doesn't work like this either. You brain is not a computer stepping through linear processes. Quite the contrary, your head contains a network without a center, a complex chemistry set where sparks between neurons form patterns that are always morphing, recombining, and influencing one another. Before we get into re-defining learning, here's my framework for boosting brainpower.

Learning begins with a desire to accomplish something. This applies to both individuals and organizations. While the outcome may be murky, learning always begins with an end in mind.

The Future Shape of Business

The structure of business, the role of workers and the architecture of software are changing before our very eyes. Business is morphing into flexible, self-organizing components that operate in real time. Software is becoming interoperable, open, ubiquitous and transparent. Workers are learning in small chunks delivered to individualized screens at the time of need.

Learning is becoming a core business process measured by key performance indicators. Taken together, these changes create a new kind of business environment—a business singularity.

Businesses are evolving into networks. What happens inside the walls is not nearly as important as the flow of value from raw material to customer. Networks shared among suppliers, partners and customers integrate the business into a commercial ecosystem—a larger network.

Software is evolving into networks. The internet is the new model for organization. Open networks that can talk with one another are far more valuable than yesterday's proprietary fortresses. As on the net, enterprise software evolves, routes around damage and reaches out to form new connections.

People are nodes enmeshed in networks with one another. Our bodies and minds are networks with built-in firewalls and filters. Outboard memory in the form of PDAs and personal data stores supplement human wetware. The biggest factor in individual success is the quality of one's social networks.

In any thriving network, tentacles reach out to snare new members. Growth begets growth until a tipping point is reached. Then, expansion becomes explosive. The rewards of membership become so high that everyone must join.

We are about to witness a spectacular convergence of networks of people and businesses. Workers and their work are becoming synchronous and inseparable. Colleagues and customers collaborate seamlessly. Transparent software eliminates the business-IT divide. Organizations focus on what they do best, outsourcing everything else to the greater commercial ecosystem. Network efficiencies eradicate the largest drag on corporate performance: slack. Business becomes instantaneous.

The environment in which people improve their performance in this future business landscape is called a *workscape*. It is what corporate learning can become in three to five years. It takes place in a virtual workplace where workers interact, learn and control the process of creating value in real time. The virtual workplace results from the internetworking of changes in business, software and learning.

Networks are defined by the quality of their connections. The successful business has people and connections so good that value flows without friction. The successful software environment connects so well that no one notices it's there. The successful worker is so synchronized with the challenges of work that she enters a state of flow.

Back Matter

Bibliography

Aldrich, Clark. (2009). *The Complete Guide to Simulations and Serious Games.* Pfeiffer

Aldrich, Clark. (2010). *Unschooling Rules: 50 Perspectives and Insights from Homeschoolers and Unschoolers on Deconstructing Schools and Reconstructing Education.*

Alexander, Christopher (1977). *A Pattern Language: Towns, Buildings, Construction.* Oxford University Press, USA

Alexander, Christopher (1979).*The Timeless Way of Building.* Oxford University Press, USA

Allee, Verna. (1997). *The Knowledge Evolution: Expanding Organizational Intelligence.* Butterworth-Heinemann

Allee, Verna. (2002). *The Future of Knowledge: Increasing Prosperity through Value Networks.* Butterworth-Heinemann

Brinkerhoff, R. O. & Gill, S. J. (1994). *The Learning Alliance: Systems Thinking in HRD.* Jossey-Bass

Brown, John Seely & Duguid, Paul. (2000). *The Social Life of Information.* Harvard Business School Press

Brown, John Seely & Hagel, John. (2005). *The Only Sustainable Advantage.* Harvard Business School Press

Brown, John Seely & Hagel, John. (2010). *The Power of Pull.* Harvard Business School Press

Brown, John Seely et alia. (2004). *Storytelling in Organizations.* ButterworthHeineman

Brown, Juanita, and Isaacs, David. (2005). *The World Café.* Berrett-Koehler Publishers

Conner, Marcia & Bingham, Tony. (2010). *The New Social Learning.*

Conner, Marcia & Clawson, Jim. (2004). *Creating a Learning Culture*. Cambridge University Press

Conner, Marcia. (2004). *Learn More Now: Ten Simple Steps to Learning Better*. Wiley.

Cross, Jay. (2001*). Implementing eLearning*. ASTD Press.

Cross, Jay. (2003). *Informal Learning, the Other 80%.* White paper found at http://internettime.com

Cross, Jay. (2005). *Informal Learning: Rediscovering the Natural Pathways that Inspire Innovation and Performance.* Pfeiffer.

Cross, Jay and O'Driscoll, Tony. (2005, September) *Gloria Gery In Her Own Words.* Performance Improvement Quarterly. ISPI

Cross, Rob (2005). Network Roundtable at the University of Virginia. On the web at: https://webapp.comm.virginia.edu/networkroundtable/

Csikszentmihalyi, Mihaly. (1991). *Flow: The Psychology of Optimal Experience*. Harper Perennial

Davis, Stan & Meyer, Christopher. (2003). *It's Alive : The Coming Convergence of Information, Biology, and Business*. Crown Business

Geary, Gloria. (1991). *Electronic Performance Support Systems*. Ziff Institute.

Illich, Ivan. (1999). *Deschooling Society*. Marion Boyars Publishers, Ltd.

Institute for Research on Learning. (1999) *Seven Principles of Learning.*

Kelly, Kevin. (1995). *Out of Control: The New Biology of Machines, Social Systems and the Economic World*. Perseus Books

Kelly, Kevin. (1999). *New Rules for the New Economy: 10 Radical Strategies for a Connected World*. Penguin Books

Lehrer, Jonah. (2010) *How We Decide.* Mariner

Lehrer, Jonah. (2008) *Proust Was a Neuroscientist*. Mariner

Leonard, George. (1968). *Education & Ecstasy*. Delacorte Press

Leonard, George. (1992). *Mastery: The Keys to Success and Long-term Fulfillment.* Plume Books

Locke, C., Weinberger, D., Levine, R., & Searles, Doc. (2000). *The Cluetrain Manifesto: The End of Business as Usual.* Perseus Books

Mager, Robert. (1992). *What Every Manager Should Know About Training.* CEP Press

Malone, Tom. (2004). *The Future of Work: How the New Order of Business Will Shape Your Organization, Your Management Style and Your Life*. Harvard Business School Press

Medina, John. (2009). *Brain Rules.* Pear Press

Pink, Daniel. (2005). *A Whole New Mind: Moving from the Information Age to the Conceptual Age*. Riverhead

Pink, Daniel (2009). *Drive.* Riverhead.

Quinn, Clark (2005). *Engaging Learners.* Pfeiffer.

Rummler, Geary and Brache, Alan. (1995). *Improving Performance, How to Manage the White Space on the Organization Chart*. Jossey-Bass

Seligman, Marty. (1991). *Learned Optimism: How to Change Your Mind and Your Life*. Free Press

Shirky, Clay. (2009). *Here Comes Everybody: The Power of Organizing Without Organizations.* Penguin

Siemens, George. (2006). *Knowing Knowledge.* web

Stafford & Weiss. (2005). *Mind Hacks*. O'Reilly Media

Stewart, Tom. (2003). *The Wealth of Knowledge: Intellectual Capital and the Twenty-first Century Organization*. Currency

Weinberger, David. (2008). *Everything is Miscellaneous*. Holt

Wenger, Etienne; McDermott, Richard; and Snyder, William M. Snyder. (2002). *Cultivating Communities of Practice*. Harvard Business School Press

Wenger, Etienne; White, Nancy; and Smith, John D. (2009). *Digital Habitats, stewarding technology for communities*. CPSquare.

People

I am in debt to the inspiring people I've met and at least chatted with since forming Internet Time Group, among them Donald Clark, Marcia Conner, Dan Pink, Don Norman, John Hagel, John Seely Brown, Jon Husband, Malcolm Gladwell, Robert Scoble, Doug Engelbart, Ted Nelson, Stewart Brand, Ellen Wagner, Stephen Downes, Dave Wilkins, Howard Rheingold, Peter Fingar, Howard Gardner, Chris Pirillo, Ray Kurzweil, Wil Wright, Jaron Lanier, Paul Saffo, Regis McKenna, Ellen Langer, John Medina, Dave Gray, Kevin Wheeler, Bob Horn, Jerry Michalski, David Weinberger, Marty Seligman, Clay Shirky, David Sibbet, Andy McAfee, Juanita Brown, David Cooperrider, Etienne Wenger, Nancy White, George Siemens, Mark Oehlert, Tom Stewart, Verna Allee, and maybe you as well.

Jane Hart, Clark Quinn, Harold Jarche, Charles Jennings, and I participate in a braintrust we call Internet Time Alliance. We learn from one another and collaborate on projects. Our multi-disciplinary group never ceases to push my thinking on working smarter.

Special Thanks

Lori Thompson voluntarily edited an earlier version of text, and it reads much the better for it. Clark Quinn read the September 2009 manuscript; his suggestions tightened things up. Janet Laane Effron cleaned up scads of typos and awkward spots.

In March 2010, both Jane Bozarth and Sahana Chattopadhyay reviewed the January 2010 edition of Working Smarter, helping to publicize the effort.

The web introduced us all. Long live the web.

About the primary authors

Jay, Jane, Harold, Charles, Clark
(not pictured: many of you)

Jay Cross is the Johnny Appleseed of informal learning. His calling is to help business people improve their performance on the job and find satisfaction in life. The Internet Time Alliance, which he chairs, helps corporations and governments use networks to accelerate performance.

Jay has challenged conventional wisdom about how adults learn since designing the first business degree program offered by the University of Phoenix. He is author of *Informal Learning: Rediscovering the Natural Pathways that Inspire Innovation and Performance* and numerous other books and articles.

Jay served as CEO of eLearning Forum for its first five years, was the first to use the term eLearning on the web, and has keynoted such conferences as Online Educa (Berlin), I-KNOW (Austria), Research Innovations in Learning (U.S.), Emerging eLearning (Abu Dhabi), Training (U.S.), Quality in eLearning (Bogotá), LearnX (Melbourne), and Learning Technology (London).

He is a graduate of Princeton University and Harvard Business School. Jay and his wife Uta live with their miniature longhaired dachshund in the hills of Berkeley, California.

Jane Hart is founder of the Centre for Learning and Performance Technologies, where she keeps track of existing and emerging technologies. Jane has recently implemented more than a dozen social learning environments in Europe – in universities, non-profit and profit making organisations.

Harold Jarche is not afraid to challenge conventional wisdom. Through his blog and consulting practice, people look to Harold for innovative ideas on business, technology, social networks and learning. He helps make sense of the complexities facing organizations today with creative approaches for working smarter that are grounded in analytical thinking. As a pioneer who has worked and learned online since the dawn of the Web, Harold continues to develop his practice and help his clients face life in perpetual Beta.

Charles Jennings served as CLO of Reuters and Thomson Reuters for eight years until the end of 2008 and *knows* organizational learning. Prior to that posting he had roles as head of the UK national centre for networked learning, as a professor at Southampton Business School and senior business roles for global companies. He has also been an evaluator for the European Commission's learning, performance and eCommerce research initiatives.

Charles sits on steering groups and advisory boards for national and international bodies including the European Learning Industry Group and the Institute for IT Training. He is a Fellow of the British Institute of Learning. In 2008 he was honored with the UK World of Learning 'Outstanding Contribution to the Learning Industry' award in recognition of his work on performance improvement, and 'just-in-time' and informal learning.

Clark Quinn is a leading advocate of design that respects how people really learn, courtesy of a PhD in applied cognitive science at UCSD. He has a track record of providing strategic solutions to Fortune 500, education, government, and not-for-profit organizations, including mobile, performance support, simulation game, social, and intelligent learning systems.

An internationally respected scholar and speaker, he is the author of *Engaging Learning: Designing e-Learning Simulation Games*, and the forthcoming *Designing mLearning: Tapping into the Mobile Revolution for Organizational Performance*, as well as numerous articles and chapters. He has held management positions at Knowledge Universe Interactive Studio, Open Net, and Access CMC, and academic positions at the University of

New South Wales, the University of Pittsburgh's Learning Research and Development Center, and San Diego State University's Center for Research in Mathematics and Science Education.

Where Jay is coming from

In 1998 I fell so deliriously in love that I neglected my work and lost my job. My mistress was the web. I love her still. She never ceases to amaze me.

Cozumel is an island twenty miles offshore from Mexico's Yucatan Peninsula and sixty miles south of Cancun. People have made pilgrimages to Cozumel to receive wisdom and become more fertile for more than two thousand years. I flew there to lick my wounds and sort out my priorities.

Sitting on a stone bench amid Mayan ruins in the jungle, I gave myself permission to think freely. Hanging out in this ancient seat of wisdom reinforced my nascent belief in the power of the web to fuel ever-greater collective intelligence.

The net was going to connect people faster, better, cheaper, more often and more openly. Virtual was merging with actual. People would be able to learn and innovate faster and deeper than ever before.

Human networks were the key to collaboration. The net could make everything happen faster. I envisioned new ways of bringing workers, customers, and partners together. The net would make it simpler for like-minded individuals to build upon one another's ideas.

I decided then and there that my calling was to help business people improve their performance on the job and find satisfaction in life. I would challenge the conventional wisdom about how adults prosper in and for organizations.

Phoenix

In the late seventies, a group of renegade academics hired me to research the market potential of an off-campus degree program in business. After a few years in Europe as an Army officer, I'd earned an MBA at Harvard, so I could speak the lingo.

Tech firms up and down Silicon Valley and banks in San Francisco were enthusiastic. I signed on with John Sperling's venture to create a profit-making college and spent the next two years developing interactive workshops in management, marketing, finance, accounting, business law, and similar topics that led to an accredited Bachelors degree in business administration.

When Sperling and his associates moved from San Jose to Phoenix to become the University of Phoenix, I quit to head up marketing and sales for a start-up in California. I'd learned that learning is a process, that adults don't have much patience for classrooms, and that practitioners make the most effective teachers.

Our little start-up trained bankers how to make sound loan decisions. We boiled complex financial decisions down to job aids, performance support, algorithms, and case examples. For a dozen years I worked with senior loan officers, training directors at banks, and instructional designers. More than half of the 100 largest banks in the U.S. became customers. We helped a million bankers learn their trade.

Enter The Web

In the mid-eighties, a pioneering online conferencing system called the Well (Whole Earth 'Lectronic Link) was my doorway to thousands of conversations among digerati, deadheads, dabblers, degenerates, and do-gooders.

Conversing on the Well taught me about community and online culture. The Well introduced me to email early on and gave me an on-ramp to the internet. I began surfing the web when the entire thing ran on Tim Berners-Lee's NeXT machine at CERN.

When Marc Andreesen at the National Supercomputing Center released the Mosaic browser, I was ecstatic. This web thing was magic. Connections for free! Graphics and text. No limits to scale! And as the name said, "worldwide."

I recognized that the web would change lives. Not only that, my customers at the time would pay big money for scant work in this new medium. A new rocket was leaving the launch pad. I could hardly sit still.

Good-bye to organizations
Over the course of a dozen years, the staff of the start-up for whom I managed sales and marketing had grown from six people to a hundred and fifty.

If you think you can do a thing, or think you can't do a thing, you're right.

Henry Ford

My fanaticism about the power of the net did not endear me to co-workers, who were flat out chasing other rainbows. The more charitable of them said it was sad to see such a talented guy like me go off the deep end. The firm did not have time to deal with this web stuff. We parted company.

Early to the party
Human resources had become more important than natural resources, brains more important than brawn. Networks were connecting everyone and everything. Time ran faster.

Increasing brainpower had become a corporate survival skill. Learn or die. Machine-age managers complained when employees had downtime because they were in training. Tomorrow's leaders would understand that learning is not just another discretionary item. In the information age, innovation is the competitive advantage. In the Information Age, learning *is* the business.

I wrote those paragraphs soon after I returned from Cozumel in 1999. It seemed revolutionary back then. To some people, it still does.

Oddball stuff is often regular stuff making a premature appearance. When I began blogging (in the last century), my friends didn't "get it." When I started writing about eLearning, Brandon Hall emailed me that he didn't like the term; it wouldn't stick.

Traditionalists were not pleased with my observation that "Courses are dead." People put down informal learning, saying it lacked rigor, even though informal learning works better than its formal cousin. After all, how did you learn to talk, walk, and kiss?

Not that I'm always prescient. My wife reminds me that in the mid-sixties, I had predicted that we'd all be watching flat-panel televisions that hung on the wall like pictures... by 1975. I was off by more than thirty years.

About Internet Time Group

When I returned from Cozumel, I talked with more smart companies about how they were thinking about using the power of the web to close gaps between the talent their industry required and the abilities their people possessed.

"Living the web lifestyle," I posted my findings about what I called eLearning to the internet. When the CEO of the largest CD-ROM training company decided his firm needed to switch to hosted distance learning, he scoured the web for someone who knew something about the topic. My name came up 1, 2, 3, and 4, on the most popular search engine of that time and for the better part of two years, I researched the market, read the tea leaves, and wrote the white papers for SmartForce, the eLearning Company.

I started Internet Time Group to further the conversation about using networks and cognitive science to boost organizational brain power, make work more fulfilling, create an atmosphere of continuous improvement, and improve performance. I became CEO of eLearning Forum to champion my beliefs.

Jay Cross | Jane Hart | Harold Jarche | Charles Jennings | Clark Quinn

Jay

Jay Cross
Internet Time Alliance

September 2010 Edition

Berkeley, California

Reviews of the January 2010 Edition:

Jane Bozarth: “Cross leads the reader on a tour of informal, networked learning and performance support, and helps move the conversation from 50,000 feet to 50. This ‘unbook’ is a compilation of his own ideas as well as interjections from his colleagues in the Internet Time Alliance (Harold Jarche, Jane Hart, Charles Jennings, and Clark Quinn), with chime-ins from many others. There are checklists, tools, and images, charts and provocative questions. And there are honest remarks about the state of learners, many of whom need to stop waiting for directions and start becoming self-directed.”

Sahana Chattopadhyay: “Just as learning never ends, knowledge is never static and thus not “capturable” in the true sense… And hence, the need for informal learning–the only way that the constantly changing nature of today’s business, knowledge, content, context, needs, can be shared, utilized for growth, innovation, development—both organizational and personal. Informal learning adds that much-needed context to an ever-growing volume of information, adds meaning to the data, and thereby facilitates efficient decision- making.

Working Smarter is a must read, as is *Informal Learning*.

Acknowledgements
Some of this material first appeared in Jay’s column on Effectiveness in Chief Learning Officer magazine, in the resources sections of Learning Light, the magazines Training and T+D, and our blogs.

They are able because they think they are able.

Virgil

Evolution of The Working Smarter Fieldbook

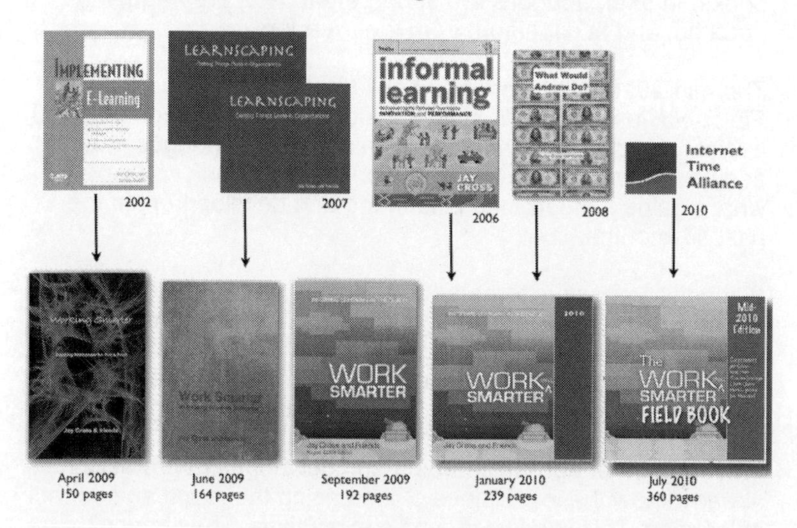

Issues? Email Jay Cross at jaycross@internettime.com

Join the movement? Sign in at InternetTimeAlliance.com/book

Evolution of the Unbook
by Jay Cross

from Chief Learning Officer magazine, September 2010

"Reality is an endless stream of knowledge, culture and ideas that flows faster and faster. Traditional books are snapshots of that stream. The swifter the stream, the shorter the life of the book. A book is an event. We need a process that outlasts the moment — a movie in place of a photograph." I wrote that two years ago in CLO, and I've been working on a solution -- the unbook.

The "un" prefix highlights how unbooks differ from traditional books. In brief, unbooks are in perpetual beta, are frequently updated, and accept input from their readers,

The mid-2010 edition of an unbook titled *The Working Smarter Fieldbook* just came out. It is the successor to the January 2010 edition of *Working Smarter*. Let's examine the changes and additions to show both the evolution of the unbook concept and what's gained importance in learning and development in the past six months.

Since this unbook is targeted at business managers, the word *learning* does not appear in the title. Learning is the means, not the end. To managers, the L-word triggers thoughts of schooling, classrooms, boredom, and the cessation of work. Learning has become the work. Hence, we talk of working, not learning.

Why target managers? Learning and development professionals already know the importance of increasing the reach and impact of learning. This is news to many executives. They haven't thought of learning as a component of executing strategy. Our aim is to speak directly to managers -- or to provide L&D professionals with the ammunition to make their case.

In nonfiction, the single-author concept is a conceit. "All of us are smarter than any of us." Hence, my colleagues Jane Hart, Harold Jarche, Clark Quinn, and Charles Jennings wrote many of the words here. Our thoughts are inextricably intertwined; we couldn't separate them if we wanted to. Most of the book is written in a single voice.

Like all unbooks, The Working Smarter Fieldbook is not finished. It's beta. This is the sixth edition in less than two years. We'd rather be current than polished. We warn readers to expect some rough edges and redundancy in this version. Furthermore, readers learn more from tentative material than from text that's set in stone. This goes for all learning events, not just unbooks.

Informal learning, social networking, and interactive web technologies make learning and development a richer but more complex field. The mid-year unbook is 120 pages longer than in

January, much of it addressing web 2.0, and that's after chopping out fifty pages deemed irrelevant.

The current edition focuses on how-to rather than theory. We've entered an age of do-it-yourself. Forty-five examples show how organizations are working smarter. We have included a new way of assessing social and informal learning.

The ongoing economic meltdown has tested the patience of business managers everywhere. They want results *now.* A new chapter on making the business case describes how to assess productivity and business results, propose to management, evaluate intangibles, when to replace learning with performance support, and when *not* to use training. We share the job aids from our workshop on developing a pragmatic elevator pitch for senior management.

Everyone is short of time these days, so rather than bulk up the Fieldbook with another five chapters, we provide collected thirty cheat sheets and job aids that summarize motivation, natural learning, unmeetings, psychology, retention, enterprise 2.0, and more.

Traditional instructional design frameworks come unglued in the face of uncertainty, peer learning, collaboration, granular content, and roving mobile learners. We propose new ways of looking at instructional design. It's high time to rise above training programs and focus on learning environments.

When you don't understand or disagree with a traditional author, there's not much you can do about it. You might write a review but you're not going to have a dialog. Hence, most books are frozen in time. They don't change. Authors don't benefit from suggestions from readers.

The site that accompanies The Working Smarter Fieldbook encourages readers to discuss the issues raised in the book. We are committed to addressing their every concern. Furthermore, we encourage our readers to contribute material, provide examples, and introduce new topics. (You can see this in action at http://bit.ly/96NOM4.)

September 2010 Edition

For more about unbooks, visit http://theunbook.com

Turn your organization on to Working Smarter

About Internet Time Alliance

The five Internet Time Alliance partners help organizations solve performance problems.

Our toolkit contains collaborative intelligence, network optimization, performance support, informal learning, and a hundred years of practical experience.

Join us at *http://bit.ly/avDnKO (http://internettimealliance.com/book)*

Together, we can help you make your workers and partners more proficient, in less time, and often for lower cost. See what we're thinking and read our white papers at http://internettimealliance.com

September 2010 Edition

Printed in Great Britain
by Amazon.co.uk, Ltd.,
Marston Gate.